WHO OWNS ANTIQUITY?

JAMES CUNO

With a new afterword by the author

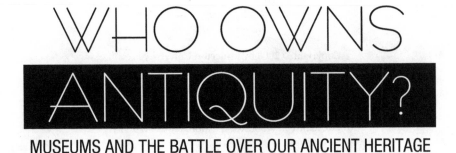

WHO OWNS ANTIQUITY?

MUSEUMS AND THE BATTLE OVER OUR ANCIENT HERITAGE

PRINCETON UNIVERSITY PRESS • PRINCETON AND OXFORD

In the United Kingdom: Princeton University Press,
6 Oxford Street, Woodstock, Oxfordshire OX20 1TW

press.princeton.edu

Fourth printing, and first paperback printing, with a new afterword
by the author, 2011

Paperback ISBN: 978-0-691-14810-6
Cloth ISBN: 978-0-691-13712-4

Library of Congress Control Number: 2008922048

British Library Cataloging-in-Publication Data is available

This book has been composed in Minion with display font in Bernhard Fashion

Printed on acid-free paper ∞

Printed in the United States of America

5   7   9   10   8   6   4

For Sarah, Claire, and Kate

Nationalism becomes self-reproducing in a world of nation-states. For once the world has defined "normality" as national solidarity and national statehood, every nation must be vigilant against signs of cultural assimilation and must produce nationalists whose self-appointed task is to strengthen national identity and uniqueness in order to increase social cohesion and solidarity. In a world of nation-states, nationalism can never be ultimately satisfied.

—Anthony D. S. Smith, *Nationalism in the Twentieth Century* (1979)

Economic integration, and with it cultural globalization, has far outpaced our global mindset, which is still rooted in nationalist terms. We benefit from all that the world has to offer, but we think only in narrow terms of protecting the land and people within our national borders—the borders that have been established only in the modern era. The barbed wire, chain-link fences, security forces, and immigration and customs agents that separate us from the rest of the world . . . cannot change the fact that we are bound together through the invisible filament of history.

— Nayan Chanda, *Bound Together: How Traders, Preachers, Adventurers, and Warriors Shaped Globalization* (2007)

CONTENTS

PREFACE

It is the magic of nationalism to turn chance into destiny.
— Benedict Anderson[1]

I. Through the first decade of the nineteenth century, Thomas Bruce, 7th Earl of Elgin, British ambassador to the Ottoman court in Constantinople from 1799 to 1803, had numerous sculptures removed from the Parthenon in Athens and shipped to London. He did so, we are told, with permission from the governing Ottoman authorities. The original legal instrument has disappeared and is said to exist only in an Italian translation made for Elgin by the Ottoman court. Some then and now question the legality of Elgin's actions. The Italian language document gives Elgin the right to draw, measure, and make plaster casts of the sculptures, and dig for others that might have been buried. It also allows for "some pieces of stone with old inscriptions and figures" to be taken away. Did this refer to the sculptures on the building or only the fragments found on the ground? The document is not clear. And without greater clarity (and, at this point, probably even with it), no legal case can be made against Britain's ownership of the marbles. Still, the modern government of Greece has consistently called for their return.

Whatever the legal circumstances of Elgin's actions, they could hardly have been surreptitious. The sculptures, both freestanding and in relief, were numerous and heavy and had to be taken off the building and down from the temple's considerable height. They then had to be transported to ships, where, for fear of sinking the ships themselves, Elgin's agents sawed off the backs of the thickest relief slabs before loading them. They then sailed slowly away from the coast of the then Ottoman territory, out to sea, and for weeks toward Britain. Considerably impoverished as a result, Elgin offered to sell the sculptures to the British nation. A Select Committee of the House of Commons received testimony from leading British artists as to the sculptures' quality, importance, and value. Pronounced worthy of acquisition in 1817, the Elgin Marbles, as they were called, were placed on public display in Montagu House. Thirty-five years later, they were transferred to their first permanent gallery in the new, Robert Smirke–designed British Museum.

Byron famously criticized their acquisition by the British government, including in verse: "Cold is the heart, fair Greece! That looks on thee,/ Nor feels as lovers o'er the dust they lov'd;/ Dull is the eye that will not weep to see/ Thy walls defac'd, thy mouldering shrines remov'd/ By British hands … " Keats wrote positively of them in a sonnet, "On Seeing the Elgin Marbles." And Goethe celebrated their acquisition as "the beginning of a new age for Great Art." In the meantime, what remained of the Parthenon—which was much depleted not only from Elgin's actions, but also from years of damage, architectural accretions, vandalism, and, most dramatically, the destruction of much of the building in 1687 when Venetian forces of a Christian Holy League formed against the Ottomans bombarded the building with more than seven hundred cannonballs, ultimately igniting the ammunition stored there in a vast explosion that killed as many as three hundred people—became an emotional symbol of a newly independent Greece.

A first attempt at an independent Greek government failed when its president was assassinated in 1831. Two years later, after independence was finally achieved with help from international forces, a monarchy was established with the seventeen-year-old son of King Ludwig of Bavaria on the now Greek throne. Plans were drawn up to rebuild Athens as the new state's national capital. Maximilian, the king's brother, commissioned the Prussian architect Karl Friedrich Schinkel, who had never been to Athens, to design a royal palace for the Acropolis. But for reasons in part of cost, security, and lack of water supply, the plan was never completed. Another, perhaps more influential reason was that Schinkel's rival, Leo von Klenze, the king of Bavaria's favorite architect, was convinced that the entire hill of the Acropolis should become an archaeological zone. And so it did, on August 28, 1834.

Klenze oversaw the lavish ceremony marking the occasion. The young German prince (now Greek king) rode up to the Acropolis on horseback. There he was met by young girls dressed in white, carrying myrtle branches. As a band played, he took his place on a throne within the Parthenon and in front of soldiers and courtiers listened to a speech delivered by Klenze in German. "Your majesty stepped today," Klenze thundered, "after so many centuries of barbarism, for the first time on this celebrated Acropolis, proceeding on the road of civilization and glory, on the road passed by the likes of Themistocles, Aristeides, Cimon, and Pericles, and this is and should be in the eyes of your people the symbol of your glorious reign. . . . All the remains of barbarity will be removed, here as in all of Greece, and the remains of the glorious past will be brought in new light, as the solid foundation of a glorious present and future." The material remains of the years when the Parthenon served as a Byzantine church and an Ottoman garrison, complete with a small mosque, were removed. The Acropolis became the political symbol of the new Greece. As one archaeologist put it, speaking at a meeting of the newly formed Archaeological Society of Athens in 1838, "it is to these stones [the sculpture and architecture of classical Greece] that we owe our political renaissance." Or, as another archaeologist wrote more than a century later, in 1983, the Parthenon is "the most sacred monument of this country . . . which expresses the essence of the Greek spirit."

It is on this basis that the Greek government is calling for the Parthenon marbles to be returned, and not just from the British Museum but from all the foreign countries in which they reside. They have come to be treasured as critical to the identity of the modern nation-state, a vital link with its imagined ancient past from which it claims to have been unjustly separated by more than one thousand years. It is not because they are to be restored to their original location on the Parthenon itself (they are to be shown in a museum newly built on a site across from the Acropolis), nor because they can not be studied equally well in London. It is because they are said to *belong* to Greece and to hold within them the very spirit of its people. They are political symbols first, not archaeological artifacts of scientific value.

But if they are political symbols for the Greeks, important to their national identity, they have also been claimed as symbols of and vitally important to the cultural values of modern Britain, where they have resided and been seen publicly now for nearly two hundred years, longer even than there has been a modern state of Greece. As the British Minister for the Arts said in 2000, at a meeting of the Select Committee for Culture, Media, and Sport investigating the illicit trade in cultural property, "I understand the emotional importance . . . to the Greek people of this case. I would also say with respect that we too in this country are heirs to the classical tradition. I would say that the diffusion of the classical culture of ideas, values and of physical relics and monuments over two millennia, has contributed in profoundly important ways to the history that has led to the emergence of the world that we have. It seems to me unthinkable that we would wish to reverse that process."[2]

II. In the summer of 1799, French troops in the Egyptian city of Rosetta were hard at work rebuilding the walls of a fifteenth-century fort in an effort to secure the Egyptian coastline against the British fleet. A French officer named Pierre François-Xavier Bouchard came across a fragment of a stone with writing on it. Sensing that it was important, he showed it to his superiors who sent it to the Institut d'Égypte in Cairo, where it remained until it fell into the hands of the victorious British, who removed it (together with other "nationalized" antiquities from the Institut) to London in 1802.

The text inscribed on the stone's surface is in three scripts: Egyptian hieroglyphs ("the writing of the divine words"), Egyptian demotic ("the writing of documents"), and ancient Greek ("the writing of the Ionians"). It documents the terms of an agreement between a synod of Egyptian priests and the Macedonian ruler of Egypt, Ptolemy V, on March 27, 196 B.C. It promises that a copy of the text in the three languages will be placed in every temple of the first, second, and third divisions in the land "alongside the statue of the king who lives for ever." The Rosetta Stone, as it has come to be called, is less important for its content than for its being deciphered (other Egyptian texts of equal or greater importance exist; and there are even other copies of the Stone's text itself, the so-called "Decree of Memphis"). It unlocked the door to the ancient Egyptian language and allowed for the history of that ancient land to be written.

The two key figures in the history of the Stone's deciphering are Thomas Young, a British, Quaker polymath, who even on his death-bed was working on his Egyptian dictionary, and Jean-François Champillon, a brilliant and precocious student of languages and a dedicated Egyptologist. In many ways they could not have been more different.

Young was educated in Edinburgh, Göttingen, and Cambridge. He was a Fellow of the Royal Society by the age of twenty-three; he would later become its foreign secretary. Although he worked as a doctor of medicine, he lived off a generous inheritance and wrote on any number of scientific topics, from anatomy to mechanics, the wave theory of light, navigation, and longitude. As a student of languages, he invented the term "Indo-European" for the family of languages that included most European languages as well as Persian and many dialects of modern India. He was introduced to Egyptian in 1814 and five years later published in the *Encyclopedia Britannica* what he had come to know about the equivalents between demotic script and hieroglyphic groups.

Champillon, seventeen years Young's junior, was born into a shop-keeper's family in December 1790. With an older brother he moved to Grenoble when he was nine, and there began his studies of languages, including Hebrew, Arabic, and Syriac. At age sixteen, he announced to the Grenoble Society of Sciences that he intended to decipher Egyptian and reconstruct the history of the Pharaohs, which he did eight years later with the publication of *L'Égypte sous les Pharaons*, a copy of which he sent to the Royal Society in London where Thomas Young came across it. Over the next eight years, Champillon concentrated on Egyptian hieroglyphs and in 1822, at a meeting of the Académie des Inscriptions et Belles Lettres, and in the company of Young and Alexandre von Humboldt, he read his famous paper, which has since been known as the *Lettre à Monsieur Dacier*. In it he outlined the hieroglyphic alphabet he developed from the Rosetta Stone. Two years later, he published his summa—*Précis du système hiéroglyphique des anciens égyptiens*—which earned him a curatorial position at the Louvre. In 1826, Champillon made his first trip to Egypt, where he studied obelisks at Luxor and the inscriptions in the Valley of the Kings. In 1831, he was elected to the world's first chair of Egyptology, at the Collège de France.

The two men met only a few times, but knew each other's work well; Champillon begrudgingly admitted the importance of Young's earlier, more tentative discoveries, and Young acknowledged the extraordinary, groundbreaking discoveries of his younger colleague. Ultimately, their work made possible the deciphering of hieroglyphs and is, as one Egyptologist has written, "the creator of the entire *Historie* of ancient Egypt, because it has enabled us to read the texts which led us to start writing [the history of Egypt itself]." And it all began with the Rosetta Stone, and its chance find, reused as building material in a wall of a medieval fort.

The Egyptian government has called for the Stone's return, claiming that it is important to Egyptian identity, although at the time of its taking there was no independent state of Egypt and wouldn't be for more than one hundred years. Nor was there a local regard for the land's ancient heritage. Until the final decades of the nineteenth century, Egyptians showed little interest in their ancient past, and this despite the extraordinary evidence of it all around them. They believed that their significant history began with the advent of Islam many centuries later. It was only through European interest in the remains of ancient Egypt, in great part provoked by the finding of the Rosetta Stone and the deciphering of its hieroglyphs, that the Egyptians also became interested. And then their interest was as much for the current political value of those remains as for their scientific importance. Almost immediately they were used to strengthen Egypt's separatist ambitions within the Ottoman Empire, making the claim that Egypt was an old, venerable land, older and more venerable even than the Ottoman Empire itself.

The Rosetta Stone was found without archaeological context. In the terms of the current argument between museums and archaeologists over the relative value of unexcavated antiquities, the Rosetta Stone would be pronounced meaningless. Were it to come on to the art market today without provenance (knowledge of where it was found and the history of its recent ownership) and/or without legal, export documents issued by its "country of origin," museums would be discouraged from acquiring it. If a museum did, it would be criticized in the international community. Archaeologists criticize museums for acquiring antiquities without documented provenance prior to 1970 (the date of the UNESCO Convention on the Means of Prohibiting and Preventing the Illicit Import, Export, and Transfer of ownership of Cultural Property) or without export license. They would rather allow an unexcavated, undocumented antiquity to remain on the private market than to have it be brought "inappropriately" into a public museum collection.

If by chance a scholar came across the Rosetta Stone in a private collection, she would be discouraged from publishing it in today's leading English-language, archaeological journals. Those journals have policies against serving "as the initial place of publication or pronouncement" of any unprovenanced object acquired by an individual or institution after December 30, 1970, unless it was in a collection prior to that date, or there is evidence that it was legally exported from its country of origin. Such policies are intended to support national cultural laws of "source" countries to discourage the looting of archaeological sites and illegal trafficking in antiquities. Not being acquired or published, and thus neither studied nor deciphered, the Rosetta Stone would be a mere curiosity, Egyptology as we know it would not exist, and modern Egyptians would not know it to claim it as theirs.[3]

III. Chen Mengjia, a leading Chinese scholar of ancient bronzes and Chinese writing, committed suicide in 1966 during the Cultural Revolution. He had been accused of being a Rightist and hounded by colleagues and students. He had published his first article on ancient Chinese bronzes in 1936: "The Sacrificial Systems of Shang and Zhou as Found in Ancient Inscriptions." He was appointed instructor at Yanjing University that same year, and a year later was appointed research professor at Qinghua University. When war broke out with Japan, he moved with his university to Kunming in Yunnan Province, where he continued to publish on inscriptions found on ancient oracle bones and bronzes. In 1944, he was among the first to receive a grant from the Rockefeller Foundation under a new program to encourage Chinese scholars and advance the study of Chinese language and history in the United States. He arrived in Chicago in November and assumed his position in the Department of Oriental Languages and Literatures at the University of Chicago. A month later, while touring through the Metropolitan Museum of Art in New York, he stated in an interview with the *Shanghai Evening Post* his intention to survey American collections of Chinese bronzes and speculated that the United States would become the center of the study of Chinese art and Sinology and that the greatest collections of Chinese art would be preserved here after the war.

Chen was already familiar with Chinese bronzes in foreign collections and had written a two-volume catalogue of them for a commercial press in Shanghai in 1941, although with the disruption of the war it was never published. In 1945, he was invited by the Art Institute of Chicago to survey its collection of bronzes. His work was published a year later, under the authorship of both Chen and Charles Kelley, the museum's curator of Oriental art. Chen's contribution can be found in the catalogue's extensive, scholarly entries, which are introduced by a succinct account of the history and function of ancient bronzes, from the Shang through the late Western Zhou dynasties and Chan Kuo period. Where the bronzes have inscriptions, those are reproduced. And where there are similar examples in the United States, those are noted.

A year later, Chen was back in China at Qinghua University. He had recently completed his study of Chinese bronzes in American collections and was seeking a publisher. In 1952, he accepted a position at the Institute of Archaeology, Chinese Academy of Social Sciences. There he continued to publish actively on inscriptions, bronzes, and oracle bones. By 1957, however, he was being attacked by the anti-rightist movement in part for having lived in the United States. And in 1963 he was made to wear "the hat," by which he was publicly denounced. His American study appeared in 1960, without his participation, in two volumes under the title, *Shang and Zhou Bronzes Stolen by the American Imperialists*.

Chen's political troubles began when he disagreed publicly with Mao's campaign to modernize the Chinese writing system in the 1950s. The Chinese leader hoped even to replace Chinese characters with an alphabet. Chen spoke openly of his opposition to the proposed reforms. He was a scholar of ancient writing and admired its beauty and rich allusiveness. He was also a distinguished, published poet. In 1957, a young scholar, who had once worked closely with Chen, published an article critical of the older scholar's (until then) definitive writings on oracle bones, the foundation of our knowledge of earliest China. The article's author, Li Xueqin, wrote that Chen "has not presented anything substantial enough to match his arrogance . . . [and that] he neglects many essays and theories of other scholars, instead collecting only his own ideas. . . . This self-boasting attitude should not be accepted by us."

Li Xueqin remains a major figure in Chinese archaeology and early history. He has written widely on oracle bones and ancient bronzes. And he is the director of the Xia-Shang-Zhou Chronology Project, funded by the central government to establish exact dates for China's early cultures. The project is controversial inside and outside China. While it funds important archaelogical work, it is thought to be politically motivated and many of its conclusions are judged spurious at best. Previously, the earliest date in Chinese history for which there is sufficient archaeological and textual evidence had been 842 B.C. Using new scientific analyses, Li's project has established an earlier date of 1046 B.C. But this is only a start. The Chronology Project is preparing for a new initiative on the origins of Chinese civilization, which it expects to be able to date much farther back. Li admits that some critics believe he and his group are trying to extend Chinese history for political reasons. "But this isn't true. We just want to figure out how China developed. It's no different from studying ancient Greece, or Egypt, or Israel. These other ancient cultures have all been studied more than China. And China has a special characteristic: it still exists, whereas the others have all disappeared."

Li Xueqin is also head of an advisory committee to the Poly Art Museum, a private museum with ties to the People's Liberation Army. His is the final voice in approving the museum's acquisition of Chinese antiquities. The museum is dedicated to buying back for China what it believes to be important national cultural treasures. The museum has an extraordinary, if small, collection of early bronzes as well as an exquisite collection of mostly Northern Wei and Northern Qi stone sculptures. It is serious about its installation standards, having just moved into new space in a new Poly Group headquarters in Beijing. Its cases and lighting are standard setting for Chinese museums and the equal of the best museums in the world, and its publications are thorough and exacting. In both its installation labels and published catalogues, it takes pains to reproduce ancient inscriptions found on its bronzes. But it almost never publishes an object's provenance, because its collections do not come from excavations and almost never have provenance. They are "bought back" for China from foreign collections, the sources of which remain unknown. Many of the bronzes have been purchased from European dealers who bought them from Hong Kong dealers who got them from "old collections." None of this is documented, however. And none need be. The important thing is that the Poly Art Museum is bringing them home to China, returning them "to their native place, putting an end to their wicked fate of wandering without proper shelter," as the museum proclaims.[4]

❋ ❋ ❋

I recount these stories to make a simple point. The real argument over the acquisition of undocumented (unprovenanced) antiquities is not what it appears to be. It is not really between art museums and archaeologists, about the protection of the archaeological record from looting and illicit trafficking in antiquities. It is between museums and modern nation-states and their nationalist claims on that heritage. Archaeologists are part of the argument as allies of those states (or "source" nations; those with ancient remains within their jurisdiction). Archaeologists encourage the institution of nationalist retentionist cultural property laws, believing them to be important to the protection of archaeological sites. That their work is used by source nations for nationalist political purposes is the price archaeologists pay for excavating within national jurisdictions.[5]

When I have made this point at various conferences, archaeologists have objected, arguing that they can not be held accountable for how national governments misuse their work; they are mere scientists, disinterested scholars using scientific methods to uncover the early history of humankind. Some have even argued that the misuse of their work is no different than the way national governments misuse museum work. After all, national museums are important instruments in the formation of nationalist narratives: they are used to tell the story of a nation's past and confirm its present importance.

That may be true of national museums, but it is not true of encyclopedic museums, those whose collections comprise representative examples of the world's artistic legacy. National museums are of local interest. They direct attention to a local culture, seeking to define and legitimize it for local peoples. Encyclopedic museums direct attention to distant cultures, asking visitors to respect the values of others and seek connections between cultures. Encyclopedic museums promote the understanding of culture as always fluid, ever changing, ever influenced by new and strange things—evidence of the overlapping diversity of humankind. Take, for example, just six objects in the collection of the Art Institute of Chicago.

1. This *fangding*, or rectangular caldron, made of bronze and dating from the Shang dynasty, ca. 1700–ca. 1050 B.C., was acquired by the Art Institute in 2004 (fig. 1, p. xx).[6] Especially striking for its stately dignity and architectonic elegance despite its diminutive size (8.5 inches high), the caldron's decoration includes a pair of profile birds with long, trailing tails and feathers cast in high relief against a background of squared spirals or *leiwen* above a margin of rounded forms that frames a panel of squared spirals resembling interlocked Ts. Its round, stout legs are decorated each with relief ogre masks (*taotie*). In form and quality and bold character of its casting, the caldron is typical of the late bronze art of the Shang, who ruled north central China along the lower reaches of the Yellow River during the second half of the second millennium B.C.

Bronze casting requires an abundance of copper and a highly developed technology for converting the natural material into bronze and casting it into the resulting forms (excavations have unearthed more

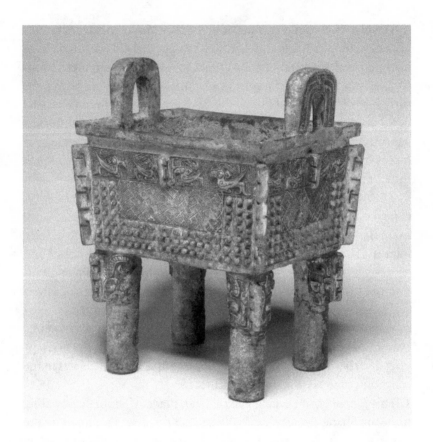

Figure 1. *Fangding*, 12th/11th century B.C. China, Shang dynasty Bronze (8 %₁₆ × 6 ¾ × 5 ½ in.) Avery Brundage, Russell Tyson, and Alyce and Edwin DeCosta and Water Heller Endowments; General Acquisitions Fund, 2004.701

than 350,000 metric tons of slag from a single, ancient mine!). During the Shang, vessels like this were typically cast from ceramic cast molds. First a model of the vessel was sculpted from high-quality clay, then pieces of molds were pressed onto its surface. The decoration's broad design was carved on the model and transferred onto molds and further refined. After the inner model and the outer model were reassembled, molten bronze was poured into the cavity between the model and the mold. When the bronze was cool, the assembled model was removed and the resulting bronze vessel filed and polished. The advantage of this technique was the superb clarity in the cast bronze, but it required high-quality materials, aesthetic sense, and sophisticated technology. The disadvantage of the ceramic mold technique was that it left small seams of bronze between the parts. For this reason projecting flanges were elaborated into highly decorative features, such as those we see on this *fangding*.[7]

The excavations at Anyang, the richest area thus uncovered for our understanding of the Shang, were the first major excavations undertaken in China, beginning in 1928. Earlier discovery of oracle bones—found in urban medicinal shops, far from any archaelogical context—allowed scholars to document Shang life, including the important role played by ritual.[8] Among the most important rituals were those that sanctioned the kinship organization. These used bronze vessels as symbols of aristocratic authority. At the highest levels they were made to symbolize the dynastic rule of a state. Most of the bronzes found in Anyang were excavated from grave sites, where they once served in the burial rites for the deceased's ancestors, who are thought to have derived their strength in part from offerings of wine, flesh, and blood presented in bronze vessels. Just what the decoration on the vessels means is unknown and much debated. It may simply register a regard in the ritual of honoring the deceased and one's ancestors. This caldron bears an ancestor dedication cast on the interior, noting that it was made for Father Yi, and is marked with a noble clan sign.

2. A year later, the Art Institute acquired a much larger *ding* vessel, dating from the Western Zhou, the successor to the Shang (fig. 2, p. xxii). It includes an extensive inscription cast on the caldron's interior bowl and is decorated with patterns of recumbent c- and s-shapes with narrow, trailing ribbons with frilly hooks derivative from zoomorphic designs of dragons or birds on early Shang bronzes, and suggests an important symbol of statehood and royal power. Its inscription reads:

> The Grand Captain's young son Captain Wang says:
> "Illustrious august
> deceased-father Duke Jiu was beautifully capable of making
> accordant his heart and making wise
> his virtue, with which he served the past kings, and gained purity
> without flaw. Wang for the first time has gone on to emulate

xxi

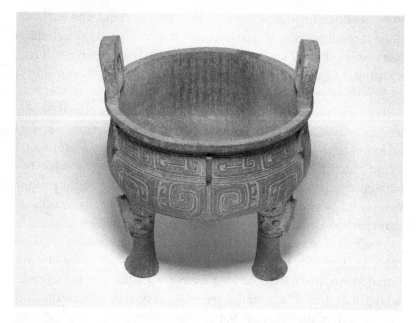

Figure 2. *Shi Wang Ding*, early 9th century B.C. China, Western Zhou dynasty Bronze (19 ¼ × 16 ⅞ in.) Major Acquisitions Centennial Fund, 2005.426

his august-deceased father, respectfully
morning and night taking out and bringing in the king's
commands, not daring not
to follow through or to manage. Because of this, the king has
not forgotten the sagely man's
descendant, and has greatly praised his accomplishments and
awarded him beneficence. Wang dares
in response to extol the Son of Heaven's illustriously fine
beneficence, herewith
making for my august deceased-father Duke Jiu this offertory
caldron; my Captain
Wang for ten thousand years have sons' sons and grandsons'
Grandsons eternally to treasure and use it."

Sometime in the eleventh century B.C., the Zhou overthrew the Shang royal house and founded a dynasty that lasted for eight centuries. Inscriptions on Zhou bronzes, like the one just quoted, are important for our knowledge of the dynasty's history. They document social and dynastic relations and ritual practices, such as Captain Wang's commissioning of this large bronze to commemorate the honor of his deceased father, Duke Jiu.[9] As with the Shang *fangding*, the importance of this Zhou vessel lies in its size and quality of manufacture—the thickness of its wall, strength of its structure, and crispness and clarity of its casting—in the beauty of its design and decoration, and in the contents of its inscription. Centuries—and in the case of the Shang, millennia—before the Greeks, bronze makers in the central river valleys of China possessed a sophisticated understanding of metallurgy and a refined sense of aesthetic form and were making bronze vessels of astonishing range and quality.

3. Just steps away, in a neighboring gallery, is this bronze plaque from the Royal Kingdom of Benin, in the west of Africa (fig. 3, p. xxiv). Dating from the late sixteenth or early seventeenth century, the plaque (commonly referred to as bronze but actually made of leaded brass; brass being an alloy of copper and zinc rather than copper and tin as bronze is), probably once decorated a pillar in a courtyard of the royal court.[10]

Much of the Benin Kingdom was located in what is now the Edo State in the southwest of Nigeria. According to oral history, the kingdom was founded in mythological times by the Ogiso rulers, the first royal dynasty of Benin (until ca. A.D. 1200). The earliest European reports date from three centuries later, with the arrival of the Portuguese. Over the next five hundred years, Benin carried out a prosperous trading relationship with the Portuguese, British, Dutch, and French, exchanging pepper, ivory, cotton, textiles, redwood, palm oil, ivory, and slaves for a diverse set of European luxury goods, including European and Indian textiles and fine silks, hats, and Mediterranean coral. In the late nineteenth century, the Benin coast was dominated by the British. In 1897, violence erupted between the British and forces loyal to the Benin king. As retribution for the deaths of members of the British mission, a punitive exhibition was organized, which occupied the royal city of Benin in 1897 and led to the removal of hundreds of Benin bronze plaques, brass sculptures, and ivory tusks to Britain. The British Museum acquired a number of them and the rest

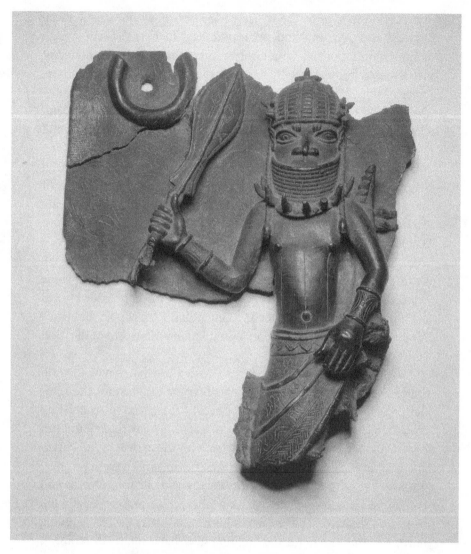

Figure 3. *Plaque with Courtier*, 16th/early 17th century Edo, Court of Benin Bronze
(13 ⅜ × 11 ⅜ × 1 ⅞ in.) Samuel P. Avery Fund, 1933.782

were distributed throughout Europe, mostly to museum collections
in Germany and Austria, while a few made their way to the United
States, including this one in the Art Institute, which was acquired by
the museum in 1933.

The bronze reliefs have no parallel in African art. Their quality of manufacture and formal elegance even led some European intellectuals to propose very early contacts between Benin and Europe; how else, it was asked, could Africans have produced them? (The celebrated, early-twentieth-century German mathematician, Frobenius, even argued on the evidence of a passage in Plato, which describes an island far beyond the straits of Gibraltar surmounted by a large castle ornamented with bronzes, that the Benin bronzes derive from—and even *prove* the existence of—Atlantis!) The bronze plaques typically portray figures who, by their clothing and attributes, can be identified by their specific function in the Benin court hierarchy. The court's power structure, of which much is known through oral and written history and recent anthropological research and studies, was characterized by a complex system of hereditary and nonhereditary titles. The king, or Oba, was distinguished from a courtier, drummer, hornblower, or other kind of attendant by his costume, decorative attributes, and handheld elements. He sat at the top of a hierarchy which included multiple layers of chiefs (Uzama chiefs—closest to the Oba—town chiefs, and palace chiefs), a state council, district administrators, and affiliated guilds. In this plaque, the male figure wears a coral-studded cap and high coral-beaded collar, indications of his courtly rank, and carries an *eben*, or ceremonial sword. Typically, a courtier would carry an *eben* in court rituals, tossing and twirling it many times to pay homage to the king and and show fealty to him. Similar rituals were performed before the Oba's ancestral shrines.

4. Such royal ancestral shrines included carved elephant tusks, often inserted into pedestals in the form of bronze heads of Obas. This mid-nineteenth-century tusk, acquired by the Art Institute in 1976, was among more than hundred that came from ancestral shrines in Oba Ovonramwen's palace (fig. 4, p. xxvi).[11] It would have protruded upward from the center of the crown of a bronze head and served as a focal point for a commemorative celebration of sacrifice dedicated to the spirt of the Oba's deified father. Carved on the length of its surface are nine rows of motifs, the most important of which are in the center of each row, which would have been clearly visible from the altar. The most significant motif in the second row is the Oba Ewuare the Great,

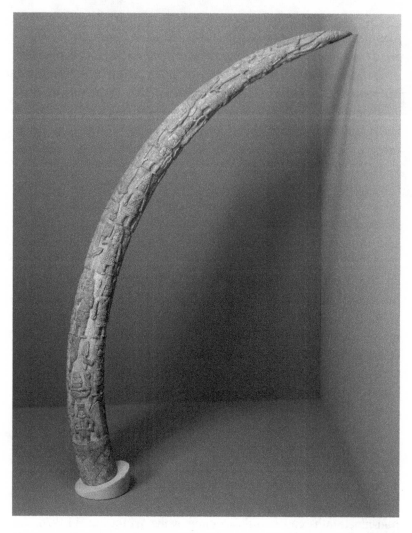

Figure 4. *Royal Altar Tusk*, 1850/1888 Edo, Court of Benin Ivory (58 ¼ × 77 × 5 in.) Gift of Mr. and Mrs. Edwin Hokin, 1976.523

who ruled Benin in the late fifteenth century. He is often associated with a leopard and viper, which respectively gave him strength and good fortune. Here he is shown holding a coiled mudfish in each hand, symbolizing his connection to Olokun, the lord of the great waters of the world, from whom he derived his powers of creativity and destruction.

The ancestral altars provided models of the life well-lived. They commemorate a life and a reign. This is especially important in royal altars, for a king's place in history is central to the sense of identity and continuity of the Edo as a people and a nation. The combination of the ivory—with its narrative imagery—and the likeness of the Oba's head in bronze, in which the ivory is inserted, connect that particular ruler with the continuity of the dynasty and protect his role in it for all who follow him. It establishes the deceased monarch as one who once shaped—and through the power of ritual continues to shape—events important to the history of the Edo.

5. Ivory like this tusk was a much prized export commodity from Africa, and had been for centuries. An ivory box in the Art Institute, acquired in 1926, was probably made in Sicily early in the thirteenth century (fig. 5, p. xxviii). Its thin ivory plaques were carved from a thick African elephant's tusk probably obtained from Muslim traders from the Swahili coast of east Africa (who had traded for it in the interior of South Africa; likely exchanging silk and cotton obtained from trade in the Indian Ocean).[12] The Swahili lived (still live) along the coast of eastern Africa, from what is now Somalia in the north to Mozambique in the south. Their culture is ethnically diverse, largely urban, with a common language and shared Islamic faith, and is marked by a long history of commercial trade with distant ports. By the eighth and ninth centuries, contact with the Islamic world meant contact with an enormous network of trade routes along the African and Arab coasts, up the Persian Gulf and across the Indian Ocean to what is now India and Indonesia, and beyond to China. By the thirteenth and fourteenth centuries, the trading ports of Malindi, Mombasa, Zanzibar, and especially Kilwa were marked by beautifully built structures described in 1331 by the famous Moroccan traveler Ibn Battuta.[13]

Through a network of exchanges northward, trade between the Swahili coast and the Mediterranean Sea flourished during Europe's medieval period. The strategically placed island of Sicily, which was held successively over the centuries by Byzantine emperors, Fatimid

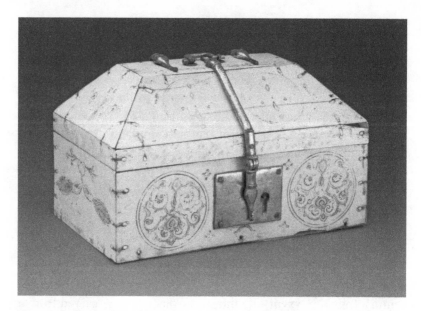

Figure 5. *Casket*, 1200/25 Sicily Ivory, brass, tempera, and gold leaf (3 ⅞ × 6 ¼ × 3 ¼ in.) Samuel P. Avery Endowment, 1926.389

rulers, and Norman kings, participated actively in this trade. The decorations on this box are evidence of the island's rich and diverse artistic inheritance. Its arabesques, gazelles, peacocks, and the formulaic inscription in Arabic ("May glory endure") derive from Islamic metal works and ceramics; as does its use of gold and vivid tempera colors, now visible only in traces. Such Islamic works were typically traded from the Levant or Egypt—especially metal bowls, buckets, and caskets decorated with inlaid metal arabesques—and were especially prized for their exoticism and magnificence. That this box was likely first used to hold jewelry or other domestic valuables and later used as a Christian reliquary (many similar ones still remain in church treasuries) is no contradiction. Its status as a luxury good, made of costly materials and exquisitely ornamented, made it a perfect receptacle for the relics of a saint, the most precious of all items for its Christian owner. And its decorative references to the Biblical east (the Levant and the Islamic lands, generally) made this point all the stronger.

6. The transformation of objects through trade between Europe and Islamic Egypt is evident in this beautiful fourteenth-century German monstrance, once a highly prized part of an ecclesiastical treasury, known commonly as the Guelph Treasure (fig. 6, p. xxx).[14] The term "monstrance" derives from the Latin *monstrare*—to show. During this period, changes in the church's liturgical practices called for the public display of relics during the celebration of the Mass, giving monstrances pride of place on altars.

Made of gilt silver, the Art Institute's monstrance is in the shape of a medieval church building, complete with two buttresses and a small chapel surmounted by a delicate crucifix. At its center is a translucent, rock crystal bottle, within which is said to be a tooth of Saint John the Baptist (identified by an inscription on a small piece of paper in the relic's linen wrapping). The bottle itself was originally a perfume bottle made in Fatimid—Muslim—Egypt. There rock crystal was especially prized as the most precious of stones, celebrated for uniting "the fineness of air with the quality of water."[15] When the eleventh-century Fatimid rulers fell on hard economic times, much of the caliph al-Mustansir's palace treasury was looted, sold, or disappeared. Chronicles of the day report that tens of thousands of gold, silver, precious stone, and rock crystal objects either left Cairo or were melted down during the crisis of 1070–71. The Byzantine court in Constantinople was probably the foremost recipient of these goods, no doubt many of which, in turn, came to Europe when Venetian ships sacked Constantinople during the Fourth Crusade in 1204. (The Islamic rock crystal and cut glass objects in Venice's Saint Mark's Treasury were probably acquired in this fashion.) Others made their way on to the European market, where they competed with others circulating having been purchased directly in the bazaars of Cairo during the preceding two centuries.[16]

When the maker of the Art Institute monstrance was looking for a beautifully crafted, transparent object into which he could place the saintly relic, he turned to this piece of rock crystal. Its multifaceted surface refracts lights and enhances the glimmer of the gilt metal surround. It is as if a boundless aura of light lies at the center of this miniature church building. And within it, seemingly held by the

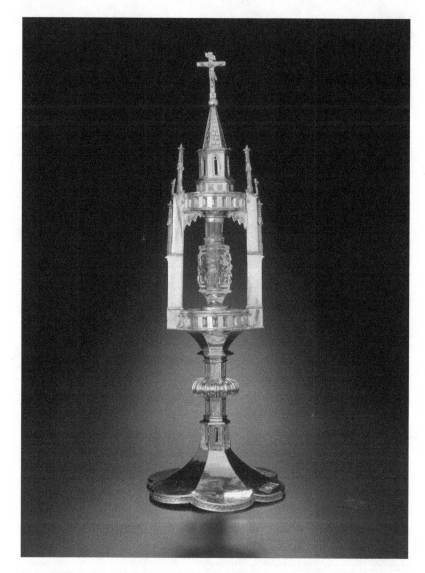

Figure 6. *Monstrance with Tooth of Saint John the Baptist,* 1375/1400 Germany, Lower Saxony, Brunswick Gilt silver (17 ⅞ × 5 ¼ in.) Rock crystal, 900/1000 Egypt, Fatimid dynasty Gift of Mrs. Chauncey McCormick, 1962.91

power of magic and belief itself, is the precious relic of the Baptist. Nothing could be more appropriate for housing such a precious thing, or better represent the later Medieval church's regard for beautiful things in and of themselves and for how they further endow holy things with visual power. That this rock crystal bottle, which probably originally held perfume, was made in and for a Muslim culture, was either of no interest or of very special interest indeed. Its origin in Fatimid Egypt—or generally, as with the ivory box, from the East, the Biblical lands—was reinforcing of the relic's claim to be from the Baptist himself: container and its contents, one and the same.

❊ ❊ ❊

What have we learned from this brief glimpse at six objects installed in just three neighboring galleries of the Art Institute? We have traveled halfway around the world and over thousands of years, from what is today China to Nigeria, Egypt, Sicily, and Germany. We have seen how bronze is worked magnificently in two, seemingly very different cultures; and how in each of the courts of the Zhou and Benin, objects were used to document courtly history and dynastic relations. We have also seen how in these courts, as in Medieval European Christian communities, precious objects were central to ritual practices, and how these rituals venerated, sometimes included pieces of, or were buried with human bodies. We have seen how objects move about the world through trade or because of economic hardship, looting, and violence. And we have seen how different cultures use, reuse, and transform other cultures' objects or decorative motifs, either indifferently or because they add value to the object in its new cultural setting. And in each instance, we have admired the beauty and workmanship of the object and the sophistication of the culture within which it was produced. Unsuspected connections were made between cultures, and great distances in space and time were overcome.

This is the promise of the encyclopedic museum: the museum as a repository of things and knowledge, dedicated to the dissemination of learning and to the museum's role as a force for understanding, tolerance, and the dissipation of ignorance and superstition, where the artifacts of one time and one culture can be seen next to those of other times and other cultures without prejudice. This is the concept of the museum dedicated to ideas, not ideologies, the museum of international, indeed universal aspirations, and not of nationalist limitations, curious and respectful of the world's artistic and cultural legacy as common to us all.

Nationalist cultural politics and their legal instruments—nationalist retentionist cultural property laws—argue against these values and call for the return of cultural artifacts to national jurisdictions. They claim ownership of the world's ancient heritage. They declare antiquities found within the borders of modern nations as the cultural property of particular nations. And they claim cultural, spiritual, even racial descent from the ancient peoples who made those antiquities. The Parthenon Marbles should be returned to Greece because they are *of* Greece; they embody its spirit and connect modern Greeks to their ancient ancestors and confirm ancient legitimacy on their modern government. The Rosetta Stone should be returned to Egypt because "it is the icon of our Egyptian identity" (in the words of Zahi Hawass, director of the Supreme Council of Antiquities in Cairo). Its importance lies in the role it played in deciphering ancient Egyptian hieroglyphs from which the history of ancient Egypt has been written as the origins of modern Egypt. And Chinese antiquities belong in China. They are evidence of China's long and glorious history, which lives still in the present, in the living culture of modern China. That they are currently outside China is a sad reminder of the nefarious doings of foreign imperialists and of treasonous politicians who removed much of the Imperial collection to Taiwan on the eve of the Communist victory. Greece, Egypt, and China have each enacted strict cultural property laws investing ownership of antiquities found or thought to have been found within their state jurisdiction: they are state property and their export is forbidden without state permission.

The international archaeological community has allied with national governments in encouraging such laws (and the bilateral treaties and international conventions which reinforce them) because it believes they protect archaeological sites from looting and destruction.

And yet, by any measure, they have failed to do so. Archaeological sites continue to be looted and destroyed at an alarming rate. All of the cultural property laws in force over the past four decades have not stopped—*cannot* stop—this. They are a failed regime. Calling for more and ever more restrictive laws will make no difference. Archaeological sites will continue to be looted so long as there are people anywhere in the world willing to pay money for looted antiquities, and so long as there are people living in poverty and the chaos of war and sectarian conflict who are willing to break the law to uncover and sell them. Looting is not a leisure time activity. It is an act of desperation. And people living desperate lives will continue to loot. And archaeological sites will continue to be destroyed. And not only through looting, but through war itself, rampant development, and environmental catastrophes.

The question then is: should the fate of the archaeological record—and of antiquities alienated from their archaeological context—remain under the jurisdiction of national governments? Is there an alternative? Yes. And it was once in place and encouraged the scientific excavation of the archaeological record and the preservation and sharing of ancient artifacts between local governments and international museums. It is called *partage*. Under that policy, foreign-led excavation teams provided the expertise and material means to lead excavations and in return were allowed to share the finds with the local government's archaeological museum(s). That is how the collections of archaeological museums at the University of Chicago, the University of Pennsylvania, and Harvard and Yale Universities were built; as well as important parts of the collections of the British Museum and the Metropolitan Museum of Art. It was also how the collections in archaeological museums in Egypt, Iraq, Afghanistan, and Turkey were built. Foreign museums underwrote and led scientific excavations from which both the international archaeological and local political communities benefited. While local tensions increased over time as nationalist aspirations took hold, *partage* served both communities well. It was only with the flood of national retentionist cultural property laws in the second half of the twentieth century that *partage* all but disappeared. The collections of the university museums mentioned above now could not be built, and the directors and faculty curators of those museums, many of whom are the loudest proponents of national retentionist patrimony/cultural property laws, could not teach and research as they do now. Much of their work is dependent on a policy no longer legal in the countries with jurisdiction over the archaeological materials they study.

If the ancient past and antiquities are important—and we can all agree they are—they are important to all of us and not only to the governments (and some citizens or subjects) of modern nations with jurisdiction over them. I will argue that the best way to preserve the archaeological record and unprovenanced or "alienated" antiquities is to encourage scientific excavation of the archaeological record, protect archaeological sites, broaden access to their finds through the restoration of partage, allow for the reasonable acquisition of unprovenanced antiquities, strengthen existing and establish new encyclopedic museums, and develop programs for sharing and exchanging collections and scholarly and professional expertise broadly.

Some readers will interpret my argument as favoring museums in the developed, first world at the expense of those in the developing, third world. Nothing could be farther from the truth. That encyclopedic museums are currently predominantly in the developed world is not an argument against the idea of the encyclopedic museum. Indeed, the promise of the encyclopedic museum is an argument for their being everywhere, in both the developed and developing world, wherever people are broadly curious about our common past, from New York to London, Berlin, Istanbul, Cairo, Lagos, Mumbai, and Tehran, Beijing; everywhere.

Neil MacGregor, the director of the British Museum, is articulate about the cosmopolitanist aspirations of the encyclopedic museum. He likes to point out that the British Museum was established for the whole world on the premise that the study of things gathered together from all over the world would reveal the truth and "not one perpetual truth," in MacGregor's words, but "truth as a living, changing thing, the truth constantly remade as hierarchies are subverted, new information comes, and new understandings of societies emerge. And as such truth emerged, it was held, it would change those societies and the result would be tolerance." The British Museum's collection was formed as a means to knowledge and a way of creating a new kind of citizen for the world. That it was in London was only because London met its founder's terms: his collection would be kept together and would be open, free to any and all interested persons. It could easily have been in another European capital but at the time, London was the most cosmopolitan and largest city in all of Europe. It was presumed that more—and *more different*—people would experience the collection in London than anywhere else. And that was most important to the museum's founder. "Sir Hans Sloane gave his collection for a purpose, more than to a place," MacGregor points out. "The place was important only in so far as it advanced the purpose for which Sloane gathered and gave his collection of wonderful things. He wanted the museum to be where it would best be used by a large number of people, international people as much as possible."[17]

This is why the British Museum was founded in London. And just as it is important to engage with the diversity of the world's cultures under one roof in London, it is important to do so everywhere. Building encyclopedic collections in itself, wherever it can be done, is important for the preservation of the world's artistic culture and for the encouragement of global understanding. And not just global understanding in terms of other people and other cultures elsewhere, but in terms of other people and other cultures here, where we live, at home. The world is becoming increasingly diverse, although not everywhere, of course. Economic and political circumstances conspire against open and free migration across the globe. But wherever the patterns of human migration are taking people—to Paris, London, Rome, New York, Chicago, and smaller cities in every hemisphere (about 3 percent of the world's population, or nearly 200 million people, lived outside the country of their birth in 2005)—living conditions are becoming more and more diverse and are requiring ever greater and more sensitive understanding of and respect for the differences and similarities between cultures.[18]

This is why I am arguing against nationalist retentionist cultural property laws. They nationalize and fail to protect our ancient heritage, and they conspire against a greater understanding and appreciation of the world's many, diverse cultures. No culture of any consequence is free of influences from other cultures. All cultures are dynamic, mongrel creations, interrelated such that we all have a stake in their preservation. National retentionist cultural property laws deny this basic truth. They depend on the myth of pure, static, distinct, national cultures. And not just about living cultures, but about ancient cultures, too. They define and seek to regulate access to ancient cultures on the grounds that they belong to the modern nation as the work of its descendents and the origins of its modern culture and identity. They promote a sectarian view of culture and encourage the politics of identity at a time when nationalism and sectarian violence are resurgent around the world.

Museums and archaeologists can agree on this: the argument over antiquities is not between us. It is really between us and nation-states with nationalist retentionist cultural property laws. We, museums and archaeologists and the public we serve, all have an equal stake in the matter. The situation is grave, to be sure. We are losing ground against the destruction of the archaeological record through war, environmental damage, economic development, looting, and acts of nature, and against the rise of nationalism and its claim on antiquity and on culture, generally. We cannot afford to waste time debating the same tired question of whether or not museums should acquire unprovenanced antiquities. That just won't do. We can do better. We have to.

Many people deserve mention for their invaluable assistance with this project, more than I can acknowledge here. Hanne Winarsky and Brigitte Pelner of Princeton University Press shepherded this book through editing and publication with care and diligence. At the Art Institute of Chicago, Maureen Ryan, Lisa Burback, Dorothy Schroeder, Julie Getzels, Robert Sharp, and Jack Brown and his staff at the Ryerson and Burnham Libraries helped in numerous ways, as did Jay Xu and Elinore Pearlstein. Colleagues with whom I have discussed this topic over the years, including Kwame Anthony Appiah, Jonathan

Bloom, Sharon Cott, Steven Kinzer, Josh Knerly, James Lally, Neil MacGregor, John Henry Merryman, Philippe de Montebello, and Timothy Potts, and colleagues with whom I have disagreed on conference panels, in print, and in hallways at meetings, as well as students in seminars and lectures, and friends and colleagues who have read parts of this manuscript, and the perceptive anonymous readers commissioned by Princeton University Press; all have refined and helped shape my understanding of the intellectual and professional principles and practices that inform art museums and archaeologists in their work, and just what is at stake in seeking common ground for the resolution of our differences.

James Cuno

WHO OWNS ANTIQUITY?

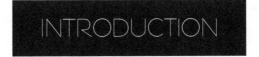

INTRODUCTION

The Crux of the Matter

Consciously or subconsciously, archaeological interpretation and the public presentation of archaeological monuments are used to support the prestige or power of modern nation-states.
—Neil Asher Silberman[1]

For years, archaeologists have lobbied for national and international laws, treaties, and conventions to prohibit the international movement in antiquities. For many of these years, U.S. art museums that collect antiquities have opposed these attempts. The differences between archaeologists and U.S. art museums on this matter has spilled over into the public realm by way of reports in newspapers and magazines, public and university symposia, and specialist—even sensationalist—books on the topic.[2]

At the center of the dispute is the question of unprovenanced antiquities. In conventional terms, an unprovenanced antiquity is one with modern gaps in its chain of ownership. As it pertains to the United States, since in most cases we are an importer of this kind of material, this means there is no evidence that the antiquity was exported in compliance with the export laws of its presumed country of origin (these are always *modern* laws, hence the qualification above, *modern* gaps). Archaeologists argue that unprovenanced antiquities are almost always looted from archaeological sites or from what would become archaeological sites. But strictly speaking, since provenance is a matter of ownership and not archaeological status, and as some countries allow for the ownership of antiquities but not their export, it is possible to illegally export a legally owned, unprovenanced antiquity. (It would have to be either an excavated antiquity that could be legally owned, or a found or looted antiquity owned by someone, if not by its current owner, before the implementation of anti-looting laws.) For nationalist reasons, some countries—we will see this is the case with China—allow for the legal import and ownership of unprovenanced and even suspected looted antiquities, but not their export.

Because it can make complex matters appear simple, and attractively controversial, the public discourse around the acquisition of unprovenanced antiquities has focused largely on the legal aspect of their ownership: either they are owned legally or they aren't. This does not mean, of course, that legal disputes over ownership are easy to resolve. As is always the case in matters of law, everything turns on evidence. Is there convincing evidence that the unprovenanced antiquity was removed from its country of origin in violation of that country's laws? Indeed, is there convincing evidence that allows us to identify its country of origin? Just because an antiquity looks Roman, do we have any evidence that (1) it was unearthed within the borders of the modern state of Italy, as opposed to elsewhere in the former Roman Empire; and (2) that it was unearthed since the implementation of restrictive Italian export and ownership laws? And what would constitute convincing evidence? An eyewitness's testimony? A confession? Some kind of convincing documentation? Rarely does such evidence exist. And since unprovenanced antiquities, like all works of art in the collections of U.S. art museums, "belong" in fact or principle to the public, U.S. art museums are obliged to keep the unprovenanced antiquity until a preponderance of evidence convinces both parties that it should be turned over to the claimant party.

In a few recent cases, U.S. art museums have been charged by foreign state authorities with having in their collections unprovenanced antiquities alleged to have been illegally removed from their (presumed) country of origin. After a review of the evidence in three of those cases, and without going to court, the art museums either returned the antiquities in question or came to an agreement to

2

return some of them.[3] In other cases, claims were made only through the press, with evidence hinted at but not shown to the charged museums. The museums rushed to deny the allegations and called for a review of the evidence. But by then the damage had been done: the public had read that the museums were in the possession of stolen property and that somehow, somewhere, a theft had occurred.[4]

Most often it falls to the museum to prove that it has the right to keep the questioned unprovenanced antiquity. A foreign authority— often a ministry of the government, such as the judicial or cultural ministry; rarely, if ever, the executive or legislative branches, what we might more accurately call the foreign *government*—makes a claim and implies that it has evidence to back it up. In the court of public opinion, the burden of proof falls to the museum to show that it has positive evidence to the contrary: that the unprovenanced antiquity entered its collection legally. And proving one's innocence in the blinding light of a public dispute can be very difficult, especially when "convincing" evidence is likely never to be found.

By far most unprovenanced antiquities were acquired by museums long before the adoption of international agreements between nations and/or the implementation of those agreements by the U.S. government and before the U.S. courts enforced foreign patrimony laws under the U.S. National Stolen Property Act. The United States only signed on to the UNESCO Convention on the Means of Prohibiting and Preventing the Illicit Import, Export, and Transfer of Ownership of Cultural Property in 1983, thirteen years after it was adopted. Before 1983—and even for some years after—it was enough for U.S. art museums to perform due diligence and make a good faith effort to ascertain whether or not an antiquity had been legally removed from its presumed country of origin. Without documentation testifying to its legal status—an export license, bill of sale, or some other kind of evidence of its being in a private or public collection outside the likely source country prior to the date of the relevant law in that country—a U.S. art museum had only to inquire of antiquities authorities in the likely source country as to any evidence they might have that the antiquity was illegally removed from their country, seek a review by IFAR and the Art Loss Register for any evidence that the antiquity might have been stolen, and consider the museum's relations with the donor or dealer offering the antiquity: was the donor's or dealer's reputation positive? had the art museum a long-standing relationship with him or her? did the art museum have reason to believe that the donor or dealer had the museum's best interest in mind, rather than his or her own? and ultimately, did the art museum *trust* the donor or dealer? If the art museum found no reason not to proceed with the acquisition, it could do so and then was obliged to publish and exhibit the antiquity for the public's benefit.[5] By acquiring it, the museum brought the antiquity into the public domain for the delight and instruction of everyone. If it indeed had been removed illegally from its country of origin, this would more likely be determined by its being in a public museum than by its circulating in the private realm of dealers and donors.

Things changed in 2001, when the New York antiquities dealer Frederick Schultz was indicted for (and later convicted of) conspiring to receive stolen Egyptian antiquities that had been transported in interstate and foreign commerce in violation of U.S. law, with the underlying substantive offense of violating the National Stolen Property Act. His conviction on the latter charge was a marked departure from previous cases involving similar accusations. Schultz argued that the U.S. National Stolen Property Act, under which it is against the law to import or subsequently come into the possession of stolen property, did not apply to an antiquity removed in violation of a national patrimony law like Egypt's, since such an object was not "stolen" in the commonly used sense of the word in the United States. The court disagreed and found in favor of the 1983 Egyptian patrimony law, which declares all antiquities found in Egypt to be state property and thus owned by the Egyptian nation. Anyone, or any institution, coming into possession of such articles without state authorization is necessarily in possession of stolen property and in violation of the law.

Due diligence and good faith inquiries are no longer sufficient. When weighing the risks of acquiring an antiquity for which there is no positive evidence of its legal removal from its presumed country of origin, U.S. art museums have to be much more careful. It is not simply that the antiquity might be returned. It may be that individuals within U.S. art museums will be held criminally liable.[6] As a consequence, the acquisition of antiquities by U.S. art museums has declined dramatically over the past five years. This does not mean that illegal trafficking in antiquities or the looting of archaeological sites has declined; in fact, archaeologists claim that both have increased. It means only that unprovenanced antiquities are not being acquired by U.S. art museums to the extent that they were in the past. Instead, undocumented antiquities are going elsewhere in greater numbers, either remaining in the private domain of private collectors and dealers or being sold or donated to museums in countries that do not enforce foreign patrimony laws as the United States does.[7] If undocumented antiquities are the result of looted (and thus destroyed) archaeological sites, that there is still a market for them anywhere is a problem. Keeping them from U.S. art museums is not a solution, only a diversion.

A second criticism of the acquisition of unprovenanced antiquities is that it is unethical: unprovenanced antiquities are likely to have been looted from a (now) damaged archaeological site and the destruction of archaeological sites and the loss of the knowledge they contain is bad and those who encourage it are bad as well. But archaeologists consider almost any context in which an old object is found an archaeological site. And they consider every archaeological site important, for it will likely tell us something we wouldn't otherwise know, and that is good.

Was every unprovenanced antiquity at some point in an archaeological site? It depends on the definition of an archaeological artifact, what I am calling an antiquity. The general, political definition of an antiquity (as it is used in political agreements and national laws) is an object that is more than 150 years old. Often they are included among all manner of things more properly called "cultural property." Recent requests by the governments of Italy and the People's Republic of China to have the U.S. government impose blanket restrictions on the import of a range of materials were based on the premise that such restrictions would protect archaeological sites, since they would not allow for the import of looted and illegally exported antiquities.

But the requests were very broad. In Italy's case, it included stone sculpture, metal sculpture, metal vessels, metal ornaments, weapons/armor, inscribed/decorated sheet metal, ceramic sculpture, glass, architectural elements and sculpture, and wall paintings dating from approximately the ninth century B.C. to approximately the fourth century A.D.; that is, virtually every kind of object produced in or imported to the land we now call Italy over 1,200 years of recorded human history. In China's case, it was even more broadly defined, covering all manner of things from the Paleolithic period through the end of the Qing dynasty (A.D. 1911); by its own estimation, some 20,000 years of human artistic and material production, including everything from bronze, gold, and silver vessels to textiles, painting, calligraphy, lacquer, wood, and bamboo objects, and ceramics of all kinds. Clearly, these items are not all equally ancient in the common use of the term, nor are they all archaeological artifacts. Many of them were made for the trade and circulated in the trade for hundreds if not thousands of years. It is unlikely that each artifact was removed from an archaeological site. The promiscuous slippage between the terms "antiquities" and "cultural property" in the public and governmental discourse on the acquisition of unprovenanced antiquities is unhelpful, and, as I discuss below, is intended to support a nation's nationalist aspirations rather than the stated goal of protecting archaeological sites.

Why are archaeological sites looted and unprovenanced antiquities sold? Because, the archaeologists' argument has it, antiquities have commercial value. If they had no commercial value, they would not be looted and sold. They would remain in the ground for archaeologists to excavate, and would enter local site or national museums with knowledge of their archaeological context intact and would be there for people to enjoy as sources of inspiration and learning. But of course, until such time as antiquities have no commercial value, it is reasonable to assume that archaeological sites will be looted and unprovenanced antiquities sold. How to deprive antiquities of their commercial value, and thus how to protect archaeological sites and preserve the knowledge they contain? Stop buying them. Of course, people should also stop looting and selling them, but that falls to source nations to enforce. And that is extremely difficult: they would have to police all known and suspected archaeological sites within their borders and fully police their borders to prevent illicit export of antiquities. It is unlikely that this can be done: there are too many sites, national borders are too porous, and the nations themselves are too poor. Rather, it should be up to the acquiring (sometimes called "collecting") nations to enforce restrictions against importing and buying unprovenanced antiquities. And when these countries no longer allow for the import or purchase of unprovenanced antiquities, all other nations will follow; then there will no longer be a market for such artifacts and archaeological sites will no longer be looted. Of course there may still be people and institutions willing to risk looting and buying unprovenanced antiquities illegally. But one day even they will no longer take these risks, since all acquiring and source nations will enforce export, import, and ownership laws equally and the risks will be just too high (and the rewards too low). The market will finally dry up. What happens until then?

No museum has ever endorsed the looting of archaeological sites and the loss of the knowledge they contain. But in many respects, when faced with the choice whether or not to acquire an undocumented antiquity, the looting of the archaeological site has already occurred and the knowledge that may have been gained from the careful study of an antiquity's archaeological context has already been lost. Now the museum is faced with the choice of acquiring a work and bringing it into the public domain for the reasons cited above, or not acquiring it.

It is a fact that the archaeological site will not be restored or the lost knowledge recovered by a museum's decision not to acquire the antiquity. Then, putting aside the legal risks for a moment, why shouldn't a museum acquire it? Critics of museums emphasize the benefits of a "clean hands" approach. Even if it were legal to acquire unprovenanced antiquities, and even though not acquiring them will not restore archaeological sites nor recover any loss of knowledge, a museum should not acquire such works but should instead set an example for others to follow. Although in the interim archaeological sites will be looted and knowledge lost, *eventually* that will no longer

7

be the case. It is more ethical, according to this argument, to allow looted antiquities from damaged or destroyed archaeological sites to remain unknown in private hands or in museums elsewhere in the world.[8]

Often, archaeologists argue that antiquities belong to the source nations where we presume they were found; they are their property and important to the identity and self-esteem of that nation and its citizens. If a foreign museum were to acquire them, it is only because it can afford to do so as an heir to an imperial and colonial past. The argument that acquiring nations should stop acquiring unprovenanced antiquities because they are rightfully one or another source nation's cultural property (important to its national identity) is, as I have heard it once said, a means of redressing the historical imbalance of power between first- and third-world nations.[9] But power relations often have a long history. There are "source" nations in the first world (Italy, Greece, and increasingly China) and former colonizing empires in the third world (notably Turkey, as the heir to the Ottoman Empire, with its museums filled with antiquities from former imperial territories). There are even former imperial territories with rich remains of the empire's culture (Turkey, with its Greek and Roman remains; Egypt, Lebanon, Libya, Syria, and Tunisia, with their Roman remains).

The argument not to acquire unprovenanced antiquities on these grounds—because they are meaningful to the identity of the source nation and its citizens and thus in a profound way "belong to them"— would require museums with collections of provenanced antiquities to return them to their known source countries. (I'm thinking of archaeological museums with collections deriving from excavations, like those at the University of Chicago and the University of Pennsylvania.) For these too would be meaningful to the identity of the source nation and its citizens and thus would equally redress the imbalance of power that not buying unprovenanced antiquities is said to do. One can compromise in legal matters and find acceptable compromises to resolve disputes, but how can one compromise on ethical matters? Politically, one can draw a line, say 1983, having passed legislation implementing an international agreement, and behave differently going forward. But ethical reasoning would require going backward as well. Doing what is right is different than doing what is legal.

Sometimes archaeologists argue that antiquities have no meaning outside their archaeological context. If we don't know where they were found, antiquities are meaningless; of aesthetic value only. But of course antiquities have meaning outside their specific, archaeological context, all kinds of meanings: aesthetic, technological, iconographic, even, in the case of those with writing on them, epigraphic. Indeed, most of what we know about the Ancient Near East we know from unprovenanced cylinder seals and cuneiform tablets; the same is true as well of Mayan history, which we know primarily from unprovenanced ceramics. Antiquities also certainly have political meaning. They give modern nations a claim on an ancient past and legitimize politically dominant cultures as national cultures. The specifics of their archaeological contexts—of where precisely they were found, within which strata of their sites, and next to which other objects—are not necessary to these ends. Antiquities need only be claimed by one government as its cultural property. Of course, the claimant government needs to have the sovereign authority to regulate and enforce its claim. And that's the stuff of politics and political power.

Cultural property is a political construct: whatever one sovereign authority claims it to be (*property*, after all). Cultural property is presumed to have a special meaning to the powers that claim it (also to the people governed by those powers). It is said to derive from them and to be a part of them. It is central to their identity. And they are attached to it emotionally. But is that possibly true of antiquities? Antiquities are often from cultures no longer extant or of a kind very different from the modern, national culture claiming them. What is the relationship between, say, modern Egypt and the antiquities that were part of the land's Pharaonic past? The people of modern-day Cairo do not speak the language of the ancient Egyptians, do not practice their religion, do not make their art, wear their dress, eat their food, or play their music, and they do not adhere to the same kinds of laws or form of government the ancient Egyptians did.

9

All that can be said is that they occupy the same (actually less) stretch of the earth's geography.

But these differences didn't prevent the rise of "Pharaonism" in Egypt in the last decades of the nineteenth century. Until then, and despite easy contact with extraordinary remains of ancient, Pharaonic Egypt all around them, Egyptians were uninterested in their land's pagan past. Their country's significant history, so its people reasonably believed, began with the advent of Islam. Yet this all began to change with their increased awareness of outsiders' (Europeans') interest in Egyptian antiquities. In 1868, Rifā'a Rafi' al-Tahtāwī, an Egyptian scholar who had spent years in France, published a book on the history of Egypt from the beginnings to the Arab conquest. As Bernard Lewis has written, "[I]t was an epoch-making book, not only in the self-awareness of the Egyptian historiography, but also in the self-awareness of the Egyptians of themselves as a nation."[10] Many books followed, adding thousands of years to what the Egyptians knew about their own history, and a new kind of history-teaching was introduced in the schools.

This movement coincided with Egypt's separatist ambitions, as an increasingly independent province of the Ottoman Empire. It also marked a dichotomy in the Egyptian identity: between its Islamic, even Arabic language and culture, defined by its religious and communal life, and its imagined, descendent relationship from a Pharaonic past, which was defining itself in national and political terms. It also sparked opposition within the Arabic-speaking, Islamic world. The Arabic word for Pharaonism is *tafar'un*, which literally means pretending to be Pharaonic. Other Arabic countries denounced the movement as a separatist attempt to create an independent Egypt within the greater Arab or Islamic world. And religious elements criticized it as neo-pagan. Nevertheless, it encouraged newfound cults of antiquity in other Islamic countries, especially Iraq and Iran, where it reached its height in 1971. In that year, the Pahlavi shah held a great celebration in Persepolis to commemorate the 2,500th anniversary of the foundation of the Persian monarchy by Cyrus the Great. He was heavily criticized for both exalting the monarchy and proclaiming a common identity with a pagan past. As Lewis notes,

"For the shah's religious critics, the identity of Iranians was defined by Islam, and their brothers were Muslims in other countries, not their own unbelieving and misguided ancestors."[11] The shah was overthrown in an Islamic revolution eight years later and the Egyptian President Anwar Sadat was assassinated by a devout Muslim who declared afterward, "I have killed Pharoah."[12]

To include antiquities within the political construct of cultural property is to politicize them. It is to make them part of modern, national cultural politics. What is a national culture in this modern age, when the geographic extent of so many cultures does not coincide with national borders, and when national borders are often new and even artificial creations with sovereignty over the cultural artifacts of peoples no longer extant or no longer in political power? What, we are reminded over and over again while reading reports of the war in Iraq, is Iraqi national culture? Some claim there is not one, but three: Shiite, Sunni, and Kurdish. Some even claim that there is not one Iraqi nation but a weak national authority trying to govern over three nations: of Shiite, Sunni, and Kurdish character. Whatever it is, Iraqi national culture certainly doesn't include the antiquities of the region's Sumerian, Assyrian, and Babylonian past.[13]

A Lebanese man was quoted as saying recently, in the midst of the sectarian violence within his country and the conflict between Hezbollah and Israel, "If you cut me, you see Lebanon. You see the prophet Muhammad, you see Imam Ali, you see the cedars. You see everybody in my country in my heart."[14] He didn't say the ancient Roman ruins or antiquities within Lebanon's borders. The stuff of his culture—*his* cultural property—does not include antiquities before the Muslim conquest. And his culture is not the same as a Lebanese Sunni's or Christian's culture. Culture after all is personal; it is not national. People make culture, nations don't. And in particular parts of the world, especially the Middle East—including Lebanon—non-national aspects of identity, especially religion or membership in a religious community, are far more determining than national ones.

Just as national claims on identity are political claims, so are national claims on antiquities. They serve the purpose of the modern, claiming nation. When regimes change, the parameters of the claims change as well. The claims of the Ottoman Empire were different than those of the Turkish Republic, just as the claims of Iran were different before and after its revolution of 1979. National, cultural identity claims are made by those in power and reflect the interests of the powerful over those of the powerless. I explore this in some detail in the following chapters; it is enough here to note that this is as true in the United States as it is anywhere in the world. If there were a single national, U.S. cultural identity, why have we been fighting culture wars for years? We can't agree whether the U.S. cultural identity descends from Europe or from many countries, includes only the English language or many languages, is Christian or of many confessions, allows for heterosexual unions or any or all sexual unions, is pro-life or pro-choice, stands for economic liberty or economic fairness.[15] But we are clear about one thing: it does not include the antiquities found on the land within our modern borders. Those in power here over the two and one-quarter centuries we have been a nation have either ignored or dismissed these antiquities, considered them the artifacts of other, primitive cultures, or given them up to other sovereign entities within our borders: the nations of the Native American peoples.

National cultures are contested within and from outside a country. They are defined by and are meant to sustain the powerful elite within a nation, and they are defined by others as a way of distinguishing one national culture from another: ours from theirs. Antiquities play a role in this, either because the people of a modern nation feel a direct, racial link to those earlier peoples, or because more frequently a modern nation derives a particular (modern) benefit from them. That benefit may be financial, in terms of tourism, or political: important archaeological remains give a modern nation a place of prominence at international forums (such as UNESCO) that it might not otherwise have for its lack of political, economic, military, or strategic importance in the world's affairs. So, even if we agree that antiquities can play a role in the formation of a modern nation's identity, we should acknowledge that in by far the most cases it is a politically constructed role and not, as it is often argued or presumed, a "natural," indelible, almost mystical role, akin to race, language, and religion; something "felt" by all of the citizens of that nation.

The emotional, "national, cultural identity" card played by some proponents of nationalist retentionist cultural property laws is really a strategic, political card. It is used, together with the legal and ethical cards, to argue against the acquisition of unprovenanced antiquities for the reasons I have outlined above. But are these the right principles on which to regulate the acquisition and international movement of unprovenanced antiquities? The eminent legal scholar John Henry Merryman has proposed alternative principles, what he calls a "triad of regulatory imperatives." The first and most basic is preservation. How can we best protect the object and its context from impairment? Second is the quest for knowledge. How can we best advance our search for valid information about the human past, for "the historical, scientific, cultural, and aesthetic truth that the object and its context can provide"? And the third is access. How can we best assure that the object is "optimally accessible to scholars for study and to the public for education and enjoyment"? He calls this triad "preservation, truth, and access."[16]

Merryman's triad shifts our attention from the "ownership" of antiquities to their stewardship. Does it really matter who owns a particular antiquity—whether it is a museum in the first world or a nation in the third world? Museums own antiquities (and all works of art in their collections) only insofar as they hold them in trust for the public they serve. They are not in the collections of the art museum *for* the art museum. They are there for the public. And that public, which of course in the first instance is local, ultimately comprises anyone and everyone who might in some way come into contact with the museum's collections or with knowledge informed by those collections. This is why museums preserve antiquities.

So, does it mean that antiquities can best be preserved only in their presumed countries of origin? We have too many examples where that has proven not to be the case: Afghanistan and Iraq, only most recently. Critics, of course, will rightly point to the destruction of antiquities in Berlin museums during the Second World War. But is that an argument not to allow for the removal of antiquities from their place of origin? Isn't it more reasonable to allow for the maximum dispersal of antiquities, along the lines of general risk management: disperse rather than concentrate the risk? For many decades in the late nineteenth and early twentieth centuries, archaeological finds were shared between the excavating party and the local, host country through *partage*. This is how the great Ghandaran collection got to the Musée Guimet in Paris (shared with Afghanistan), the Assyrian collection got to the British Museum in London (shared with Iraq, before the formation of the modern, independent government of Iraq), the Lydian materials from Sardis got to the Metropolitan Museum of Art in New York (shared with the Ottoman Empire, now Turkey), the Egyptian collection got to the Museum of Fine Arts in Boston, a number of collections got to the State Hermitage Museum in St. Petersburg, and of course how the great collections were formed at the university archaeological museums, like the Peabody Museums at Harvard and Yale, the Oriental Institute at the University of Chicago, and the University Museum at the University of Pennsylvania. But this principle is no longer in practice. With the surge in nationalism in the middle decades of the twentieth century, it has become almost impossible to share archaeological finds. All such finds belong to the host nation and are its property. Only the state can authorize the removal of an archaeological artifact to another country, and it almost never does. Even when one lends antiquities abroad, it is for severely restricted periods of time.[17] Antiquities are cultural property, and cultural property is defined and controlled by the state for the benefit of the state.

Merryman's second principle—the quest for knowledge—would ask us to consider whether it serves our best interest in searching for knowledge to have the antiquity remain in its presumed country of origin, or to be housed elsewhere. In other words, is there a compelling reason, in terms of research and scholarship, why an antiquity should be in a particular place? One can imagine cases when it makes most sense for an antiquity to be with like things: similar artifacts from the same culture and time period. But of course this could mean that a newly discovered Ottoman ceramic ought to be in New York rather in Istanbul, or a Khmer sculpture in Paris rather than in Phnom Penh.

One can also imagine cases when it makes sense for an antiquity to be with similar artifacts from different cultures: Han Chinese ceramics with Roman and Mayan ceramics in London, and Greek classical bronzes with Han bronzes and even much later Benin and Italian Renaissance bronzes in New York. Why should we want to see an antiquity only within the country of its presumed origin? Why does it have its greatest meaning there? Why shouldn't we want to see the art and antiquities of China, for example, also in New Delhi, Athens, Rome, or Mexico City (or London or Chicago, for that matter) with examples of comparable cultural artifacts from India, Greece, Rome, and Mesoamerica?

Merryman's third principle is access. Does it serve anyone's interest to limit access to antiquities? Of course, there are preservation reasons why one might impose restrictions: they are far too fragile or susceptible to sudden changes in environment to allow their being moved around the world. But, assuming that they can be moved safely, and that the place to which they are being moved is secure, doesn't it make sense to increase access to such artifacts? Does it serve anyone's best interest to have stockpiles of antiquities inaccessible to the public, as they are in Italy and China, among other places?

Possession is power, and notions of property include notions of control. Increasingly, that control lies in the hands of governments and governments have their own, nationalistic reasons for wanting to exercise control themselves. The international agreements into which nations have entered regarding antiquities (as control property) reinforce the principle of national control. Merryman has pointed out that the 1970 UNESCO Convention defines "cultural property" in Articles 1 and 4 as, in effect, anything the authorities of a state so designate, and that skeptics might conclude that in the name of cultural property internationalism, the Convention actually supports a strong form of cultural property nationalism, leaving states free to make their own self-interested decisions about whether to grant or deny export permission in specific cases. "In this way," he concludes, "the Convention condones and supports the widespread practice of over-retention or, less politely, hoarding of cultural property."[18]

We live in a time of resurgent nationalism and sectarian violence. The United Nations was founded sixty years ago with fifty-one member nation-states. It now has 191. UNESCO grew out of a U.N. conference held in London in 1945, which was attended by forty-four countries. It now has 190 member nation-states and six associate members. A majority of these nations have either ownership laws, export laws, or some hybrid laws such as preemption rights. Nations with ownership laws, and many of those with hybrid laws, can bring charges of possession of stolen property against people and institutions holding objects covered by the relevant laws.

The world is increasingly divided: more nation-states than ever before, and more nation-states with laws that restrict the international movement in archaeological and cultural property found within their borders. The archaeological community is allying with the nationalistic programs of many of these nations, many of which are imposing tighter restrictions on the international movement in antiquities, including unprovenanced antiquities.

⊠ ⊠ ⊠

In the following chapters, I consider the political circumstances that inform the drafting of national and international laws and agreements governing the practice of archaeology and the international movement of antiquities. More often, one reads of such laws, agreements, and practices as if they were entirely free of politics: the stuff of objective science, reasoned best practice, and indifferent government regulations.

Nothing could be farther from the truth. Governments issue archaeological permits and regulate the ownership and export of antiquities, and they do this in their own interest. Which archaeological excavations are encouraged and which antiquities are deemed important to regulate and collect in national museums depends on the perspective of national governments. What keeps you and me from doing what we want with archaeological sites and antiquities is government.

And government always serves the best interest of those in power. This is as true in the United States as it is anywhere. What our government defines as worthy of regulation is what it believes to be important to the nation. Throughout this book, I use the terms country, nation, and state in the conventional sense. "Country" is used to mean a place, as in "country of origin," to refer to where on earth an antiquity was found or presumed to have been found. "Nation" refers to both the sovereign authority governing a country and the group of people held together by their identification with the nation, whether they live in the particular country or not. And "state" is used to refer to the governmental apparatus of the nation; that which enforces and of course regulates the program of a nation, which in turn rules over a country.

Nations are made, not born. They are the result of the political ambitions of a powerful group of people who seek—and succeed in gaining—control over a certain territory and its population. Once in power, leaders have to breed loyalty among their subjects or citizens (power alone is never enough, for long). And loyalty comes in great part from identifying with the nation. Identity is where one's loyalties lie. One can be a citizen of a nation for reasons of expediency (my job is good here, I prefer the educational opportunities for my children, I am dependent on its health-care system, etc.). But one can never, really, be *loyal* on those terms, and nations cannot last long on those terms. We have to believe in our nationality, and identify with nations if they are to survive. This is the source of nationalism: identity with and loyalty to a nation. And national culture is at once the means and manifestation of that belief, identity, and loyalty.

Of course, in this sense, I mean culture broadly stated: language and religion, for example, also patterns of behavior, dress, and artistic production. But I am particularly concerned with the way antiquities are used as cultural property to serve the purpose of the nation. How is it that antiquities—as artifacts of cultures no longer extant and in every way different from the culture of the modern nation—are used by the modern nation to substantiate its claim on power? On what bases and for what purposes can a modern nation claim an identity

17

with a nonexistent culture that only happened to have shared (and often only more or less) the same stretch of the earth's geography? What makes antiquities one nation's cultural property and not the world's common artistic and cultural legacy? There's only one answer: power. And power comes from a government's state authority. It's all a matter of politics.

In the chapters that follow, I offer a perspective on the politics of archaeology and antiquities. I begin with an account of the laws, agreements, and policies that govern the international movement in antiquities, especially those that regulate the acquisition of antiquities by U.S. art museums. Then I consider the larger question of the politics of archaeology, internationally and historically. In the third and fourth chapters, I consider two specific cases: Turkey and China. Archaeology and the regulation of antiquities are new to both countries, and have been regulated differently according to the changes in their national governments over the past 150 years. In Turkey's case, the once polyglot and multiethnic Ottoman Empire, in which the mix of past and current, different cultures were once celebrated and a defining characteristic of the empire itself, has given way to a republic struggling to come to terms with its Islamic past and secular ambitions and in the process become almost monolingual and monocultural. What does it mean, then, that its archaeological regulations and antiquities laws privilege certain past cultures over others? What role do these regulations and laws play in the formation of the modern Turkish national, cultural identity?

In China's case, the People's Republic of China is struggling to contain what it considers to be the separatist ambitions of minority ethnic populations by controlling (some would say diluting) their cultures. And with the rise of the Chinese economy and the newfound wealth of Chinese citizens and corporations, they are buying back "for China" antiquities—even unprovenanced antiquities—offered for sale abroad. Why does the People's Republic of China allow its citizens and corporations to purchase antiquities in ways it doesn't allow foreign citizens and corporations? And why does the archaeological community in the United States support the Chinese efforts in this regard, even when they so obviously contradict its stated professional practices, those which it seeks to impose on U.S. art museums?

In the fifth chapter, I consider the question of nationalism and national and cultural identity. Much has been written on this topic recently by fiction writers, philosophers, literary critics, and university professors—and especially by those from countries we call the third world. Given that these countries comprise the primary theater for the debate over the acquisition of antiquities and the role of antiquities and archaeology in the formation of national, cultural identities, a review of these writings is of primary importance. I thus emphasize these writings, while I also consider the literature on the history and concept of nationalism itself, especially as it pertains to identity.

Finally, in an epilogue, I reflect back on identity politics and their implications for inhibiting our regard for the rich and fecund diversity of the world's culture. For this I believe is the true context in which to consider the current argument over antiquities. Nationalist retentionist cultural property laws conspire against our appreciation of the nature of culture as mongrel, overlapping, and a dynamic force for uniting rather than dividing humankind. And they dangerously reinforce the tendency to divide the world into irreconcilable sectarian, or tribal, entities. As the journalist and novelist Amin Maalouf has written:

> If the men of all countries, of all conditions and faith can so easily be transformed into butchers, if fanatics of all kinds manage so easily to pass themselves off as defenders of identity, it's because the "tribal" concept of identity still prevalent all over the world facilitates such a distortion. It's a concept inherited from the conflicts of the past, and many of us would reject it if we examined it more closely. But we cling to it through habit, from lack of imagination or resignation, thus inadvertently contributing to the tragedies by which, tomorrow, we shall be genuinely shocked.[19]

Nationalist retentionist cultural property laws perpetuate this view of the world, and the preservation and access to antiquities is governed by them. This is the *real* argument over antiquities. And this is what we should be talking about. Sadly, instead we—museums and archae-ologists and the governments of retentionist nation-states—have been arguing for years about the acquisition of unprovenanced an-tiquities, and whether or not this is a threat to the integrity of the archaeological record. I am arguing that this is not the real argument, but a diversion; a surrogate argument that will, even if settled in favor of archaeologists and nation-state governments, not protect the archaeological record but only preserve nation-states' claims of ownership over antiquities found or presumed to have been found within their jurisdiction. And it will do this just as the world is being increasingly divided along nationalist, sectarian lines. And that's the danger.

Antiquity cannot be owned. It is our common heritage as repre-sented by and in antiquities and ancient texts and architecture. We should be working together to preserve and share it broadly as what is surely our common ancient heritage. That discrete antiquities have been found within the borders of a particular modern nation-state is a matter of chance. There is no natural and indelible connection between antiquities and modern nation-states. The battle over our ancient heritage today is over false claims of ownership. It is a matter simply of politics.

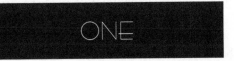

ONE

Political Matters

Since its inception as a field of study and later as a discipline, archaeology has been immersed in, and conditioned by, the economic, political, and governmental institutions of nation states.
—Don D. Fowler[1]

At my job interview for the directorship of the Harvard University Art Museums in the summer of 1990, a panel member called me aside during a break and asked my position on acquiring antiquities illegally exported from other countries. Caught off guard, primarily because it was such a hurried and almost informal question, I gave an honest, and the obvious, answer: I would never approve of acquiring objects that were illegally exported from other countries.

That was pretty much the last I thought of the matter for a few years. Then in 1996, we organized an exhibition of large-scale Roman bronzes, some of which were loaned from private collections.[2] The colleague who had queried me at my interview objected to our borrowing a work from a particular private collection and claimed that it had been purchased in contravention of international law. The work in question had been part of a controversy involving the British Museum and when I sought that museum director's advice, he assured me that so far as the British government and British Museum were concerned, the controversy was resolved and he had no objection to our exhibiting—and publishing—the Roman bronze, which we did.

Then, in 1998, we mounted an exhibition of Greek vase fragments, which we had acquired three years earlier. The fragments comprised a collection that had been assembled by Robert Guy, former curator of ancient art at Princeton University and at the time a research fellow at Oxford University. When I first saw them, I was struck by their astonishing beauty and intimacy: they were of a size to be held easily and turned in raking light to reveal the thickness of the vase body and to show the different sheens of the black slip with which they were painted and the diluted composition lines that guided the painters. In short, they were like fragmentary drawings: mysterious and beautiful things in their own right, but also aids for further study into the making of antique vases and the stylistic markings of their makers. We agreed on a price and proceeded to purchase them for the museum. A year later, we mounted an exhibition and published a catalogue of them. Every fragment was described and reproduced. Their provenance, such as we knew it, was indicated. And the objects became the subject of study in seminars and other classes.[3]

Not everyone was happy, however. I began to hear that some people "in the field" were criticizing us for acquiring unprovenanced and "obviously looted" objects. I was taken aback. To be honest, I had not thought the matter through on those terms when I agreed to purchase them. They were as I have described them: beautiful in themselves, aids for teaching, and stimuli for further study. Still, very few had any provenance and those that had any had very little (vase fragments, by their small, fragmentary nature, have been exchanged frequently and informally for centuries). We discussed the matter with the dealer and collector and got more provenance, but only some; all that could be found. We sent copies of the catalogue off to relevant Italian authorities informing them of the whereabouts of the collection and asking them for any information that might make illegitimate our having acquired the fragments. We heard nothing in response.

In the meantime, I got a telephone call from a reporter at the *Boston Globe*, inquiring about the purchase of the vase fragments. He had been contacted by scholars elsewhere (he didn't say who, how many, or where they were) who had expressed alarm at our acquiring them. I told him why we had acquired them and that they were better in our hands, in the public domain, and published for the world to know than in a private collection somewhere, whereabouts unknown. He was not convinced and seemed to take the side of the argument that we were aiding and abetting looters of archaeological sites by acquiring unprovenanced antiquities. Nothing I said moved him from this position, nor would he agree to talk with other scholars who might have a view different than the one his sources had.[4]

I was determined to learn more about the question of museums and the acquisition of antiquities. That I was late in doing so was obvious. I could still answer my colleague who asked me during the break in my job interview if I would ever acquire antiquities illegally exported from other countries: the answer was still "no." But now the question was more complex. How much information and evidence would I have to have before I could answer that question? And what if I never got complete information, or no more than I originally had? Should I acquire the antiquities anyway? If so, would I necessarily be contributing to the looting of archaeological sites or the loss of another country's cultural property? What is the relationship between antiquities and cultural property? Are all ancient objects allegedly found on or in a country's soil valued cultural property of that modern country? What laws govern this and what is the position of the United States in this matter? Is it really a scientific question or a political one?

I discussed these questions with colleagues in the hallway, at conferences, and at professional meetings. I heard some things that astonished me. The colleague who had queried me during my job interview said that she'd rather an unprovenanced antiquity be destroyed than acquired by a museum. (The same colleague removed from display in our bookshop a copy of the Royal Academy, London, exhibition catalogue *In Pursuit of the Absolute: Art of the Ancient World from the George Ortiz Collection*, 1994, on "moral" grounds because she said it encouraged the looting of archaeological sites; I had to retrieve it from her office.) Other colleagues—university colleagues, only—said that antiquities had no meaning without knowledge of their findspots (where they were found; their archaeological context).

23

Still others said that museums (and their directors) were pathologically addicted to collecting and were knowingly colluding with criminals, many of whom had ties with international organized crime and drug dealers. Nothing I said seemed to make a difference. The world was divided on this question: museums, private collectors, and art dealers were on one side and archaeologists, academics, and source nation cultural ministers were on the other. And the debates were heated.

I found myself speaking publicly on the matter, most often in law schools (they were the venues most interested in the question).[5] But I found discussions about the law—strictly speaking, about the legality or illegality of acquiring unprovenanced antiquities—insufficient, and in the end even uninteresting. They were too narrowly focused; too technical. They didn't ask why such laws were written in the first place, or what they represented about the ambitions of the nations whose laws they were. Laws are human creations. They express the social and political values of a people. And as their jurisdiction is politically determined, they represent the values of a nation. If there are laws against the acquisition of unprovenanced or undocumented antiquities, it is because politicians have judged them to be in the best interests of their citizens (or subjects).

I wanted to know what it meant that in 1983 the U.S. Congress passed (and the president signed into law) legislation enabling the 1970 UNESCO Convention on the Means of Prohibiting and Preventing the Illicit Import, Export and Transfer of Ownership of Cultural Property; why was it in the best interests of the United States and its citizens to have done so; and why it took our government thirteen years to implement the Convention. Insofar as these questions were addressed in the conferences I attended and the papers I read, it was always assumed (taken for granted) that the interests of archaeologists—the preservation of the archaeological record—are in the best interests of everyone. But are they?

Laws change. One day the majority votes differently. Governments change. Nations get divided up and borders redrawn. What was valued yesterday is no longer valued today, or at least not valued in the same way and not by the same people. I am interested in the intellectual and political context of antiquity laws. I see the law as part of a larger, political narrative: laws governing the trade in and possession of antiquities are always part of a larger narrative about the formation of modern national political identities.

This chapter—indeed, this book—is an attempt to broaden the discussion of museums and antiquities beyond a narrow consideration of what is or is not technically legal. Perforce, however, we begin with the law.

※ ※ ※

The first universal convention to deal solely with the protection of cultural property was held in 1954: the Hague Convention for the Protection of Cultural Property in the Event of Armed Conflict. Born of the trauma of World War II, its language and principles set forth an internationalist or cosmopolitan view of the value of cultural property: "Being convinced that damage to cultural property belonging to any people whatsoever means damage to the cultural heritage of all mankind since each people makes its contribution to the world;/ Considering that the preservation of the cultural heritage is of great importance for all peoples of the world and that it is important that this heritage should receive international protection;/Being of the opinion that such protection cannot be effective unless both national and international measures have been taken to organize it in time of peace."[6] Although the United States signed on to the Convention in 1954, it has never ratified it. In all, ninety-three States Parties have signed and ratified or acceded to the First Protocol of the Convention, which entered into force on August 7, 1956. Forty-four States Parties have signed and ratified or acceded to the Second Protocol, which was intended to strengthen the enforcement terms of the First Protocol and entered into force on March 9, 2004.

In 1994, Etienne Clément of UNESCO noted that among the five Permanent Members of the U.N. Security Council, only France and Russia were Parties to the Convention.[7] Since then, China has signed on as a Party to the Convention. On March 13, 2009, the United States became the 123rd nation-state to ratify the Convention.

When in times of interstate conflicts both nations are Parties to the Convention—India and Pakistan in 1971, Cyprus in 1974 (as both Greece and Turkey are States Parties), Iran and Iraq in 1980, Iraq and Kuwait in 1990, and Yugoslavia in 1991, the Director-General asks both Parties to comply to the terms of the Convention. Of course, nations can ignore these entreaties. In the end, nations make their own decisions with regard to protecting cultural property. The Second Protocol (2004), which was intended to strengthen the implementation of the Convention fifty years on, has not been signed on to or ratified by the major military powers in the world or by any of the Permanent Members of the U.N. Security Council. Archaeology and antiquities are often subject to the violence of international warfare and the maneuverings of domestic, sectarian politics. This should come as no surprise. It has always been so. No international convention—neither Hague 1954 nor any other—and no U.N. Security Council resolution can prevent this from happening.[8]

❀ ❀ ❀

Nationalism and nationalist politics bedevil international initiatives. In 1970, UNESCO passed its Convention on the Means of Prohibiting and Preventing the Illicit Import, Export and Transfer of Ownership of Cultural Property. Nationalist in perspective, UNESCO 1970 organizes the importance of cultural property ("one of the basic elements of civilization") around its value to modern nation-states:

> Considering that cultural property constitutes one of the basic elements of civilization and national culture, and that its true value can be appreciated only in relation to the fullest possible information regarding its origin, history and traditional setting,/ Considering that it is incumbent upon every State to protect the cultural property existing within its territory against the dangers of theft, clandestine excavation, and illicit export,/Considering that, to avert these dangers, it is essential for every State to become increasingly active to the moral obligations to respect its own cultural heritage and that of all nations, ... /Considering that the illicit import, export and transfer of ownership of cultural property is an obstacle to that understanding between nations which it is part of

26

UNESCO's mission to promote by recommending to interested States, international conventions to this end,/Considering that the protection of cultural heritage can be effective only if organized both nationally and internationally among States working in close co-operation.[9]

Perhaps this is inevitable. UNESCO, like the United Nations itself, exists only as a cooperative venture between nations. Nations become members of international bodies like UNESCO because they believe it is in their self-interest to do so. Any conventions written by UNESCO can only be entered into force if ratified by a sufficient number of national governments. National governments determine the fate of international conventions, both whether or not they come into force and whether or not they are adhered to. A nation can always ignore UNESCO 1970, or choose officially to denounce it: Article 23, 1–3, "Each State Party to this Convention may denounce the Convention on its own behalf or on behalf of any territory for which territorial relations it is responsible./The denunciation shall be notified by an instrument in writing, deposited with the Director-General of the United Nations Education, Scientific and Cultural Organization./The denunciation shall take effect twelve months after the receipt of the instrument of denunciation." In the end, the principles of the Convention cannot be enforced internationally. When nations ratify the Convention, they implement it by passing legislation with national jurisdiction. To the extent that individual citizens or institutions contravene the terms of the national legislation, they can only be held accountable locally, not internationally.

The United States did not pass legislation enabling UNESCO 1970 until 1983, when Congress passed and the president signed the Cultural Property Implementation Act (CPIA). France signed on to the Convention only in 1997 and the United Kingdom in 2002; Germany and the Netherlands have yet to do so. (During the 1970s, 42 nations signed on the Convention, with the highest concentration in the first years; to date 118 nations have signed.) What was the context for the United States' consideration of the Convention?

In 1969, a young art historian, Clemency Coggins, at the time a Ph.D. candidate at Harvard, now a professor of archaeology and art history at Boston University specializing in the ancient cultures of Mesoamerica, wrote what she herself calls "a jeremiad directed at my own profession, which seemed to me implicated in the burgeoning traffic in plundered Pre-Columbian antiquities." In an article in a professional journal, she traced the rise in ancient monuments stolen, mutilated, and illicitly exported from Guatemala and Mexico and declared that "not since the sixteenth century has Latin America been so ruthlessly plundered."[10] As a professional, she argued that the rights of individuals to own Pre-Columbian antiquities—which often meant, given the nature of removing and transporting them and the economics of the market, *fragments* of antiquities—did not outweigh the rights of humankind (or at least local peoples and interested scholars) to have them preserved intact and in place:

> Unlike many natural resources, our archaeological resources are not renewable. Once a site has been worked over by looters in order to remove a few salable objects, the fragile fabric of its history is largely destroyed. Changes in soil color, the traces of ancient floors and fires, the imprint of vanished textiles and foodstuffs, the relation between one object and another, and the position of a skeleton—all of these sources of fugitive information are ignored and obliterated by archaeological looters. . . . The collector buys a beautiful object about which he knows virtually nothing, and no one ever mentions to him the devastation that was created in order to deliver it.[11]

Of particular importance was Coggins's cataloguing of recent thefts of major monuments from Guatemala and Mexico (her concern was specific, not general) and its tracing of stolen and mutilated art into American museums, specifically the Cleveland Museum of Art, the Museum of Fine Arts, Houston, the Minneapolis Institute of Art, the Brooklyn Museum, and the St. Louis Art Museum, as well as to private dealers, collectors, and European museums. As the Harvard law scholar Paul Bator noted in 1982, "Dr. Coggins's account of the 'Maya crisis' played an important role in giving credibility to the contention that the illegal traffic in art treasures is a problem that has to be taken seriously."[12] U.S. art museums could no longer claim to be unaware of the problem, even if they disagreed on how best to address it.

The looting and pillaging of archaeological sites and the destruction of ancient monuments were now documented. And it was the subject of international conventions, agreements, and treaties.

At the same time, at the annual meeting of the College Art Association—the U.S. professional organization of scholars and teachers of art and art history—"eighty concerned Harvard faculty and graduate students" tried to get passed a resolution or a statement prohibiting the "increasingly destructive trade in antiquities." This broadened the issues raised in Coggins's article to a general concern about antiquities as such. But it was not immediately compelling. As Coggins reported on the meeting, "Relatively few people were even aware of the problem and when it was described many art historians doubted that it could be serious enough to warrant interfering with an art market which had operated in the United States, virtually without hindrance, or regulation for a century or more."[13]

University museums were among the first museums in the United States to address the concerns raised by Coggins. This was for obvious reasons: university museums are part of a larger set of scholarly interests and programs, any one of which might be compromised, suspended, or terminated by a foreign national body because of the university museum's alleged or actual inappropriate acquisition of an antiquity claimed by that nation as its cultural property. Among these scholarly interests or programs are archaeological excavations, teaching, training, and/or research programs, even student fellowships and faculty support. Any action by one part of the university that might affect the progress of another is subject to enhanced scrutiny and oversight.

The University of Pennsylvania Museum of Archaeology and Anthropology, renowned for its research on and collections of antiquities from the Near East and the Americas, formally adopted "The Pennsylvania Declaration" on April 1, 1970. It stated that the museum "would purchase no more art objects or antiquities for the Museum unless the objects are accompanied by a pedigree—that is, information about the different owners of the objects, place of origin, legality of export, and other data useful in each individual case." Further, it obligated the Museum to make this information public. The Declaration acknowledged the increasing illicit trade in cultural objects, "particularly antiquities, which is causing major destruction of archaeological sites in many countries throughout the world," and noted that UNESCO was discussing an international convention which would call for stricter import restrictions by the major importing countries, like the United States, United Kingdom, [West] Germany, and France (this would become UNESCO 1970). It then acknowledged that source countries would also have to impose stricter regulations on trade in antiquities within each country, for "the preservation of the cultural heritage for mankind as a whole is, in fact, a domestic problem for all nations." It concluded by declaring that "The staff of The University Museum hope that their actions taken today will encourage other museums not only in the United States but in other nations to follow a similar procedure in the purchase of significant art objects, at least until the United Nations succeeds in establishing an effective convention to control this destructive trade."[14]

The Pennsylvania Declaration was just that: a declaration. It was not a collections policy. It simply stated that the Museum director and curators needed to gather information useful in determining the pedigree of an antiquity before it could be acquired. Six years later, on May 2, 1978, the Museum adopted an Acquisitions Policy. This affirmed the principles of the earlier Declaration and those of the November 1970 UNESCO Convention, and resolutions passed earlier by the Archaeological Institute of America, the Society for American Archaeology, and the American Anthropological Association, 1973 Joint Professional Policy on Museum Acquisitions Resolution of the American Association of Museums, all of which were in support of UNESCO 1970. It then stated that its director and curators "will not knowingly acquire, by gift, bequest, exchange or purchase, any materials known or suspected to be illegally exported from their countries of origin; nor will they knowingly support this illegal trade by authenticating or expressing opinions concerning such material, and will actively discourage the collection of such material, exhibiting such material in The University Museum, or loaning University Museum objects to exhibitions of illegally acquired objects in other museums." It further stated that "The University Museum reserves the right to refuse any loans to museums or museum departments that, in its opinion, knowingly violate the UNESCO Convention."[15]

Over the next few years, claims against antiquities continued to make headlines. In 1972, the Metropolitan Museum of Art acquired the Greek vase commonly referred to as the Euphronios Krater. Almost immediately, public charges were made against the museum. The Italian government (on the presumption that it had been looted from an Italian tomb) investigated the matter but failed to produce convincing evidence; the krater would of course be the centerpiece of the 2006 agreement between the Metropolitan Museum and the Italian government resolving claims against the museum. In 1973, the California collector Norton Simon purchased a Hindu sculpture, the "Nataraja," which resulted in a high-profile claim by the Indian government, which was settled out of court in 1976. Articles documenting these and other cases attracted attention in U.S. periodicals, most notably New Yorker magazine and the New York Times.[16]

At the same time, and at the request of the U.S. State Department, the American Society of International Law formed a Panel on the International Movement of National Art Treasures to study the political and legal problems around the international trade in art objects. Paul Bator served as reporter to and a member of that Panel. In April 1970, the Panel recommended that the United States adopt certain narrow restrictions on the import of illegally exported art and "prohibit the import of illegally exported Pre-Columbian monumental and architectural sculpture and murals."[17] The Panel also studied proposed drafts of UNESCO 1970, and a lawyers' subcommittee of the Panel considered the Draft Convention and submitted a report to the U.S. Secretary of State in October. At the same time, and following Coggins's earlier article and the Panel's recommendation regarding Pre-Columbian antiquities, the United States signed a treaty with Mexico (July 1970). Two years later, Congress passed legislation prohibiting the import into the United States of monumental ancient sculptures and frescoes illegally exported from their country or countries of origin.

As Congress considered legislation implementing UNESCO 1970, legal action was taken against U.S. citizens charged with illegally trafficking in stolen antiquities. The first involved a California dealer in Pre-Columbian antiquities named Clive Hollinshead.[18] In late 1971, a curator in the Brooklyn Museum wrote the Harvard Mayanist Ian Graham, seeking his opinion on a Pre-Columbian stela that had been offered by Hollinshead. Graham had in fact discovered and documented the stela in Guatemala ten years earlier. Suspecting that the stela had been illegally removed from Guatemala, Graham notified authorities, whose investigation uncovered an elaborate smuggling network. Hollinshead was arrested and convicted in 1973 of conspiracy to transport stolen property in interstate commerce and causing the transportation of stolen property in interstate commerce, both in violation of the National Stolen Property Act. A year later his conviction was affirmed by the Court of Appeals for the Ninth Circuit.[19]

In 1977, a U.S. art dealer named Patty McClain and her four co-conspirators were convicted of conspiring "to transport and receiv[e] through interstate commerce certain Pre-Columbian artifacts . . . knowing these artifacts to have been stolen" on the basis that since 1897, "Mexican law has declared pre-Columbian artifacts . . . to be the property of the Republic of Mexico, except in instances where the Government has issued a license or permit to private persons to possess, transfer, or export the artifacts."[20] The defendants' conviction was reversed on appeal because the court ruled that the trial court had erred in charging the jury that Mexico had become the owner of all Pre-Columbian artifacts in 1897: "The court's review of the expert testimony led it to conclude that it was not until 1972 that Mexico unambiguously declared by statute that it was the owner of *all* pre-Columbian artifacts."[21] The defendants were retried and convicted for violations of the National Stolen Property Act and conspiracy to do the same. On appeal, conviction on the substantive count was reversed for reasons similar to the first appeal. But their conviction on the count of conspiracy was affirmed because of "massive" evidence that the defendants were engaged in continuing efforts to remove cultural property from Mexico; conspiracy in this case being obviously post-1972 activity. These high-profile cases raised public—and congressional—awareness of the problem of looting and illicit trafficking in cultural property, including antiquities.

The legal framework governing the trade in antiquities is basically export and ownership laws. These are meant to control the movement of cultural property, which one nation claims to be of great importance to its national identity and esteem. They are retentionist laws by intent, meant to retain a nation's self-proclaimed cultural property for itself. Export and ownership laws have increased in number dramatically over the past sixty years, just as the number of nation-states has. As I noted above, the number of member nation-states in the United Nations has almost tripled over the last fifty years. Retentionist cultural property laws exist in a majority of these nations: either ownership laws, in which antiquities found in the ground within the modern borders of the modern state are declared state property; export laws, in which specific kinds of objects, even if privately owned, can not be exported from the modern nation-state without official permission; and hybrid laws, laws that combine state ownership rights and preemption rights by which the modern nation-state has a certain period of time within which to decide to buy the privately owned object or allow its export. Half of these date since 1947; and more than half of these date from 1970. Such is the trajectory of cultural property laws that more than half of the most severe date from only the last thirty years.

Sovereign nations have the authority to define their cultural patrimony as they wish, and even to claim ownership of that property. Of course, nations may do this for a variety of reasons, but they certainly do it for nationalistic reasons. The language of UNESCO 1970 is clear on this point: "Considering that cultural property constitutes one of the basic elements of civilization and national culture, and that its true value can be appreciated only in relation to the fullest possible information regarding its origin, history and traditional setting." And when Italy requested special import restrictions by the United States under the terms of the 1983 Cultural Property Implementation Act, it emphasized this point: "These materials [covered by the request] are of cultural significance because they derive from cultures that developed autonomously in the region of present day Italy that attained a high degree of political, technological, economic, and artistic achievement. . . . [T]he cultural patrimony represented by these materials is a source of identity and esteem for the modern Italian nation."[22]

Bator criticized the broad use of a nation's power to claim anything within its jurisdiction as its national cultural property: "the national patrimony should not be defined so as to suggest that it is desirable that a nation retain all of its art, or even all of its important art."[23] John Merryman was even more critical: "[s]keptics might conclude that this Convention [UNESCO 1970], in the name of cultural property internationalism, actually supports a strong form of cultural property nationalism. It imposes no discipline on a State's definition of the cultural property that may not be exported without permission. It leaves States free to make their own self-interested decisions about whether or not to grant or deny export permission in specific cases.... In this way, the Convention condones and supports the widespread practice of over-retention or, less politely, hoarding of cultural property."[24]

But what of U.S. law in this matter? How does it regard and enforce other nations' ownership laws? Defendants—and certain legal scholars—have argued that blanket legislation "purporting to 'vest' ownership of a large class of antiquities in the state (without further steps taken to 'manifest' such ownership, whether by possession, specific designation, or otherwise) should not 'trigger' the application of the NSPA [National Stolen Property Act]." They argue that the word "stolen" should be interpreted "to cover only acts which result in the deprivation of rights of 'ownership' as that term is understood at common law."[25] This argument has been squarely rejected, however (as in the case against McClain, for example). Generally, the United States has sanctions which apply to the import or possession of stolen art; for example, the NSPA makes it a federal crime "to transport in foreign commerce goods known to be stolen, or to receive, conceal, or sell such goods."[26]

The difficulty in enforcing these laws, however, is proving that an antiquity was stolen in the absence of any evidence regarding where it was found or from which particular jurisdiction it may have been removed. Italy may claim that all antiquities found within its borders are property of the state. But how is one to know that a Roman statue came from modern Italy rather than from anywhere else in what was once the Roman Empire, especially when all that may be known about the sculpture was that it was exported from Switzerland to the United States? (It may not even be possible to determine when it was imported into the United States.)

The absence of evidence is an indication that retentionist cultural property laws—export and ownership laws—are difficult to enforce. Congress recognized this and offered foreign governments the opportunity to request emergency import restrictions on categories of material typically covered by export and ownership laws. These requests are reviewed by the President's Cultural Policy Advisory Committee, which then advises the State Department, which in consultation with the U.S. Treasury then advises the president, who decides on the matter. The review process was judged to be a fair process to weigh the implications such requests would have on U.S. interests. Congress wanted to be certain that U.S. interests in the international exchange of cultural property were maintained and that any restrictions on such trade were the result of multilateral and not unilateral action. The Senate Finance Committee report stated that U.S. import controls should be part of a concerted international effort, including the control of exports and imports, and noted that in previous years when considering various proposals for implementing legislation, a particularly difficult issue was how to formulate standards establishing that U.S. controls would not be administered unilaterally.[27]

Congress was concerned about legislating U.S. blanket enforcement of foreign ownership laws. It wanted to reconcile U.S. notions of property with those of foreign countries' ownership laws. It also wanted to reconcile foreign export laws with U.S. import laws. As Bator wrote, blanket enforcement of the former "wholly removes from the hands of the importing country both the substantive decision as to what art objects should enter the country, and the institutional decision as to the scope of the enforcement regime it is practical and desirable for it to operate."[28] Prohibiting imports in this manner is a "blank check" rule, delivering up to foreign government the decision as to what if anything the United States can import.

As it pertains to antiquities, such a policy would surrender to foreign governments the determination of what kinds of objects could enter the United States and be collected by private individuals and public institutions. Congress wanted this decision to be made locally, within U.S. jurisdiction, and not by foreign governments.

The United States finally implemented UNESCO 1970 in 1983. The enabling legislation—the Cultural Property Implementation Act—dealt with the question of local jurisdiction by instituting a review process, as mentioned above. Members of the Cultural Property Advisory Committee (CPAC), which undertakes the review, are appointed by the president for a term of three years. The process of nomination and appointment is a long and political one. Often positions on the Committee have gone unfulfilled for months, even years, compromising the intention of the law to have all interested U.S. parties participate in the review of foreign governments' requests. In 2006, the two museum positions on the Committee were filled by a retired president and the current president of the same natural history museum (the Field Museum, Chicago) with active archaeological and anthropological field research projects in foreign countries. No art museums were represented on the Committee.[29]

When the Committee receives requests from foreign governments for import restrictions on whole categories of cultural property, it holds public hearings (only summaries of the requests are made public; the full requests in the original languages are not). The Committee then deliberates in private and makes a recommendation to the State Department, which then advises the president. As the recommendation resides in the State Department, it is considered within the context of U.S. foreign policy objectives. Maria Kouroupas, executive director of CPAC, has denied to me that foreign policy has ever influenced the recommendations of the Committee; she has not denied the same with regard to the State Department's recommendation to the president. Until recently, the person in the State Department who ultimately reviews the recommendation and, in consultation with the U.S. Treasury, advises the president, was Karen Hughes, Under Secretary of State for Public Diplomacy and Public Affairs. (Hughes resigned her position in late 2007.) Hughes was appointed to her post by president George W. Bush in 2005. Her assignment, with the rank of ambassador, was to focus on ways to change perceptions about the United States abroad. Through the 1990s, she was President Bush's director of communications when he was governor of Texas, and then served as counselor to the president when he moved to Washington. In 2002, she was a member of the White House Iraq Group and was a key advisor to the Republican National Convention in 2004 and to the late stages of the president's successful re-election campaign later that year. It is impossible not to see the final determination of foreign government requests to CPAC as political: necessarily, they are part of U.S. foreign policy and must be considered together with other aspects of our nation's relations with the requesting government and that government's relations with other countries in which we have an important interest.[30]

CPAC bases its recommendations to the State Department to enter into or extend an agreement on four determinations: first, that the cultural patrimony of the requesting country is in jeopardy from pillage of archaeological or ethnological materials; second, that the requesting country has taken measures consistent with UNESCO 1970 for the protection of its cultural patrimony; third, that import controls by the United States with respect to designated objects, if applied in concert with similar restrictions implemented or to be implemented within a reasonable period of time by other market states, would be of substantial benefit in deterring such pillage; and fourth, that the establishment of such import controls in the particular circumstances is consistent with the general interest of the international community in the interchange of cultural property among nations for scientific, cultural, and educational purposes.

These are very serious considerations. They are intended to allow for the international exchange of cultural property within very specific terms: when a requesting country's cultural patrimony is not in jeopardy from pillage and when import restrictions are in keeping with the interests of the international exchange of cultural property. One can debate the application of these determinations in specific cases, and no doubt that is precisely what happens behind closed doors at CPAC meetings. But the public has no access to these debates.

They occur in private and the resulting recommendations are private; indeed, even the original request is protected information since it is received from foreign governments through diplomatic channels. All the public gets to see is an English-language summary of the request and ultimately the president's final decision. And CPAC members are prevented from revealing the content of their private *in camera* discussions by the terms of their appointment to the Committee. Some have argued that such policies are not in keeping with the intentions of Congress that informed the drafting of the 1983 legislation. Those intentions were for fair and open consideration of all requests to have the United States restrict trade in their cultural property. Otherwise, how would one know that the request met the four determinants as set forth in the law?

Take only two recent cases. In 2001, at the request of the government of Italy (and we assume on the recommendation of CPAC, although we can never know), the U.S. government imposed import restrictions on "certain archaeological material originating in Italy and representing the pre-Classical, Classical, and Imperial Roman periods of its cultural heritage, ranging in date from approximately the 9th century B.C. through approximately the 4th century A.D."[31] These materials included stone sculpture, metal sculpture, metal vessels, metal ornaments, weapons/armor, inscribed/decorated sheet metal, ceramic sculpture, glass architectural elements and sculpture, and wall paintings; that is, virtually every kind of object produced in or imported to the land we now call Italy over 1,200 years of recorded human history. It is hard to accept that *all* of these objects are worthy of restriction because they are important archaeologically or as cultural property. But this is what the memorandum essentially says. It states, for example, that "the value of cultural property, whether archaeological or ethnological in nature, is immeasurable ... such items often constitute the very essence of a society and convey important information concerning a people's origin, history, and traditional setting; these materials are of cultural significance because they derive from cultures that developed autonomously in the region of present day Italy ... [and] the pillage of these materials from their context has prevented the fullest possible understanding of Italian

cultural history by systematically destroying the archaeological record; and the cultural patrimony represented by these materials is a
source of identity and esteem for the modern Italian nation."

In other words, as the bilateral agreement would have it, the destruction of the archaeological record in modern-day Italy is prob-
lematic not because the world has lost vital information about
humanity, about the way our human ancestors lived and ornamented
their lives thousands of years ago, but because without it a full understanding of Italy's cultural history is not possible and because the lost
materials are a source of identity and esteem for the modern Italian
nation. This line of reasoning runs counter to the intention of the
U.S. 1983 legislation. It devalues the international exchange of archaeological artifacts and cultural property for the benefit of the
world's peoples, and privileges instead the retention of cultural property (of which it determines archaeological artifacts to be but a part)
by modern nation-states for the benefit of local peoples. How then
did the Italian request meet the terms of the four determinations set
forth by the CPIA legislation? Is the cultural patrimony of Italy in
jeopardy from pillage? There are reports of active looting of archaeological sites and of material resulting from accidental finds on Italian
territory. But how does one determine that the patrimony of Italy is in
jeopardy as a result? By any measure, the museums of Italy are filled
with similar antiquities, most of which are neither published nor
available on public view. Has the Italian government taken measures
to protect its cultural patrimony? Yes, actively. Would the import
controls taken by the United States deter pillaging in Italy? Not unless
similar import restrictions were in place in other major market
countries in Europe, Asia, and the Gulf States. Unless they were, the
imposition of import controls by the United States could be considered a unilateral action and not a multilateral one as called for by the
CPIA. And, finally, are import controls consistent with the general
interest of the international community in the interchange of cultural property for cultural and educational purposes? Not unless Italy
were to be more generous in lending to museums around the world
antiquities from its museums' storerooms. At the time of its request,
2001, Italy severely restricted the loan of antiquities, limiting the

number and duration of such loans to a matter of a few months at a time. In 2006, it increased that period to four years in specific cases.

Why did the U.S. government grant the Italian request? For decades the Italian government had been making high-profile claims against U.S. museums, which it accused of acquiring illegally exported antiquities from Italy. Looting of antiquities in Italy was a matter of public record. Of course, there was real concern for the loss of archaeological context. But governments rarely, if ever, make decisions based on academic arguments about scholarly pursuits. There are always political trade-offs to consider, and to consider first. Throughout the Cold War, Italy was an important ally of the United States and a strategic partner in the West's control of the Mediterranean. From U.S. military installations on Italian territory, U.S. warships and fighter planes could monitor Soviet ambitions in the Balkans and Western Asia, and of course northeastward through Yugoslavia into Hungary, and could counter Soviet influence on Socialist parties in Greece and the nonaligned countries in the Middle East, always with a watchful eye on the Suez Canal. As the Cold War gave way to the War on Terror, Italy remained an important and strategic ally, even a loyal partner in the Coalition forces attack on and occupation of Iraq: under the leadership of Prime Minister Silvio Berlusconi, Italy contributed the most forces to the Coalition after the United States and Britain. The U.S. government would have had to take Italy's request for import restrictions seriously. There was just too much at stake. (This was as true in 2001 as it was in 2006, when the bilateral agreement was renewed for five years.)

The second case in point is the government of the People's Republic of China's 2005 request of the U.S. government for import restrictions on objects including but not limited to all metal, ceramic, stone, painting and calligraphy, textiles, lacquer, bone, ivory, and horn objects from the Paleolithic period to the Qing dynasty, or nearly 2 million years of human artistic production. Once again, it was hard to justify this request at face value. The 1983 U.S. statute requires that the requesting country demonstrate that all possible internal controls on their domestic market are being diligently applied and that the requested U.S. import embargo will have a material, positive effect on the stated emergency within the requesting country. There is a thriving Chinese domestic market for the materials cited in the request, which contradicts the stated benefits of restricting imports by the United States. The statute also holds that a U.S. embargo must be implemented as only a part of a multinational response including the active participation of all other countries with a significant market for the same cultural property. This is not satisfied simply by having signed UNESCO 1970, since, as we have seen, that Convention need not be applied and cannot be enforced. (As I write, only Italy has signed a bilateral agreement with China that approaches the terms of China's request to the United States, hardly a ringing endorsement of multilateralism.) The statute also requires a qualitative standard of "cultural significance" when considering any kind of emergency, temporary restrictions such as import restrictions. No such standard was met by the request: it covered all materials over many thousands of years, without characterizing any of them as being of "cultural significance."

The request will not work because, as I note later in chapter 4, there is a booming domestic Chinese trade in precisely the materials covered in the request. The Chinese request was really an attempt to help China retain its cultural property: what the modern nation-state of China claims is *its* cultural property, even materials whose cultural heritage may not even be Chinese but Tibetan or ethnic minority, or date from when "China" was much smaller than it is now (indeed, for much of the period covered by the request, China was of varying sizes, covering a range of Asian lands: what is China today was not China during much of the time covered by the request). This request is one part of a two-pronged strategy to build mainland China's collections of what it purports to be its cultural property, having lost much of it to foreigners in the early years of the twentieth century and more again when the nationalist government transferred Taiwan during the Revolution. It is clearly an attempt to strengthen retention of what it has claimed to be its cultural property coincident with its rise as an economic, political, and military power in the world.

In the fall of 2006, the United States agreed to delay a decision on the request by the Chinese government.[32] CPAC made its recommendation to the State Department and no doubt the State Department and U.S. Treasury considered the request in the context of other U.S. concerns about and interests in China. China is very important to the U.S. government. It is a rising and powerful economic power in the world (soon, with the United States, it will be the largest economic power in the world). U.S. corporations are hungry to compete with corporations around the world for a place in the Chinese market. The U.S. and Chinese economies are increasingly interwoven. As of 2006, China was the fourth leading export market for the United States (after Canada and Japan); if one includes Hong Kong, it was the third leading export market. And it is perhaps of even greater importance militarily. China has the largest standing army in the world. It borders North Korea, which is threatening to strengthen its nuclear arsenal. It has a restless Islamist population in the far west of the country, bordering on and near to unstable Islamist regimes, like Afghanistan and Pakistan, Uzbekistan and Kazakhstan. And yet China is stubborn and independent. It has its ambitions in Africa, as well as Asia. And there is a negative view of China generally among U.S. citizens and increasingly among U.S. lawmakers: most frequently cited concerns are China's currency policy, intellectual property piracy, environmental pollution, product safety, and human rights. There is every reason for the U.S. government not to respond positively to the Chinese request—including that it would restrict U.S. citizens in ways it wouldn't restrict the citizens of almost all other market nations (Italy is the exception). But will the United States eventually approve the request? Or some large part of it? The strategic nature of our foreign policy, not archaeology or the interests of U.S. museums, will determine the U.S. response to China's request.

To date, the United States has agreed to every request for import restrictions reviewed by CPAC. These include requests from Bolivia, Cambodia, Canada, Colombia, El Salvador, Guatemala, Honduras, Italy, Mali, Nicaragua, and Peru. In addition, every request but one for an extension of an original request has been granted: these include El Salvador, Italy, Mali, and Peru: only Canada's was not extended. Is it difficult to see a political pattern here? Any time the legitimacies of cultural property requests and strategic foreign policy advantages coincide, the United States approves the foreign government's request.

So what is the value of UNESCO 1970? It set a standard for subsequent conventions and bilateral agreements, and set the bar—legal and moral—at a certain level within each State Party for the consideration of the issue of national responses to the problem of looted and illicitly exported antiquities. Within the United States, parties to the debate over the acquisition of unprovenanced antiquities can and do refer to UNESCO 1970 as if it were the determining standard governing the matter. But it is not and cannot be. It is only an international convention that can be ignored. We know from the actions of the current Bush administration that long-standing international agreements, like the Geneva Convention, can be ignored or partially adhered to in the presumed national interest of the U.S.

International conventions in themselves do not have the force of law. But they often provide the stimulus for subsequent legislative action in local, governmental jurisdictions. This is what happened with UNESCO 1970. It entered into force on April 24, 1972, was accepted or ratified by Ecuador and Bulgaria already in 1971, and then was accepted or ratified by seven nations in each 1972 and 1973, four in 1974, three each in 1975 and 1976, six each in 1977 and 1978, four in 1979, one in 1980, four in 1981, and three in 1983, the year in which the United States ratified it by passing the Cultural Property Implementation Act. Sixty-one nations have ratified it since, as of January 2007, for a current total of 111. As I've already noted, most of these nations have laws restricting the movement of antiquities across their borders (some predate 1970). But neither international conventions nor national legislations have stopped the looting of archaeological sites or the illegal trafficking in antiquities.

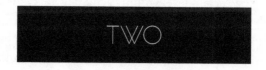

MORE POLITICAL MATTERS

The nature of archaeological research is shaped to a significant degree by the roles that particular nation states play, economically, politically, and culturally, as interdependent parts of the modern world-system.

— Bruce Trigger[1]

Over the three decades since UNESCO 1970, the organization has adopted four additional conventions that bear on cultural property, including antiquities. In 1972, UNESCO passed the Convention Concerning the Protection of the World Cultural and Natural Heritage. This developed from the merging of two separate movements: the preservation of cultural sites and the conservation of nature. The event that caused particular international concern was the Egyptian government's decision to build the Aswan Dam, which would have flooded a valley containing numerous self-declared treasures of "Egyptian civilization." In 1959, following an appeal from the governments of Egypt and Sudan, UNESCO launched an international public awareness campaign, which ultimately resulted in accelerated archaeological research in the area and the dismantling and relocation of certain, important monuments. It also joined forces with the International Council on Monuments and Sites (ICOMOS) to prepare the Convention that was finalized more than a decade later.[2]

By signing this Convention, "each country pledges to conserve not only the World Heritage sites situated on its territory, but also to protect its natural heritage." The States Parties to the Convention are "encouraged to integrate the protection of the cultural and natural heritage into regional planning programmes, set up staff and services at their sites, undertake scientific and technical conservation research and adopt measures which give this heritage a function in the day-to-day life of the community." As with UNESCO 1970, the Convention Concerning the Protection of the World Cultural and Natural Heritage pays lip service to the international value of our cultural heritage—"Considering that deterioration or disappearance of any item of the cultural or natural heritage constitutes a harmful impoverishment of the heritage of all nations of the world"—while acknowledging the importance of nations in interpreting and enforcing the Convention: natural and cultural heritage is important to the world but belongs to specific peoples (i.e., nations).

The purpose of the Convention is to encourage the establishment of an inventory of endangered sites, galvanize financial support for the protection of designated sites, and establish a fund for said purpose, funded by individuals, private and public foundations, and nation-states. The Convention has no means to prevent destruction of our cultural or natural heritage. It can only raise our awareness of what's at risk. As I write, some 890 properties—689 cultural, 176 natural, and 25 mixed properties—have been designated World Heritage sites in 138 States Parties (the U.S. ratified the Convention in 1973 and has twenty sites on the heritage list, thirteen of which are natural—national parks—and seven of which are cultural, including the Statue of Liberty). The Convention was renewed in 2006, ratified by 182 States Parties. Once again, it is only an awareness-raising Convention: it cannot prevent destruction of either national or cultural properties.

In 2001, UNESCO adopted a Convention on the Protection of the Underwater Cultural Heritage, aimed at protecting "buried treasure" that can provide important information about "life on board of ships, boat construction and trade routes," an example of which was the cache of rubies, sapphires, glass ornaments with Arabic inscriptions, and hundreds of thousands of Chinese Yue and Northern white wares found by fishermen off Cirebon on the north Java coast in 2000. The cache had been part of the cargo of a ship traveling from the Hindu Sriwijaya kingdom in Sumatra to eastern Java, then an emerging Hindu-Buddhist kingdom. The objects with Arabic inscriptions suggested that area may have had contact with the Muslim lands, possibly Syria, two centuries earlier than previously thought. Historians and archaeologists were thrilled by the discovery and wanted the cache to be kept together. "A shipwreck is a snapshot in time," a maritime historian at the University of Singapore said. "The precise nature of the cargo, the mix of commodities, would give us vital insights into the nature of commerce at this period." And a maritime archaeologist noted that the ship itself (with still more objects) was still under water and may contain important information about why the Chinese supplied the cargoes for foreign ships but didn't themselves engage in shipping. But the Indonesian government thought differently of the material's value. They were willing to keep 10 percent of the cache, but planned to auction off the rest. "It has more economic value than historical value, there is no need to take it for our heritage museums," declared Aji Sularso, a spokesman for the Indonesian Maritime Affairs and Fisheries Ministry in 2006. "The government's strategy is to choose the auction house that offers the highest price."[3]

In this instance, the government of Indonesia chose to exercise its soverign rights over the material found in its territorial waters. This is of course possible within the terms of UNESCO 2001, even if the Convention's intentions are to protect such material together for further study. It acknowledges, for example, "the importance of underwater cultural heritage as an integral part of the cultural heritage of humanity and a particularly important element in the history of peoples, nations, and their relations with each other concerning their common heritage." But it also recognizes, even asserts, the rights of individual nation-states: "Nothing in this Convention shall prejudice the rights, jurisdiction and duties of States under international law" (Article 3), and "State Parties, in the exercise of their sovereignty, have the exclusive right to regulate and authorize activities directed at underwater cultural heritage in their internal waters, archipelagic waters and territorial sea" (Article 7). And, like other Conventions, it allows for States Parties to denounce it by written notification addressed to the Director-General (Article 32).⁴ Despite the best efforts of historians and archaeologists, in the end UNESCO 2001 offers them no protection. To date, only thirty nation-states have ratified the Convention: neither the United States, nor Greece, Turkey, Egypt, India, Japan, or China has signed or ratified it.

In 2003, UNESCO adopted the Convention for the Safeguarding of the Intangible Cultural Heritage, by which it means "the practices, representations, expressions, knowledge, skills—as well as instruments, objects, artifacts and cultural spaces associated therewith—that communities, groups and, in some cases, individuals recognize as part of their cultural heritage" (Article 2). Central to the Convention is the principle that important intangible cultural property is ultimately determined not by nations but by communities, groups and, in some cases, even individuals, and is said to provide them with a sense of identity and continuity with their (non-national) culture. Nevertheless, it recognizes that States Parties enforce Conventions and therefore must have an authoritative role in its application. Article 11 obliges States Parties to work with communities, groups, and relevant nongovernmental organizations to identify and define "the various elements of the intangible cultural heritage present in its territory" and regularly update them and submit them to the Intergovernmental Committee for the Safeguarding of the Intangible Cultural Heritage (comprising representatives from eighteen States Parties to the Convention, elected by the Conventions General Assembly) (Article 12). States Parties are then obliged to adopt a general policy aimed at promoting the function of the intangible cultural heritage in society, establish ways of safeguarding it, and ensure access to it while respecting customary practices governing such access (Article 13).⁵

This is all a tricky business and difficult for political bureaucracies to manage. There has to be agreement on what is and what is not legitimate intangible heritage and on what basis a national government might recognize and protect one or another community's self-proclaimed cultural heritage. What happens when such communities are distributed across national borders? Can one imagine Turkey, Iran, and Iraq agreeing on a common policy with regard to the Kurdish populations in their countries? To date 118 nations have signed on to the Convention; no influential European nation has signed, nor has the United States; Iran and Turkey have signed, but not Iraq. Tensions between communities and cultures and host nations are just too great to be resolved by such Conventions, however well meaning they may be. No Convention alone can resolve disputed claims of political rights for communities under the jurisdiction of national governments.

Finally, in 2005, UNESCO adopted the Convention on the Protection and Promotion of the Diversity of Cultural Expressions. It acknowledges that cultural diversity forms a common heritage of humanity and should be cherished and preserved for the benefit of everyone, that it is embodied in the uniqueness and plurality of the identities and cultural expressions of peoples and societies, and that it is nurtured by constant exchanges and interactions between cultures. It reaffirms "the sovereign rights of States to maintain, adopt and implement policies and measures that they deem appropriate for the protection and promotion of the diversity of cultural expressions on their territory" and encourages States Parties "to structure administrative ways to encourage and protect cultural diversity within their territories, promote international cooperation, and resolve disputes by negotiation." This is no easier than resolving other kinds of disputed claims deriving from matters of non-national cultural identity. One hundred and eight nations have signed on the Convention, but not the United States, China, Japan, or any European nation, nor Turkey, Iran, or Iraq. And even those who signed, by terms of the Convention, can denounce and withdraw from it.[6]

While UNESCO was drafting and adopting these Conventions, the International Institute for the Unification of Private Laws (UNIDROIT)—an independent, intergovernmental organization for the study of "needs and methods for modernising, harmonising and coordinating private, and in particular, commercial law between States and groups of States"—offered up a new international convention aimed at strengthening efforts to protect cultural property by restricting its movement across national borders. The Convention on the International Return of Stolen or Illegally Exported Cultural Objects (UNIDROIT 1995), as it was called, was adopted at a Conference in Rome in June 1995.[7] Seventy nations participated, including Italy, the People's Republic of China, and the United States, with an additional eight nations observing. The Convention is in many respects similar to UNESCO 1970, but its emphasis is on the *return* of stolen or illegally exported cultural objects rather than the *prevention* of the "illicit import, export and transfer of ownership" of cultural property, and it extends its concerns beyond national interests to those of tribal, indigenous, or other communities. As with Hague 1954 and UNESCO 1970, the Convention may be denounced by any State Party by "the deposit of an instrument to that effect" (i.e., a letter). Or it can simply be ignored. UNIDROIT 1995 includes works of art of all kinds from all periods, from antiquities to the modern era and contemporary moment. Its brief was inclusive and pervasive, its reach personal, and its likely success minimal. To date, sixty nations have signed on as members of UNIDROIT, which allows them to participate in discussions about the scope and authority of its convention.

It wouldn't be an exaggeration to see these many conventions as a bouillabaisse of good intentions and bureaucratic ambitions, all of which are, in the end, unenforceable, except insofar as the States Parties themselves have imposed internal laws and sanctions governing the activities addressed by the Conventions. But they are an important indication of the international climate of political opinion as it pertains to cultural property (including antiquities) and the extent to which such property should be considered the common heritage of humankind or the local heritage of a modern nation or a people who identify themselves independently of or in opposition to a particular, legal nationality. Clearly, the claims on cultural property are getting more and more expansively defined—more and more is claimed as heritage: tangible and intangible cultural heritage, cultural heritage buried in the ground or under water, and antiquities and ancient monuments and archaeological sites—and, despite all of the rhetoric of "the common inheritance of all peoples," more and more of it is being governed by narrower and narrower jurisdictions. The purpose of these conventions is to authorize retention of cultural heritage by those who claim it and have the means of enforcing it. It is clear in the language of the three key conventions: Hague 1954 was concerned with *protecting* cultural property in times of war for the benefit of all the world; UNESCO 1970 with *preventing* the illicit transfer of cultural property between nations (for the benefit of individual nations and, thus, of all the world); and UNIDROIT 1995 was concerned with *returning* cultural property to nations for the benefit of those nations and in "the interest of all." The trajectory of retention is tightening: from protection to prevention to return.

Two years after UNIDROIT 1995, the U.N. Office of the High Commissioner for Human Rights published a report on the Protection of the Heritage of Indigenous People.[8] The Report's language extends the purview of international conventions, with regard to the material covered, almost indefinitely: As stated in the preface: 'Heritage' is everything that belongs to the distinct identity of a people and which is theirs to share, if they wish, with other peoples. It includes all of those things which contemporary international law regards as the creative production of human thought and craftsmanship, such as songs, music, dances, literature, artworks, scientific research and knowledge. It also includes inheritance from the past and from nature, such as human remains, the natural features of the landscape, and naturally occurring species of plants and animals with which a people has long been connected." And it is not just that "heritage" is virtually everything and anything a people claims it to be, but "all of the aspects of heritage are interrelated and cannot be separated from the traditional territory of the people concerned. What tangible and intangible items constitute the heritage of a particular indigenous people must be decided by the people themselves."

Earlier, international Conventions assigned ownership of cultural property—however much they may have paid lip service to its international value—to national governments. The Protection of the

Heritage of Indigenous People vests ownership of "their" heritage in "Indigenous peoples [who] are the true collective owners of their works, arts and ideas, and no alienation of these elements of their heritage should be recognized by national or international law, unless made in conformity with the indigenous peoples' own traditional laws and customs and with the approval of their own local institutions." Who defines the culture of indigenous peoples, which are now the equal of nations with regard to declared cultural property? Indigenous peoples do. It is what they say it is, and it is inevitably part and parcel of their territory (when alienated from their territory, it should be repatriated to their territory and to them). They are one with their cultural property and their territory: "Indigenous peoples regard all products of the human mind and heart as interrelated, and as flowing from the same source: the relationships between the people and their land, and with the spirit world . . . and can be considered as manifestations of the people as a whole."

Throughout the 1980s and 1990s, as archaeologists and indigenous peoples increasingly disagreed over the purpose and value of archaeological material, archaeologists reflected on the politics and ideological underpinnings of their discipline. As one author put it: "Since the 1980s there has been a growing acknowledgment in the Western discipline of archaeology that what we do as archaeologists is 'political,' and has significance beyond the accumulation of abstract knowledge about the past."[9] This acknowledgment grew in great part out of the reality of archaeological work—or Cultural Resource Management, by which is meant the scientific, legal, and political apparatus that allows and manages the practice of archaeology in a given political context—and out of a reflection on the theoretical underpinnings of the academic discipline of archaeology, especially in the Anglophone world. It was informed also by the acknowledgment that archaeology, "as a privileged form of expertise, occupies a role in the governance and regulation of identity" (with regard to both indigenous peoples and nations, especially those carved out of former empires or given their independence during the twentieth century).[10]

This reevaluation of archaeology during the 1980s took the form of a critique of the processual theory of archaeology, which was dominant in the 1960s and 1970s. It embraced logical positivism as its guiding principle and positioned archaeology as a politically neutral, scientific enterprise. Where indigenous peoples (or nations) saw archaeological artifacts as cultural heritage of special relevance central to their identity, processual archaeologists saw such artifacts as scientific data of special relevance to a universalizing database for the understanding of human behavior generally. Coming along in the 1980s, postprocessual theory criticized processual theory for its failures to understand the construction and political applications of knowledge. Influenced in part by the writings of the French philosopher Michel Foucault, postprocessual theory argued that intellectual knowledge and thought (like archaeology) is necessarily incorporated into the act of governing populations and social problems by subjecting them to analysis and becoming tools in the processes of government and administration.[11] On these terms, archaeology is practiced only through a regime of regulations and it seeks to influence that regime for its own purposes.

Postprocessual theory saw the interests of archaeology as influential over government policy, guidelines, and laws governing material and cultural heritage. The result, as one author has written, was "that the archaeological discourse which stresses objectivity, rigour and politically neutral interpretations of the past was readily embedded into bureaucracies and state institutions, and helped to 'de-politicize' heritage issues. It also ensured the priority of archaeological access to sites over public and Indigenous peoples' access through the authority invoked by the use of archaeological scientific discourse." As another author has written, the U.S. heritage legislation at this time protected sites and places from everyone except archaeologists.[12]

National governments regulate archaeologists working within their jurisdiction. They grant excavation permits, which determine which archaeological sites—*whose* ancient past—are valued by governments as important to the nation. They sometimes contribute funding and management to approved archaeological sites. They set quotas for employing local people. And they mandate what, if anything, can be removed from archaeological sites and taken back to the host institutions of participating foreign archaeologists (typically foreign universities or museums). As these regulations are in the service of the state, they inevitably have a nationalist agenda.[13]

※ ※ ※

Take Iraq, for example. In response to Kuwait's complaints that invading Iraqi forces had removed items from Kuwait museums to Baghdad, Iraqi authorities in 1990 insisted that they were storing the items to protect the totality of the cultural heritage of Iraq, "including that of its Province of Kuwait." The U.N. Security Council replied by passing a resolution requesting Iraq to return to Kuwait items exported from that country. In September and October 1991, following the cessation of hostilities and the withdrawal of Iraqi troops from Kuwait, many of the objects were returned.

The Iraq Museum in Baghdad was closed during the First Iraq War, and remained so for another ten years. It reopened only in the summer of 2000. Some of the objects on display had been looted from archaeological sites (active and inactive, some at the time unknown to archaeologists) and dispersed during the chaos of the years of warfare with Kuwait, the U.S. forces, and Iran. As *Archaeology* magazine reported:

> New to the museum are many pieces recovered from looted sites or recent excavations in Iraq. Following the Gulf War thousands of objects were stolen from provincial museums, particularly in the north and south of the country, and smuggled abroad. Iraqi officials have managed to regain at least some of the smuggled artifacts. In April, Rabi' al-Qaisi, director of the museum's Iraqi Antiquities Department, announced that he had retrieved statues and engraved jars from Switzerland.[14]

The magazine also reported that funds for archaeological research remained limited in Iraq. This had not always been the case, however. During much of the previous four decades, ever since the rise of the Ba'thist Party in 1968, archaeology had been richly supported by the Iraqi government. The first four budget years of the 1970s saw government support for archaeology in Iraq rise by 81 percent, while the cost of living rose only 35 percent. And with the boom in oil revenues beginning in 1974 and the rise to power of Saddam Hussein in 1979, support for archaeology and archaeological museums increased even more.[15]

Saddam's interest in archaeology was overtly political. In a speech to a convention of Iraqi archaeologists in 1979, he declared that "Antiques are the most precious relics the Iraqis possess, showing the world that our country, which today is undergoing an extraordinary renaissance, is the [legitimate] offspring of previous civilizations which offered up a great contribution to humanity."[16] A local journalist at the time wrote that archaeology was valued for its role in "Uncovering . . . the civilizations of the ancient forefathers . . . which is the material aspect of the culture of our [Iraqi] people and homeland . . . raising the cultural level of our toiling masses by making them familiar with our forefathers' culture which underlies our [modern] culture."[17] Such statements were common at the time and illustrate the extent to which archaeology was valued in Iraq for how it could be used by the ruling Ba'thist Party to support its claim for national greatness and ultimately, as we will see, for political primacy within the region.

The history of archaeology in Iraq has always been closely linked to the cultural and political ambitions of its governing authorities. During the late Ottoman period, Iraqi archaeology was dominated by teams of Europeans and North American excavators working on pre-Islamic sites at Babylon, Khorsabad, and Nippur.[18] They had been drawn to the area intent on confirming the historical existence of Biblical events and places and with the view that the ancient history of what they called Mesopotamia was in fact part of the West's subsequent Graeco-Roman and Judeo-Christian history. The term Mesopotamia itself was a classical Greek term used by Westerners to mark the lands known locally since the advent of Islam as al-'Iraq in the north and al-Jazira in the south. Its use by early Orientalists has been interpreted politically as a "reconstructive act severing 'Mesopotamia' from any geographical terrain in order to weave it into the Western historical narrative": Mesopotamia as a pre-Islamic source

for Western culture; Iraq as an Islamic, geographically determined—
and thus *limited*—construction.[19]

Under the British Mandate, from 1921 to 1932, archaeology in
Iraq was dominated by British teams—including the British Museum
working with the University of Pennsylvania at Ur, the fabled home
not only of Sumerian kings but of the Biblical Abraham—and regu-
lated by British authorities.[20] The Oxford-educated, English woman
Gertrude Bell, who had worked for British Intelligence in the Arab
Bureau in Cairo, was appointed honorary Director of Antiquities in
Iraq by the British-installed King Faysal in 1922.[21] A most able
administrator, having served as the Oriental secretary to the High
Commission in Iraq after the war, Bell was responsible for approving
applications for archaeologists, and thus for determining where in
Iraq excavators would work. She was also a major force behind the
wording and passage of the 1924 law regulating excavations in Iraq, a
result of which was the founding of the Iraq Museum and the legiti-
matization of *partage*:

> Article 22: At the close of excavations, the Director shall choose such
> objects from among those found as are in his opinion needed for
> scientific completeness of the Iraq Museum. After separating these
> objects, the Director will assign [to the excavator] ... such objects as
> will reward him adequately aiming as far as possible at giving such a
> person a representative share of the whole result of excavations made
> by him.

> Article 24: Any antiquities received by a person as his share of the pro-
> ceeds of excavations under the preceding article may be exported by
> him and he shall be given an export permit free of charge in respect
> thereof.[22]

The Department of Antiquities was placed within the Ministry of
Public Works, as it had been under the Ottomans. One of Bell's key
opponents, the nationalist Sat'i al-Husri, argued that the Department
should instead be within the Ministry of Education. Born and educated in Constantinople, a son of an Ottoman official, al-Husri taught
natural science in a town in the Macedonian region of Kosova near

the Bulgarian border.[23] In 1908, he returned to Constantinople to direct a teacher's college. In 1919, he was appointed Director-General of Education in Syria, and then soon Minister of Education. He grew close to King Faysal, who was elected King of Syria in 1920 but was soon ousted by the French. Over the course of the next year, he traveled with Faysal in Europe before settling in Cairo. When the British established a constitutional monarchy in Iraq with Faysal as king, al-Husri joined his patron in Baghdad. By then he had become a committed Arab nationalist and, as Director-General of Education, he worked to establish a school curriculum emphasizing the Islamic, Arab—*post-Mesopotamian*—history of the region. It was in this respect that he opposed the work of Gertrude Bell and argued to gain control of the Department of Antiquities and the Iraq Museum.

Gertrude Bell died in 1926, the year in which the Iraq Museum was founded, and was succeeded as Director of Antiquities by a number of British (and one German) administrators. Al-Husri resigned his director-generalship in the Ministry of Education that same year and taught in the Teacher's College until he was appointed Inspector General of Education in 1931, a position he kept for only a few months before becoming dean of the Law School. Finally, in 1934, eight years after Bell's death, he was appointed Director of Antiquities. In this capacity, he tightened local control over archaeological excavations. A new law was drafted allowing only those objects that are "duplicate; i.e., objects of the same kind and type and of the same historic value" to be allocated to the excavator "only by special permit."[24] Foreign archaeologists objected and the British embassy in Baghdad wrote to the Iraqi Minister of Foreign Affairs, pointing out that the new laws would discourage foreign archaeologists and cause them to pull out of Iraq—"foreign archaeological expeditions besides drawing attention to Iraq and thus adding to her prestige, bring a considerable amount of money into the country."[25] Leonard Woolley, leader of the British Museum/University of Pennsylvania excavations at Ur, wrote a letter to the editor of the London *Times*: "Twelve years of foreign excavations have given to Baghdad one of the most important museums in the world for the study of Near Eastern antiquities and that because of, not in spite of, permission given to excavators to remove objects which were sometimes unique as well as precious."[26]

Two years later, in response to these protests, new legislation was passed:

> All antiquities found by excavators shall be the property of the government. Nevertheless, as a reward for his labors the excavator shall be given (firstly) the right to make castings of antiquities found by him, (secondly) half of the duplicate antiquities, and (thirdly) certain antiquities already in the possession of the Iraq Government or included among the articles discovered by an archaeological expedition which the Iraq government can dispense with in view of the existence in the Iraq Museum of other articles sufficiently similar in respect to kind, type, material, workmanship, historical significance and artistic value.[27]

At the same time, with al-Husri's encouragement, the Museum of Arab Antiquities was founded, the Iraq Museum was limited to pre-Islamic antiquities, excavations of Ummayad and Abbasid sites were sponsored, and the government sought the repatriation of antiquities from the Islamic site of Samarra taken to British and German museums by earlier, foreign archaeologists.[28]

Al-Husri was forced to leave Iraq when he sided with the pro-German al-Gaylani coup d'etat at the outbreak of World War II. For the next six years, he worked in Aleppo, Beirut, and Damascus in various advisory positions before settling in Cairo, where he served as advisor to the Cultural Committee of the Arab League, lectured at Cairo University, and in 1953 was appointed the first director of the Institute of Higher Arab Studies. There al-Husri refined and promoted his secular, pan-Arab nationalism. He emphasized the importance of a common language among the Arabs of the modern nations: anyone who speaks Arabic was an Arab; Arabic preceded the advent of Islam; and the evidence for a pre-Islamic, sophisticated Arab civilization resides in its language, which allowed for the intricate, abstract thought in the Koran and is an indication of the high level of intellectual sophistication in the area even before Islam. He saw a common language as the basis for a noble and powerful cultural and political unity among the modern Arab nations, and the differences between them were the result of the manipulation by foreign powers:

> There is left no room to doubt that the division of the Arab provinces into several states took place because of the bargaining and ambitions of the foreign states, and not according to the views and interests of the peoples of the countries. So, too, were the borders of these states determined by the wishes and agreements of the foreign powers, and not according to the natural demands of the situation or the requirements of the indigenous interests. . . . All that I have explained indicates clearly that the differences we now see between the people of these states are temporary and superficial."[29]

Al-Husri died in 1967. Nine years earlier, the postwar Hashemite Kingdom in Iraq was overthrown. A subsequent military-supported republic met with mixed results, especially with regard to Arab-Kurdish relations and to a lesser extent Sunni-Shiite relations (the secular, Sunni elite were in power). Years of armed conflict and insurrection ensued and in 1963, with the help of powerful members of the military, the Ba'th party overthrew the government in a bloody coup d'etat. But their rule lasted only a few months. Many of their leaders were rounded up and jailed, and the party remained out of power for five years. During that time, a young, ambitious Saddam Hussein made his presence known among the Party leaders.

The Ba'th Party returned to power in 1968 and moved quickly to control the Kurds and the Shiites. The former demanded independence and fought and lost in various uprisings over the 1970s, while the latter were rounded up by the tens of thousands, imprisoned, and deported to Iran. In the meantime, the Ba'thists worked to forge a strong, nationalist political ideology. Their intention was to create "a national-territorial consciousness resting upon the particular history of Iraq and, equally significantly, of what the regime, or a powerful circle within it, presented as the history of the Iraqi people."[30] Central to this effort was an official drive to foster archaeology as a way of making people aware and proud of "their ancient past," including that of the pre-Islamic era. At the same time, the Party encouraged local folklore for the purpose of inspiring communities

with a sense of internal Iraqi unity, and emphasizing Iraq's uniqueness among the nations of the world at large.

Saddam Hussein became president of Iraq in 1979. Along with
providing generous support for archaeological research, his regime
began calling for the repatriation to Iraq of antiquities transferred to
European museums decades earlier by French and British archaeologists: "In previous periods [in Iraq, governments] did not grasp the
importance of these antiquities, taking no interest whatsoever in these
stolen treasures . . . the Iraqis and their nationalist-socialist revolution
are determined to restore the treasures which are the symbol of the
first and greatest civilizations in human history."[31] The government
even threatened to cancel projects with foreign teams whose governments refused to return archaeological finds taken under previous
regimes.[32] It also announced a program of building archaeological museums in every province and at every site of archaeological importance:
new museums were built at Basra, Kirkuk, Nineveh, and at Baghdad
University; and the Iraq Museum was renovated and expanded.

The most ambitious project was the reconstruction and cultural
revitalization of the ancient city of Babylon. Plans were announced
for the construction of three museums on the site, to be named after
Nebuchadnezzar (for the finds of the later Babylonian period), Hammurabi (the earlier Babylonian period), and Alexander the Great
(Hellenistic period). By 1981, on the first anniversary of Iraq's war
with Iran, throngs of Iraqis marked the occasion with a festival amidst
the ruins of Babylon under the slogan, "Yesterday Nebuchadnezzar,
today Saddam Hussein." Speaking on behalf of the president, a minister spoke to the crowd:

> O the masses of our great nation, O victorious sons of Iraq, O grand-
> sons of Nebuchadnezzar and al-Qa'qa'. . . . O sons of the middle Eu-
> phrates, and O masses of al-Hilla, your salute to the battle of Saddam's
> Qadisiyya [the war with Iran] under the slogan Yesterday Nebuchad-
> nezzar, today Saddam Hussein establishes the link between the histori-
> cal contributions of this country . . . and the heights of today and the
> flags of victory fluttering under the leadership of the fearless and in-
> spired leader Saddam Hussein.[33]

Similar themes were struck in speeches by the country's vice president ("When the mighty kingdom of Akkad and Sumer was founded, as an expression of the first Iraqi internal patriotic unity in history") and by the region's governor ("The festival's celebration in this *muhafazah* expressed the faithfulness of this city, which witnessed the civilizational genius of the Arab man, and an illustrious role in building up the unity of the Arab nation and liberation of its lands").[34] In 1988, the Babylon International Music Festival took place under the slogan "From Nebuchadnezzar to Saddam Hussein, Babylon Arises Anew!" and plays and pageants were performed, making ever clearer the regime's association with its ancient "predecessor." All of this was accompanied by the proliferation of images throughout Iraq showing the profiles of Nebuchadnezzar and Saddam. At the same time, Iraqi provinces and other administrative units were renamed to reference the ancient past: the province of al-Hilla was renamed Babylon, for example; even the Parliament building was renamed the "Hammurabi Building."[35]

A key impediment to linking modern Iraq with ancient Mesopotamia, however, was the skepticism of important parts of the Iraqi intellectual community, who did not see ancient Babylonians as Arabs. They tended instead to locate the source of Iraqi nationalist pride in the land, itself: "Our beloved homeland, Iraq, the cradle of many civilizations and cultures ... where many nations ... and religions lived from the time of the Sumerian and Akkadian civilization."[36] Saddam, however, saw it differently. In an address to the Bureau of Information in 1978, he laid the framework for the Arabization of Mesopotamia: "The history of the Arab nation does not start with Islam. Rather, it reaches back into ages of remote antiquity.... All basic civilizations that emerged in the Arab homeland were expressions of the personality of the sons of the [Arab] nation, who emerged from a single source."[37]

In Saddam's view—and as he would become president of the Republic the following year he had an important view—it was not only the land that the historical and modern peoples of the region of Iraq had in common, it was also the character of the people themselves, those who had occupied that land for millennia and who shared an

Arab personality. Attempts were made to locate this personality in a shared racial source: Arabs were said to derive from the ancient Semites who emigrated from the Arab peninsula northward to Egypt and the Biblical lands. Other attempts argued for clear, unbroken cultural ties from the ancient peoples to modern Iraqis. All of these efforts were difficult to justify, but some intellectuals took refuge in a final, circular argument: because modern Arab Iraqis absorbed all earlier "branches" of the region's culture, all earlier peoples of the area were Arabs.[38] It was left only to claim a unique—even senior—role for Iraq among other Arab countries.

Iraqi historians viewed the temporary ruptures in Iraq's long, continuous history as but temporary challenges which their predecessors had always overcome to advance Arab/Iraqi culture over all others. Ahmad Susa saw this as distinguishing Iraqi from Egyptian culture, the one other Arab nation which claimed a glorious ancient past: "This gave it continuity and purity of origin, as different from Egyptian civilization which ... ended with the end of its ancient era. [The fate of the Egyptian] was similar to what befell the Sumerian civilization, which perished as a result of the Semites ... in Mesopotamia."[39] And this, together with the "unique," harsh, and challenging physical conditions of Iraq—cold winters, hot summers— forged Iraq's "sharpness of perception and great intellectual capacity" and convinced Susa and others that "the civilization of the Arab nation, the mother of ancient civilizations ... necessarily will flourish again as happened in the past" and would do so at the expense of Egypt.[40]

Ba'thist ideology held Iraq to be first among all Arab nations and Arab history to be continuous with the origins of civilization itself. This encouraged a sense of Iraqi supremacy among Arab nations and emboldened Iraq in its attack on Kuwait and war against Iran. Archaeology—governmental sponsorship of excavations, reconstructions (more often than not, *recreations*) of ancient sites, founding of new museums and renovation and expansion of existing ones, and reforming of university and school curricula—and the political manipulation of its finds was crucial to this. It served the ends of the Ba'thist Party in the latter's efforts to hold and strengthen its power at home (against the always troublesome Kurds and Shiites) and advance the cause of Iraq abroad. Thus it was with great pride that the Iraq Museum reopened in 2000 after a decade of war, celebrating not only its well-known holdings gathered from a century of excavations but also looted and stolen antiquities reclaimed from abroad as well as new finds by the Iraqi Antiquities Services. The archaeological community at home and abroad was optimistic. Foreign archaeologists were beginning to work in the country again. *Archaeology* magazine trumpeted the day with the headline, "Good News from Iraq."[41]

A short three years later, Iraq was again at war—this time with the United States and Coalition Forces—and in April the Iraq Museum was attacked, partially destroyed, and thousands of its objects damaged and/or stolen. It was a chaotic situation. The international community condemned the attack. The accuracy of news reports was questioned. The number of objects lost varied by the tens of thousands. Some reported that it was an inside job: the thieves knew what they wanted; it wasn't merely wanton violence by poor, angry mobs but the work of professional thieves. Even the museum's director was accused of misconduct. UNESCO asked all countries to prohibit the importation of cultural, archaeological, and bibliographic objects that had recently been in Iraq (the National Library had also been looted). At a UNESCO-sponsored meeting, agreement was reached on six measures for immediate action:

1. That all museums, libraries, archives, monuments and sites in Iraq be guarded and secured immediately by the forces in place,
2. That an immediate prohibition be placed on the export of all antiques, antiquities, works of art, books and archives from Iraq,
3. That an immediate ban be placed on the international trade in objects of Iraqi cultural heritage,
4. That a call be made for the voluntary and immediate return of cultural objects stolen or illicitly exported from Iraq,
5. That there be an immediate fact-finding mission under UNESCO coordination to assess the extent of damage and loss to cultural property in Iraq, and

6. That there be the facilitation of international efforts in assisting cultural institutions in Iraq.[42]

The Oriental Institute of the University of Chicago began to build a Web site documenting the museum's collections as an aid in the identification of stolen objects. The U.S. State Department Bureau of Educational and Cultural Affairs provided the International Council of Museums with funding to establish a "red list" of Iraqi artifacts that were likely to be on the market illicitly. Objects were reportedly being returned, many by local Iraqis as a sign of respect for the importance of the museum. Rumors surfaced claiming that perhaps only a small proportion of the 170,000 objects in the museum's vaults were in fact looted. Very little about the state of the museum and its collection was certain. But then again, in the first few months of the war very little was certain except that things would get worse.

And yet, despite the chaos on the ground, the U.N. Security Council passed resolution 1483, Section 7 of which reads:

[The Council] decides that all Member States shall take appropriate steps to facilitate the safe return to Iraqi institutions, of Iraqi cultural property and other items of archaeological, historical, cultural, rare scientific, religious importance illegally removed from the Iraq National Museum, the National Library, and other locations in Iraq since the adoption of resolution 661 (1990) of 2 August 1990, including by establishing a prohibition on trade in or transfer of such items and items with respect to which reasonable suspicion exists that they have been illegally removed, and calls upon the United Nations Educational, Scientific, and Cultural Organization, Interpol, and other international organizations, as appropriate, to assist in the implementation of this paragraph.[43]

Things have only gotten worse in Iraq. Four years on, the Coalition war has become a full-fledged civil war, and the destruction of archaeological sites and illicit trafficking in antiquities is said to have increased exponentially. Some blame the lack of protection at the sites: the Marine officer/U.S. prosecutor/self-styled-antiquities policeman, Matthew Bogdanos, is on record claiming that it would take 50,000–75,000 security and support staff and supplies, vehicles, weapons, radios, fuel, training, and living quarters for the staff to protect the sites.[44] Is this likely to happen? Fighting against this is the economic and political circumstances that incite people to loot and take part in illicit trafficking of activities in times of war.

In 2006, three years after the passage of U.N. Security Council resolution 1483, the director of the Iraq Museum, Donny George, fled Iraq for Syria and then the United States, where he is teaching in the Department of Anthropology, Stony Brook University. The museum had been reassigned to the Ministry of Tourism and Antiquities (under Gertrude Bell in the 1920s, it had been under the Ministry of Public Works; under Sat'i al-Husri in the 1930s, it had been under the Ministry of Education). The Ministry of Tourism and Antiquities was under the control of the "radical Shiite cleric" Moktada al-Sadr, whose followers have been linked by some journalists to looting and illicit trafficking (they did lead the two uprisings against the Americans in 2004; al-Sadr's party holds at least thirty seats in Parliament, making him one of the most powerful political forces in Iraq). On August 28, 2006, George was reported to have said that it was no longer possible to work at the museum: "I can no longer work with these people who have come in with the new ministry. They have no knowledge of archaeology, no knowledge of antiquities, nothing."[45] A group of international archaeologists wrote in protest to the Iraqi authorities, asking that the museum's collections be kept together and not split up and distributed around the country, that "Antiquities Guards" at archaeological sites be increased and continued to be paid, and that "cultural heritage either be independent or that it be administered by the Ministry of Culture" and "implemented by a professional, unified State Board of Antiquities and Heritage." The letter concluded by declaring that "only a strong, national, non-political State Board of Antiquities and Heritage, backed fully by the force of the State, can preserve the heritage that is left."[46]

Striking is the request by the letter's signatories—the letter is addressed to Iraq's president, prime minister, Minister of Foreign Affairs, Minister of Culture, and two members of Parliament—that

"Iraq's cultural heritage be treated as a part of the rich culture of Iraqi people, to be preserved for future generations." In the politics of cultural property, national governments have the authority to decide what is and what is not a nation's cultural property. Typically, foreign archaeologists defend this authority against cultural property internationalists like myself by saying that we foreigners should respect a national government's claim on its cultural property. After all, it is said, the government represents the people and has the people's—the nation's—best interest in mind when it defines, protects, and retains cultural property for the nation. In this instance, clearly, a group of archaeologists did not trust the Iraqi national government to make the "correct" decision with regard to its cultural property. And they concluded their letter with the admonition: "All persons who work in Antiquities should be above politics and allegiance to any party. . . . You are in positions to save the Cultural Heritage of Iraq for everyone, and we hope you do so."

Nothing is certain about archaeology in Iraq except that, when once it served the political agenda of the prevailing authorities, now it is victim to the unpredictable violence of foreign invasion and civil war in a failed state. As the *New York Times* columnist Frank Rich wrote recently:

> It's symbolic of the anarchy throughout Iraq's capital that the museum's entrances are now sealed with concrete to keep out new hordes of killers and thieves. But the violence, which seems to spiral with each declaration of a new security crackdown, is old news. More revealing is the other half of the museum's current plight: it is now in the hands of Iraq's version of the Taliban. . . .

> The fortunes of [Iraq's] museum, once considered the finest in the Middle East, have been synonymous with the fate of Iraq ever since. . . . That America has stood helplessly by as Mr. Sadr folds the museum into his orbit of power is as ominous a predictor of what lies ahead in this war as was our callous reaction to the looting of 2003. For all of America's talk of stamping out a "murderous ideology" and promoting civilization and democracy in Iraq, we are now handing the very devil the keys.[47]

It was back to this, back to the Iraq Museum and to the Iraqi government—the government that three years later put Moktada al-Sadr and his forces in charge of the museum—back to Iraq and the chaos and violence of civil war, that UNESCO and the U.N. Security Council wanted the world to return Iraqi antiquities.

⊠ ⊠ ⊠

I began this two-chapter consideration of the political circumstances surrounding the question of art museums and the acquisition of unprovenanced antiquities by recalling a question put to me at a job interview more than sixteen years ago: what was my position on acquiring antiquities illegally exported from other countries? I replied that I would never approve of acquiring objects that were illegally exported from other countries. At the time it seemed like an obvious answer to a straightforward question. But in the years since, I have come to realize that the question is far from straightforward. Rather, it is inevitably inflected by the national and international politics of antiquities, archaeology, and museums. As the relations between the three phenomena are framed by politics, and politics is always motivated by a national, if not a nationalist, agenda, we need to ask why laws regarding the export, import, ownership, and possession of antiquities were written as they were, what they mean, and what purpose and whom in power they serve. That is a far more complicated set of questions than the simplistic one asked of me some sixteen years ago. And in the current debate between museums and archaeologists over the acquisition of antiquities, these questions are not being asked.

THREE

THE TURKISH QUESTION

The pace that archaeology took in Turkey is much more related to the ideology of the modern Republic than to the existing archaeological potential of the country.
                    —Mehmet Özdoğan[1]

We saw in the example of Iraq how the consideration of a nation's cultural property laws must take into account that nation's cultural politics—how, that is, it sees its culture as a source of its identity and esteem—within the context of its contemporaneous political circumstances. This chapter and the next will consider in depth how the cultural property laws of Turkey and China are embedded in the politics of modern nation building, and the consequences of this for the practice of archaeology in those countries.

🎴 🎴 🎴

Turkey's history is a palimpsest of different cultures. When conquered by the Muslim Ottomans in 1453, its inhabitants had long called themselves *Rūm*, or Romans in Greek. They lived under what we call the Byzantine Empire but what they themselves called the Roman Empire (Byzantine is a term of modern scholarship taken from the name for the much earlier Greek city-state, Byzantium, founded in the seventh century B.C.). The Roman Emperor Constantine moved the empire's capital to Constantinople, in the second decade of the fourth century A.D., and there it remained for more than one thousand years. By the time the Ottomans came, *Rūm* denoted the Eastern Roman Empire, the empire in which Greek was the official language and Greek Orthodoxy was the established church.[2] The name Turkey was chosen only in the twentieth century to distinguish the peoples of the new, Anatolian republic from the Arab peoples of the other former, Ottoman lands.[3]

From the beginning, the Ottoman court was in contact with the leading courts and trading cities of Europe and Asia. In 1479, Mehmet II requested from the Venetian Senate the services of an important painter and was sent Gentile Bellini, the city's most prominent artist.[4] Bellini came to paint the sultan's portrait, now in the National Gallery, London, and perhaps other pictures for the New Palace (now the Topkapi Palace) including a *Madonna and Child*. Although the latter paintings do not survive, a group of pen and brown ink drawings depicting a Greek woman, a seated Janissary, and various Turkish men and women in contemporary dress do, and can be attributed to Bellini and his workshop. There is also an exceptionally beautiful watercolor of a young man, probably a page at the Sultan's court, drawn by Bellini in Constantinople between 1479 and 1481.[5] It was later sent to the Aqqoyunlu court in Tabriz and then on to the Persian Safavid court by 1544–1545. There it was put into an album with several Chinese Ming dynasty drawings and a sixteenth-century Italian portrait of a young boy. The album was sent on to the Ottoman court, but not before it was copied by at least two Persian artists.[6]

Mehmet II's court library contained manuscripts from the earlier Byzantine court, including an Octateuch with 352 miniatures, but also other manuscripts likely acquired by Mehmet II himself, as well as Arrian's *Anabasis* and *Indica*, the primary sources for the life of Alexander the Great, a copy of Homer's *Iliad*, Hebrew and Latin manuscripts, and of course numerous Arabic and Persian texts.[7] The sultan's allegorical portrait, engraved by the so-called Master of the Vienna Passion around 1470, was presented or sold to him with fourteen other Italian engravings and later bound into an album with two watercolor portraits painted by Turkish artists, one of which was modeled after a bronze medal of the sultan by the Italian Costanzo di Moysis (or Costanzo de Ferrara).[8]

By the time Süleyman I became sultan in 1520, the culture of the court and the character of Constantinople was distinctly international, as befitting the character of the empire itself. Portraits of him and his successors, Selim II and Murad III, were made by the northern European printmaker Melchior Lorich and a painter in the circle of Veronese who painted twelve portraits of Ottoman sultans which are now in the Residenz Würzberg, Munich; a painted portrait of Süleyman I in the Kunsthistorisches Museum, Vienna, is attributed to Titian. And through a strip of woodcuts sixteen feet long published in Antwerp in 1553, Peter Coecke van Aelst represented the city of Istanbul in panorama (including a scene of Süleyman I riding through the Hippodrome) for the acquisitive European print, art, and book markets. Ten years later, the Venetian book publisher Domenico de'Francheschi published a series of nine woodcuts representing the sultan's Friday procession.[9] Perhaps the most extraordinary object attesting to Süleyman's regard for Europe—and how he wished to be seen by it—was the jewel-studded helmet made by the Venetians Luigi Carolini and Vicenzo Levriero and sold to the Sultan for the astonishing sum of 116,000 ducats. Recent scholars believe Süleyman used the crown to signal his superiority over both the Pope and the Holy Roman Emperor, Charles V. That it was grander than either the helmet Charles V wore at his coronation or the papal tiara has been interpreted as an indication of Süleyman's claim to universal sovereignty, a claim that wouldn't have gone unnoticed by his European challengers.[10]

Links between artistic patronage and trading agreements and political tactics had been a part of the Ottoman court's engagement with Europe from the start. And it went both ways. In 1525, the French king, Francis I, sent his ring in supplication to Süleyman before going into battle against the Emperor Charles V at Pavia. Defeated, Francis I continued to seek an alliance with Süleyman against the emperor. In 1533, Süleyman sent his great admiral, Hayreddin Barbarossa, to the French court to negotiate an alliance.

Two years later, Francis I sent Jean de la Forest to Constaninople to begin discussing campaign strategies. And in 1536, the two courts signed military and trade agreements, giving France direct trade with Ottoman ports (by 1620, French trade with the Ottomans was one-third of all French maritime trade, and would remain so for centuries). Queen Elizabeth's England was no less interested in the Ottomans. In the 1580s, Elizabeth signed trade agreements similar to those enjoyed by the French, and in the early 1590s, Elizabeth and Safiye, mother of Mehmet, heir to the sultanet, exchanged gifts of costumes and finely died textiles (some twenty-three chests were shipped from England alone). All of these trade agreements were aimed against the Venetians, who had enjoyed privileged relations with the Ottomans since the fifteenth century; and not just in Constantinople but throughout much of the empire (some sixty-eight named Venetians are known to have been in Damascus between 1455 and 1457, for example) and are but a few of the many examples of the instant and continuous links between the new court in Constantinople and the courts of Europe.[11]

Within a century after its conquest of Constantinople, the Ottoman Empire either governed or was in contact with most of the known world, and its population reflected this. The first census of the Ottoman capital was taken in 1477 and, counting only the civilian households (not those of the military or the imperial court), recorded 9,486 Muslim Turks, 4,127 Greek, 1,687 Jewish, 434 Armenian, 267 Genoese, and 332 European families from places other than Genoa. A century later, during the reign of Murat IV, Evliya Çelebi described Galata, a suburb of Constantinople, as comprising eighteen wards inhabited by Muslims, seventy by Greeks, three by Franks [probably Europeans, generally], one by Jews, and two by Armenians. "The town," he wrote, "is full of infidels, who number 200,000, according to the census taken in the reign of Sultan Murat IV, whereas the Muslims are only 64,000. . . . The inhabitants are either sailors, merchants or craftsmen, such as joiners or caulkers. They dress for the most part in the Algerine fashion, for a great number of them are Arabs or Moors. The Greeks keep the taverns; most of the Armenians are merchants or money-changers; the Jews are the go-betweens in amorous intrigues and their youths are the worst of all the devotees of debauchery."[12]

Two hundred years later, in 1886, near the end of the empire, the city's population had grown to 850,000, including 130,000 foreigners, primarily Europeans but also refugees from the empire's lost territories. Among the permanent residents counted in the census of that year, 53 percent were Muslims, 21 percent Greeks, 21 percent Armenians, and 3 percent Jews. The first census taken under the new Republic of Turkey, in 1924, showed Istanbul having a population of 1,165,866, of whom 61 percent were Muslim Turks, 26 percent Greeks, 7 percent Armenians, and 6 percent Jews. Today, the city's population is over 10 million, with all of the non-Muslim minorities making up less than 1 percent. Nationwide, the population is over 70 million, 80 percent of whom are Turkish and 20 percent Kurdish, while 99.8 percent of its citizens are Muslim, mostly Sunni, and the balance, only 1.4 million, or 0.2 percent, mostly Christians and Jews.[13]

The picture is clear. Over the centuries, with the end of the Ottoman Empire, Turkey and Istanbul have become almost only Turkish and Muslim, when once both included large populations of Arabs, Christians, and Jews. This is the natural result, at least in part, of the concentration of Turkish territory on Anatolia following the demise of the empire; the latter having included at one time or another Arab, Egyptian, North African, and Greek territories. But it is also the result of political and religious tensions during the first seventy-five years of the republic's history.

Under the leadership of its first president, Mustafa Kemal, or Atatürk ("Father of the Turks") as he came to be known, the Turkish Republic pursued a rigorous program of modernization. The National Assembly voted to abolish the sultanate in 1922, and shortly afterward Islamic courts were dissolved and religious brotherhoods banned. At the same time, the republic instituted a unified school system, effectively replacing the *medreses* with secular schools that taught a new curriculum in the Turkish language only (*medreses* had often taught in local languages, such as Kurdish), and all dervish lodges, shrines, and mausoleums were closed and their staff dismissed. In 1925, a law was passed prohibiting the wearing of the traditional hat, or *fez*, which in Atatürk's words was "a symbol of ignorance, negligence, fanaticism, and the hatred of progress and civilization." And in the same year the Muslim calendar was replaced by the European one (which begins with the presumed date of Jesus's birth), Arabic script was replaced with Latin letters, and Sunday was established as a day of rest.[14] Finally, in 1926, women were granted new rights, including the right to an equal share of inheritances; divorce at the husband's discretion was ended; religious or polygamous marriages were no longer recognized; and women teachers were permitted to work in coeducational primary and middle schools (previously they had been allowed to teach only in girls' schools), and in law, medicine, and public services.

The republic's most dramatic act of modernization was abolishing the caliphate in 1924. Upon the Prophet's death in 632, his closest companions and deputies were charged with strengthening and perpetuating the *ummah*, or community of believers. This was no easy task. The second caliph, or principal leader of the *ummah*, was assassinated in 644, and the caliphate passed to Uthman, who was himself assassinated twelve years later and whose death initiated a five-year civil war. His successor, Muawiyyah I, established the Umayyad dynasty, and moved his capital from Medina to Damascus. Upon his death a second civil war broke out, with the followers of the earlier, defeated challenger to Muawiyyah I, Ali ibn Abi Talib (a member of the Prophet's family, whereas Muawiyyah I was not), calling themselves the Shia I-Ali (or Shiites). In the middle of the eighth century, the Abassids, who had descended from the Prophet's paternal uncle, rose up against the Umayyads, fighting under the banner of the Shiah, and established the Abassid dynasty with its capital in Baghdad. By the end of the Abassid dynasty two hundred years later, caliphates no longer had temporal power. When in the sixteenth century Süleyman I claimed both temporal and religious authority for himself—both the sultanate and the caliphate—he was recalling an earlier era of the caliphate and flexing his muscles over all of Islam as the "shadow of God" on all nations.[15]

By the time the republic abolished the sultanate in 1922 and deposed and exiled Mehmet VI, the Ottoman caliphate was terminally weakened. The empire itself no longer existed. The Turkish Republic would soon be established with Atatürk as its president. And the former sultan's cousin, Abdül Mecit II, the Crown Prince, was caliph only, and not, as Ottoman caliphs had been for hundreds of years before him, also sultan. A short two years later, on March 3, 1924, with the stroke of the pen, the Ottoman caliphate itself—the traditional authority of the caliph, the deputy of God, successor of Muhammad, and historically chief civil and religious ruler of the Muslim community—was formally abolished and Abdül Mecit II deposed and expelled from the country.[16] The extent of the republic's sovereignty had been reduced to Anatolia, and the authority of *imams* in Turkey was made subject to the president of the new, secular state.

This was a critical moment in the history of the Turkish Muslim community. For the first time in centuries, they were without a caliph. They would soon have no Islamic courts and would be subject only to the secular law of the republic, their religious brotherhoods would be banned, and their theological schools replaced by a unified system of secular schools. Over the next twenty-five years, Atatürk and his successors would do everything in their power to limit the influence of Islam in the public life of the republic, but it would never go away.

In 1919–1920, Atatürk gave voice to the idea of a territorial nation-state. In the National Pact of that year, he wrote that "the Grand national Assembly of Turkey has a firm, positive, material policy, and that, gentlemen, is directed to the preservation of life and independence . . . within defined national frontiers. The Grand National Assembly and government of Turkey, in the name of the nation."[17] The Turkish national idea first appeared some five decades earlier as a result of a number of factors, chief among them the influence of European nationalism. A number of disenfranchised European nationalists were in exile in Turkey and a number of Turkish political exiles were in Europe during the height of European nationalism at mid-century. At the same time, European scholars were advancing the study of Turcology, or the history of the ancient history and civilization of the Turkish peoples. This was due in part to the rise of pan-Slavism in Russia and the eastern lands of the Austro-Hungarian Empire and took the form of Turanism, whose chief aim was the rapprochement and ultimate union—cultural, political, or both—among all peoples whose origins were said to go back to Turan, an ancient Iranian name for the country to the north-east of Persia, a kind of Shangri-La on the steppes of Central Asia. The Turkic peoples originating in this area were thought to speak related languages—Turkish, Mongol, Finnish, Hungarian—and thus be culturally and even ethnically related. While as a linguistic and ethnological classification this theory was soon abandoned, it persisted as a political idea through the early decades of the twentieth century.[18]

Meanwhile, in 1904 Akçuraoğlu Yusuf, a Tatar from Russia, whose family had settled in Turkey but who was educated in France and was living in Russia, wrote an article for *Türk*, a periodical published in Cairo for Turkish political exiles (to remind us of the international character of the development of local nationalism) which, when published as a pamphlet, would have considerable influence in Turkey. He laid out three options for a Turkish national identity in the final years of the Ottoman Empire: Ottomanism, or a common Ottoman citizenship irrespective of religion of origin; Pan-Islamism, based of course on religion; and Turkism, or a nationalism based on the Turkish "race." The first two were impossible since there was no Ottoman nation and the European powers would fiercely oppose an Islamist identity. And so he argued for the third option, or Turkism, which would rally the loyalties of the dominant Turkish peoples within the Ottoman Empire and reinforce them with Turks from Russia and elsewhere.[19] Atatürk would argue against all three options, limiting his vision for Turkish nationalism to the Turks living within the post-Imperial borders of modern Turkey: "We do not serve pan-Islamism. . . . We do not serve pan-Turanianism. . . . Gentlemen we are a nation desiring life and independence. For that and that alone may we give our lives."[20]

In 1923, the new republic established its capital in the Anatolian city of Ankara. This regional city, with a population only a fraction of the size of Constantinople's (Constantinople would not become Istanbul until 1930), nevertheless had significant symbolic value. It had been the headquarters of Atatürk's nationalist party, the meeting place of the National Assembly, and the seat of his government during the War of Independence. In every way it would be different from the historic Ottoman capital. Its master plan would be devised by the German town-planner Hermann Jansen, and its many government buildings designed by the Austrian architect Clemens Holzmeister. It was to be modern and efficient and represent the power of the state. The National Assembly would meet under the motto, "Sovereignty belongs unconditionally to the nation."

That Ankara was in Anatolia was important too. For the immediate task of the new republic was to construct a national identity distinct from that of the Ottoman Empire. Many of the republic's early elite sought a Pan-Turkic identity in alliance with the Turkic cultures of Central Asia. But the ancient homeland of the Turkish people—Turkestan—was in the possession of Russia and China, and more than half of the Turkish people of Asia, with whom the new nation might identify itself, lived there or elsewhere outside the former Ottoman Empire. It would not be easy, nor serve the immediate best interests of the republic, to build a Pan-Turkic identity as a minority part of a population under foreign domination or otherwise living in many different countries. Atatürk argued instead for an Anatolian identity, one that looked neither east nor west but historically within Anatolia to the Sumerians and Hittites as among the earliest peoples resident within modern Turkey's geographic borders.[21] These ancient peoples thus became descendents of the modern Turks; as the Phrygians, Lydians, Carians, Selçuks, and Ottomans would after them. A theory was advanced defining the modern Turkish identity as an amalgamation of thousands of years of Anatolian cultural history. In Atatürk's mind, Anatolia had been a Turkish land since antiquity. And he had a Museum of Anatolian Civilizations established in Ankara, to which at his direction Hittite artifacts from throughout the region were sent to Ankara as evidence of the "origins" of Anatolian Turkish identity.[22]

An Anatolian identity may have located the Turkish national identity squarely within the political borders of the modern state, but it did not define it as a set of commonly held assumptions about what it meant to be a modern Turk. Many of these assumptions centered on the role of religion in public life. In 1949, in anticipation of the coming elections, the government reinstated religious education in primary school on a voluntary basis. Four months later, the faculty of theology, which was closed down in Istanbul during Atatürk's time, was reopened in Ankara. These were cautious moves, made to appeal to reformists without significantly altering government policy. But they failed to prevent an upset at the polls. Numerous changes followed, each seemingly small but together amounting to a significant challenge to the secularist state. The law requiring the Muslim call to prayer be made in Turkish rather than Arabic was repealed, and mosques were equipped with loudspeakers so that everyone could hear the original Arabic. And new mosques were built throughout the country. In all, these changes began what some have called a Sunni Renaissance in Turkey, an institutionalization of more traditional religious values in public life that had been denied at the founding of the republic.[23]

Twenty years later, the Sunni Islamist leader Necmettin Erbakan and his National Salvation Party joined two coalition governments, with Erbakan serving as deputy prime minister. Increasing social and political disruptions—ignited by Islamists, right-wing nationalists, and leftists alike—brought a military coup in 1980. Seven years later, Erbakan formed a third political party, the Welfare Party, and again entered politics. He campaigned energetically throughout the nation and in 1995, in partnership with the True Path Party, formed a government as prime minister, the first Islamist prime minister in the history of the nation. This was a major victory for the Islamists, but it was to be short-lived. In the face of severe economic problems, Erbakan turned to other developing, Muslim nations to create a union of economic cooperation. This was interpreted by the military and center-right politicians as an attempt to change Turkish foreign policy toward the Middle East. With pro-Islamist demonstrations breaking out across much of the country, Erbakan was forced to surrender to the military and step down from office.

One of Erbakan's most charismatic followers, Recep Tayip Erdoğan, was the Welfare Party's chairman in the province of Istanbul and stood for mayor of the city and as a candidate for the Turkish National Assembly several times in the late 1980s. In 1994, he was elected mayor of Istanbul and president of the Greater Istanbul Metropolitan Council. But shortly thereafter he was arrested and imprisoned for having recited in public the lines of the nationalist poet Ziya Gökalp: "The mosques are our barracks, their minarets our bayonets, their domes our shields."[24] Erdoğan returned to politics after his release and formed the Justice and Development Party. A constitutional amendment allowed him to run for parliament in 2002 and, with the help of the reformist wing of Islamists, whose Virtue Party had earlier been banned by the constitutional court, he was elected and became prime minister.

Erdoğan is in office as I write. And while he is perceived by many to be an Islamist on the order of Erbakan, he is steering a close, moderate political line. Among his first orders of business is to secure Turkey's admission into the European Union. Some EU member states are skeptical of the economic stability of the country. Others are critical of Turkey's human rights record, while still others are doubtful that a Muslim nation—even a centrist one like Turkey—can share the values of the other EU members. Erdoğan argues otherwise. He believes Turkey's admission will be of benefit not only to the Union as a cooperative body but to the individual member states, since it will lead to an integration of their Muslim communities into the mainstream of national cultural and political life. He also believes it will send positive signals to other Muslim nations with regard to Europe's understanding and respect for Islam itself.

Erdoğan acknowledges the importance of religion in Turkish public life: "My government attaches importance to religion in the private sphere, but does not consider it right to pursue a policy with religion." By any measure Turks are religious people. In a survey taken in 1999, for example, 92 percent of the respondents said they kept the Ramadan feast, 46 percent said they prayed five times daily, 62 percent said they attended Friday prayers, and 7 percent said they had performed the pilgrimage to Mecca; 53 percent said they had visited shrines of holy men and 12 percent said they had purchased amulets. But only 21 percent said they wanted the Turkish state to be founded on Islamic law, and 77 percent agreed that Turkey had moved forward

as a result of the reforms introduced by the republic and its governments over the years.[25] Officially, the president of Religious Affairs
reports to the prime minister through a minister of state and controls
a network of nearly 77,000 mosques throughout the nation. It has
some 80,000 *imams* and other lesser staff members on its payroll.
Regional *muftis* represent the president of Religious Affairs and keep
an eye on local *imams* and the content of their sermons. Every politically viable effort is being made to institutionalize religion in Turkey
and to create a modern synthesis of the earlier divisions between the
government and the faithful.[26]

But the faithful themselves are not always in agreement. Most
Turkish Muslims are Sunni, including the nation's leaders. The Sunni
Renaissance begun during the 1950s is judged by many non-Sunnis
as being at their expense.[27] The heterodox Alevi community feels particularly aggrieved. Alevis—some 25 percent of Turkey's population—
practice what has been described as a syncretic religion with elements
of Shi'a Islam, pre-Islamic religions of Anatolia, and even ancient
Turkic Shamanism. They typically do not worship in a mosque but in
meetinghouses under the direction of an elder. Some Alevis emphasize
their Shi'a origins. Others see themselves as a kind of Sufi order. Still
others consider their faith a form of folk Islam. Opposition between
Sunnis and Alevis has sometimes been violent, as in 1978 around
Kahramanmaraş and in 1993 in Sivas, where Sunni fundamentalists
set fire to a hotel where pro-Alevi intellectuals were having a conference, killing thirty-five.

Sometimes the tension between majority and minority peoples in
Turkey is not based on religion. The Kurdish people, although largely
Sunni, are fiercely independent. They did not get a homeland—
Kurdistan—at the end of the Ottoman Empire as promised, and as
Iraq, Syria, and Kuwait did. And when the Turkish Republic was
established, Atatürk rejected their requests and Iran and Iraq agreed
not to recognize an independent Kurdish state. Their language was
outlawed and traditional culture repressed, and they were encouraged to move to large cities as a way to dilute their independent identity. During the 1920s and 1930s, they rose up in opposition to the
republic, and in the 1980s, the Kurdish Workers' Party (PKK) was

established calling for formal independence. Six years later, the PKK began an armed struggle, which over the years would claim 30,000 lives and create more than 2 million refugees. In 2000, the PKK announced a ceasefire and reforms were passed in 2002 and 2003 ending bans on private education in the Kurdish language and on giving children Kurdish names. But in 2004, renamed the Kurdish People's Congress, the party renounced the ceasefire. The matter of Kurdish independence, and of a greater Kurdish homeland, remains unresolved.[28]

The Greek question has a longer history in Turkey. Greeks have lived in Anatolia for millennia, especially along the Aegean coast. For a while, under Alexander, they dominated the land. And for all intents and purposes, the Byzantine Empire (the Eastern Roman Empire at the time) was Greek. When Mehmet II conquered Constantinople, he appointed a Greek monk to the orthodox Patriarch and allowed him to govern both the religious and secular affairs of the Greek community. The first Ottoman census, of 1477, counted half of Constantinople's population as Greek, and four-hundred years later, even after the Greek War of Independence, it was still 21 percent Greek. The end of the Greco-Turkish War (part of the Turkish War for Independence, 1919–1922) resulted in a population exchange, which forcibly resettled some 1.5 million Greeks from Turkey to Greece, but not the 400,000 Greeks in Constantinople (nor the 25,000 Muslims in Western Thrace). The first census of the Turkish Republic counted 26 percent of Constantinople's population as Greek.[29] (The complications of this exchange were many. The Greeks of Karaman who were repatriated to Greece were Greek Christians by religion but knew almost no Greek. They spoke Turkish, which they wrote in a Greek script. And many of the Turks repatriated from Greece spoke little or no Turkish. In many ways it was a symbolic exchange of populations instigated by national politicians, resulting in an odd form of national "purity.")[30]

Repressive government policies against Greeks in Turkey during the 1930s forced many Greeks to emigrate. In 1955, Greek nationalists in Cyprus launched a terrorist campaign against the British colonial administration there. Turkish Cypriots comprised 20 percent of the island's population but were disproportionately represented in the police force in its actions against the Greek terrorists. While the Greek and Turkish foreign ministers were in meetings in London, an Istanbul newspaper reported that a bomb had been set off in the Salonica house where Atatürk was thought to have been born. Within hours, crowds encouraged by governmental officials took to the streets of Istanbul, destroying Greek property and terrifying Greek residents who were forced to flee the city to save their lives. Ten years after the so-called "Istanbul Pogrom," the Greek population of Istanbul was only 48,000. It is said now to be a mere 5,000.

Ethnic, religious, and political differences have reduced the diversity of the city's and nation's population. Non-Muslim minorities now comprise less than 1 percent of Istanbul's 10 million residents, while 99.8 percent of the nation's citizens are Muslim. Still, Turkey's national identity remains an unresolved issue. Alevis and Kurds are opposed to Sunni Turkish domination (with the Kurds calling for their own, independent homeland); Islamists and secularists are at odds over the role of religion in Turkish public life; and the more or less progressive citizens of Istanbul are opposed to the traditionalists of the rest of the country. However much Erdoğan professes an open, democratic Turkish national identity, the nation's identity remains contested between Islamists, secularists, and the military, and between ethnic Turks and Kurds:

> [T]he national state signifies the partnership of the constituents that make up the Republic of Turkey on the basis of citizenship. Atatürk never agreed with concepts that defined a nation on the basis of race, religion or ethnic background. For him the distinguishing feature of a nation is a shared history and the will to love together. Today, Turkey is a powerful and democratic country that is comprised of constituents who have a sense of shared history and the will to live together on the basis of constitutional citizenship and who can see their differences as an enriching attribute.[31]

❈ ❈ ❈

Contemporary debate about Turkey's future and the future of its identity is constrained by politics. But so too is its consideration of its past—and especially the ancient past of the land within its modern borders.

The Istanbul Archaeological Museum was founded under the sultanate of Abdül Mecit I in 1846, when the empire's provincial governors were ordered to ship to the capital all appropriate, moveable works of art. Twenty-two years later the collection was inaugurated as the Ottoman Imperial Museum.[32] In 1881, the painter and archaeologist Osman Hamdi Bey was appointed curator-director. The Archaeological Museum as we know it today was opened in 1891, with new wings added in 1902, 1908, 1991, and 1994. From the beginning, its collection was truly an Imperial one—the *Ottoman Imperial Museum*—an assemblage for the capital of ancient works of art from throughout the empire. As director of the new Archaeological Museum, Osman Hamdi Bey recommended to the government that it continue this manner of acquisition and issue "orders to the numerous officials of the provinces in Asia Minor and Mesopotamia to guard carefully all antiquities that may exist, to report to the Ministry of Public Instruction all new discoveries, and, when required, to transport them safely to Constantinople."[33]

Antiquities found within the empire were first regulated in 1869, with the adoption of an ordinance that allowed for private ownership of antiquities found on private land, but prohibited their export to other countries.[34] The subsequent Ottoman Decree on Antiquities of 1874 prohibited the excavation of antiquities without permission of the state and consent of the landowner, and required that one-third of antiquities discovered in legal excavations on private land be kept by the state, one-third be given to the landowner, and one-third to the finder. If the finder was also the landowner, two-thirds of the antiquities were given to the finder-landowner. Antiquities given to the finder could be exported with State permission.

As curator-director of the Imperial Museum, Osman Hamdi Bey was influential in the 1884 Ottoman Decree on Antiquities, which declared all antiquities discovered or to be discovered through excavations as belonging to the state, and that one-half of any antiquities found accidentally on private land would be given to the landowner. All antiquities discovered in legal excavations became the property of the Imperial Museum in Constantinople, regardless of where they were found within the empire.

Twenty-two years later, the 1906 Ottoman Decree on Antiquities declared that all antiquities found in or on public or private lands were the property of the government of the Ottoman Empire and were not to be shared with their finder or, if found on private land, the landowner. The 1906 Decree remained in effect until 1973, fifty years after the founding of the Turkish Republic, when it was replaced by a very similar law, with only modest modifications.

The current law was enacted in 1983 and extended these protections to a wider range of cultural and natural properties, as well as to any property relating to the republic's first president, Mustafa Kemal Atatürk, and to the 1919–22 War of Independence (if only to make clear the relationship between cultural property and political ideology). The trajectory of legislation regulating the excavation, ownership, and trade in antiquities found within the sovereign borders first of the empire and then later of the republic has been toward ever tighter regulation. Once, antiquities could be privately owned but not exported without the state's permission; now antiquities are exclusively property of the state.

Of course the state itself, as we have seen, has changed over the years. For centuries it was one of the largest empires the world has ever known, stretching from the Black Sea south to the Arabian Sea, west to the Atlantic Ocean, and northwest to the gates of Vienna. By 1923, it had been reduced mostly to Anatolia. Its archaeological legacy is thus one both of a source nation (in modern terms: rich with an archaeological heritage) and a colonizing power. Antiquities from many of the former empire's territories—objects that could rightly be considered important to the cultural heritage and national identities of the modern states occupying those lands today—are now in Istanbul's Archaeological Museum. Indeed, the museum's most important and prized antiquities—sarcophagi from the royal necropolis of Sidon, especially the so-called "Alexander Sarcophagus"—were discovered in 1887 in what is now Lebanon, and their excavation and removal to Constantinople were supervised by Osman Hamdi Bey. Because Lebanon was under the sovereignty of the empire at the time (it would remain so until the end of World War I and did not become fully independent until 1936), the Imperial Museum had the legal right to bring them to Constantinople.[35]

The history of archaeology in Turkey has been subject to the pressures of modern nation building. Mehmet Özdoğan, a professor of Prehistoric Archaeology at Istanbul University, has written of the ideological foundation of early Ottoman and republican archaeology:

> The emergence and the development of archaeology in Turkey took place under constraints that are deeply rooted in history. Confrontation between the traditional Islamic framework and the Western model, the endeavor to survive as a non-Arabic nation in the Middle East while the empire was disintegrating, the hostile and occasionally humiliating attitude of Europeans, and growing nationalism have all been consequential in this development. . . . [T]he pace that archaeology took in Turkey is much more related to the ideology of the modern Republic than to the existing archaeological potential of the country.[36]

Recent critical studies of archaeological practice have shed new light on the inevitable nationalism of modern states with a rich archaeological heritage within their borders. Some studies draw on post-colonialist theory to admit that "constructions of identity for colonized groups inevitably entail a complex interweaving of past and present, which in themselves rely on the discourses of alterity, authenticity and origins."[37] What is most important about these studies is their acknowledgment of the nationalistic framework within which archaeology is being carried out today and has always been. "Such overt [nationalistic] political bias in archaeological research and interpretation is neither new or unusual: what has changed is the willingness of archaeologists to recognize such realities." And "by its nature archaeology has always had an obvious political dimension, and nationalism—like ethnic or cultural identity—makes manifest the character of archaeology as a social, historical and political enterprise."[38] The latter remarks were written by British archaeologists working in Cyprus, an island rich with ancient heritage but long subject to all of the pressures of modern nation building, and, since 1955, in often bloody dispute between Greece and Turkey.

During British control of the island in 1878, emphasis was on a Hellenic view of the island's past in contrast to its centuries of control under Muslim Ottoman rule. When it became independent in 1960, it had a Greek Cypriote majority and Turkish Cypriote minority. In 1974, a Greek government-sponsored attempt to seize control of the island was met by military intervention from Turkey (twenty years earlier, anti-Greek violence in Istanbul drove thousands of Greeks from Turkey). Nine years later the Turkish-held area declared itself the Turkish Republic of Northern Cyprus, which is recognized today only by Turkey. Although the entire island entered the European Union in 2004, E.U. Common Rights and Obligations apply only to areas under direct Republic of Cyprus control and are suspended in the areas administered by Turkish Cypriots.

The politics of archaeology on Cyprus are multiple. "The 1974 Turkish invasion and subsequent occupation of the northern part of the island precipitated a blatantly ideological, cultural cleansing of the Greek Cypriote past," archaeologists Bernard Knapp and Sophia Antoniadou have written.[39] It is charged that one group of nationalistic Cypriots ignores or willfully damages the archaeological remains important to the other, and that each accuses the other of either stealing or refusing to repatriate archaeological artifacts deemed important to, even as *belonging to*, the other.

Similar tensions exist in southern Turkey among the Turkish authorities and Kurdish minority population. The Kurds live in a region of Central Asia that crosses the modern borders of Turkey, Iraq, Iran, Syria, and Armenia. They have lived in that area, called by them Kurdistan, for millennia. They were conquered by Arab Muslims in the seventh century, Seljuk Turks in the eleventh century, Mongols in the thirteenth century, and later the Safavid and Ottoman Empires. Although promised a homeland at the end of World War I, they were not given one. It is estimated that about half of the more than 20 million Kurds living in the region today live in Turkey.

Turkey has been criticized for neglecting the Kurdish cultural heritage, both its living heritage (language, clothing, and culture) and the antiquities that lie beneath the ground in southeast Turkey. Mehmet Özdoğan disagrees and argues that there are archaeological campaigns in many areas of the region. He categorically denies that the Kurds' interests are being ignored. It is, he says, "misguided to consider that applications [for excavations] are processed according to potential ethnic import of a site." But then he wonders just what is intended by Kurdish heritage, or Kurdish archaeology, anyway:

> Kurds have lived in that region for some millennia under different tribal names, without establishing any state. The area now populated by Kurdish peoples has been part of numerous kingdoms and empires, including the Assyrian, Mittani, Urartian, Persian, Achaemenid, Roman, Byzantine, Armenian, Arab, Seljuk, Artuquid, Eyyubid, Mongolian, Ottoman, and even the Crusader kingdoms. Which one of these should be Kurdish, Turkish, or Arabic?[40]

The Kurds are stateless people. What right then, Özdoğan asks, have they to claim association with the archaeological remains beneath the lands they have inhabited, if even for millennia, but have never *governed*? Rights to make such claims, it would seem, come only with the sovereign authority to back them up. Without such authority, the Kurds have no claim to the region's past. But the Turks do, and have made those claims since at least Osman Hamdi Bey in the final years of the Ottoman Empire.[41]

But why should state sovereignty determine ownership? (Remember: antiquities found within the borders of Turkey are, and have been since 1884, state property.) Does ownership mean stewardship—the preservation of things for the benefit of all others—or does it mean "it's my property and not yours"? Özdoğan is critical of the idea that anything but state sovereignty (ownership) can determine control over archaeological remains. Are we to impose, he asks, "a biased imposition of present conflicts onto the past?" "Is it our concern as archaeologists," he continues, "to use the past as a tool either to prove or disprove racial origins and claims which agitate present conflicts? Or should we engender the notion that the past is past and, whatever its character, it belongs to all of us?"[42] But how can it belong to all of us if it belongs to the state? Do the archaeological remains found on the lands on which the Kurds have lived for millennia belong to them in any meaningful way so long as they are the property of the

Turkish state and the two peoples—the Turkish majority and Kurd-ish minority—are locked in political and even bloody conflict? And how can they "belong" to the rest of us, if they are owned by the state and kept by the state?

Turkey claims ownership of the archaeological remains found within its modern political borders, and to the archaeological remains found anywhere within the borders of the former Ottoman Empire that were removed to what is now Turkey prior to the end of the empire. Turkey is the legal and political heir to the empire. Sarcophagi removed from what is now Lebanon, when that land was part of the Ottoman Em-pire, now belong to Turkey. The Lebanese have no right to them. While in a generous moment a Turkish archaeologist might say they "belong to all of us," they do not. They are considered Turkish property, having been removed to what is today Turkey during the Ottoman period. Were archaeological remains the property of all of us, Turkey would have no right to argue for the return of "Priam's treasure" removed by Heinrich Schliemann.[43]

Archaeological remains are political property, regulated by state law. Greece has sovereignty over some of the archaeological remains found on Cyprus, and Turkey has sovereignty over others, even if the remains were deposited equally over the island during the historical periods when all of it was occupied by a single political power. And the Kurds? They have no claim to anything. The archaeological remains found on the land they consider to be their homeland belong to Turkey, and access to it is controlled by the Turkish Antiquity Ser-vice. Access is power, and power is circumscribed by modern, state-based sovereignty.

Cultures have and will always overlap and intermingle. The geo-graphic limits of political sovereignty will always change. These are the truths by which we must consider all nationalist claims on arti-facts of the past. In the case of Turkey, its diverse, polyglot past of cultures and peoples crossing Anatolia in search of commercial, political, and territorial gain over thousands of years—west along the Silk Road and from Turkistan, east from Europe, south from the Balkans and Thrace, and north from Mesopotamia and Persia—is being recast in light of modern political ambitions as the republic struggles still with the formation of a modern, secular state. "Approved" past cultures are exhibited in the Istanbul Archaeological Museum as the ancient foundation of the modern Turkish identity. The more modern Ottoman contributions are preserved and exhibited in the nearby Çinili Köşk, or tile museum, and Topkapi Sarayi Müzesi in the former Ottoman palace. A Turkish past is created. A Kurdish past is ignored. And all of the rough and tumble untidiness of the streets of Istanbul, once filled with Greeks, Jews, and Christians from throughout Europe is tidied up and left to Turks, overwhelmingly so, and mostly Sunni Muslim Turks at that. That's the nature of nation building. It subjects the past and the present to the rigors of identity control. And archaeology and national museums are used as a means of enforcing that control.[44]

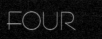

FOUR

THE CHINESE QUESTION

Foreign friends should come to China to appreciate Chinese art objects, yet too often we end up going overseas to see them in foreign museums. Our national treasures should not be flowing beyond our borders. They are ours, part of our roots.
—Spokesman, China Poly Group Corporation, Beijing[1]

Dunhuang is a small town in a poor agricultural area of northwest China. It was once a famous oasis, the westernmost outpost of China under the Han dynasty and the point of embarkation on the dangerous trek across the Taklimakan Desert along the Silk Road heading west. Just outside Dunhuang to the north is the famous Jade Gate, a stone fortress built during the second century B.C. as part of the Han dynasty's Great Wall fortification system. A few miles to the southeast are the famous Mogao caves, Buddhist frescoed cave temples carved into a cliff face above a small river in an otherwise dry, desert valley. They were first dug by wandering monks around A.D. 366 and last dug during the Yuan dynasty in the mid-fourteenth century. Their wall paintings and sculptures range in date from the Northern Liang dynasty (sixth century A.D.) to the Ming dynasty one thousand years later.

It was here that the Hungarian archaeologist and explorer Aurel Stein came in 1907, exploring and seeking to acquire antiquities on behalf of the British Museum and the British Government of India. He had been attracted to the Mogao caves by word of their extraordinary wall paintings. While there he learned of a cache of rare, early Buddhist manuscripts and paintings discovered in one of the caves by their caretaker, the Daoist priest Wang Yuanlu. After studying and documenting them, Stein negotiated a purchase of some 7,000 complete manuscripts, 6,000 fragments, and several cases of paintings, embroideries, and other artifacts, which he sent on to London and New Delhi (while negotiating their purchase, he left for two months and discovered the remains of the Jade Gate).[2] A year later the French Sinologist Paul Pelliot arrived at the caves and studied an estimated 15,000 additional manuscripts over a three-week period. Of these, he purchased a few thousand, which he shipped back to the Musée Guimet and the Bibliothèque Nationale de France in Paris.[3] Additional materials were removed by others over the next few years and are in museums and libraries in China, Japan, the United States, and elsewhere. Together, the finds from the Mogao caves comprise a rich library of Chinese, Tibetan, Uighur, and Khotanese manuscripts, ancient Buddhist sutras, and secular records, including medical records and accounts of grain and clothing from the military magazine at the Jade Gate, and silk paintings and textiles that document the overlapping religious and commercial cultures of the Silk Road.[4]

Langdon Warner, the Harvard professor of Chinese art, traveled to Dunhuang in 1924 on an expedition precisely to retrieve for Harvard an example of the art from the Mogao caves. Warner, who would become famous and celebrated two decades later for discouraging the U.S. military from destroying the Japanese cities of Nara and Kyoto, was sent to China by the director of Harvard's Fogg Art Museum on the First Fogg Expedition to China as part of Harvard's early commitment to the study of Chinese art, history, and language. Warner left Beijing for Dunhuang in August 1923 and arrived five months later, having traveled by train, camel, and pony through the Gansu corridor. It was a harrowing trip, filled with tales of physical exhaustion, illness, and even bandits; it was a time of terrifying political chaos in China with warlords seeking to fill the vacuum left by the demise of the Qing dynasty eleven years earlier. While at the caves, Warner negotiated for the purchase of a Tang dynasty, painted stucco sculpture of a kneeling, attendant bodhisattva from Cave 328. He would also remove, rather awkwardly, some painted wall fragments. The sculpture and the fragments are now in the collection of Harvard's Arthur M. Sackler Museum.[5]

It was as director of the Harvard art museums that I first traveled to the Magao caves in the autumn of 1999. Friends and I were met there by Dr. Fan Jinshi, director of the Dunhuang Academy, a center of research and conservation at the Mogao caves, founded in 1944. Dr. Fan has been at the Academy since before the Cultural Revolution and has dedicated her working life to the greater understanding and appreciation of their importance. Since 1980, when the caves were first formally opened to tourists, she and her colleagues have also managed cultural tourism at the site.

Dr. Fan is a learned, intelligent, forceful, and charming person, diminutive in size but large in stature. She greeted us as we arrived and hosted our luncheon of local delicacies: spicy noodles, vegetables, meats of various kinds, beer, and tea. She told us of her work and devotion to the caves, and she encouraged us to see as much as we could over the next two days and provided us with guides and translators. After lunch, we began our tour. At one point, as every visitor must, we broke to see a small out building with photographic displays documenting the history of the caves, the noble work of the Daoist abbot Wang Yuanlu, and the "discovery" of the caves and their contents by Stein and Pelliot. There is also a panel on the visit to the caves by Langdon Warner. Next to Warner's picture is a photograph of the sculpture he removed from Cave 328, now at Harvard.[6]

For years, both before and after my initial visit to the Mogao caves, I taught a seminar that focused on individual works of art in the Harvard art museums' collections. The Mogao stucco sculpture was always an important part of this seminar. It is a compelling work of art in itself: the wistful elegance of the Tang aesthetic, the chalky colors of the painted stucco, the profound spirit of the depicted figure's devotion to the Buddha all arrest the viewer and compel him or her to look further into the history and purpose of the individual work of art. The students and I read of the caves' history, of the significance of their content for the study of Buddhist art, the history of western China, and the Silk Road. And of course we read Warner's account of his trip to Dunhuang. We then talked about the ethics and politics of his purchasing the sculpture for the university, and of our opportunity to engage with the work first-hand in the course of our studies. I told the students of the regular letters I would get from visitors to Mogao (often erstwhile Harvard graduates) who were embarrassed and angry to see the photographic representation and description of Harvard's role in the removal of objects from the caves. But I also told them of Dr. Fan's courtesies and the frequent visits we would have from Chinese colleagues, none of whom demanded the return of the sculpture to Mogao. Often a student would declare it inappropriate that the work was at Harvard. What right after all did Warner have to disrupt the context of the caves for the purpose of bringing the sculpture to Harvard, regardless of the many students since then who have been inspired by the work to study more about China and its history and even to debate the issues of cultural property and its place in the modern world?

We often ended by discussing the definition of culture, especially national culture, and the benefits of seeing works of art exhibited among works of art of other cultures. What, we wondered, is a national culture in this modern age, when the geographic extent of so many cultures does not coincide with national borders, and when national borders are usually new and artificial creations designating sovereignty over the cultural artifacts of peoples no longer extant or no longer in political power? Why do the Chinese claim the Mogao caves and their contents as Chinese cultural property, when for many of the centuries since the caves' founding, the political authority of China did not extend as far as Dunhuang and where in addition to Han Chinese culture one finds evidence of Tibetan, Uighur, and Khotanese cultures? Wasn't Dunhuang only intermittently within China's cultural sphere of influence over the centuries until it was annexed after a successful imperialist war prosecuted by the Manchurian emperor Qianlong, who was then in control of "Han" China? And didn't the Chinese themselves, during the Cultural Revolution of the 1960s, destroy much Chinese cultural property, even in the area of Dunhuang? And isn't the contemporary Chinese government seeking to minimize the presence of Muslim cultures in the western autonomous regions to the north and northwest of Dunhuang? What after all is Chinese culture today and how does one reconcile it, as one sees it in Shanghai, with what one sees in Dunhuang, Turpan, Urumqi, or Kashgar? Does everyone in the People's Republic of China agree with what is said to be Chinese culture? Or is it, as with national cultures everywhere, the culture of the elite and powerful as opposed to the local and powerless?

There is culture and there is national culture. The former has always been a porous, constantly evolving and dynamic human creation, the result of numerous and endless influences from generations of contact with "foreign" people. No culture of any significance has ever occurred or will ever occur in isolation. And no culture of any consequence has ever been or will ever be free of distant influences.

National culture is always a political construction. It is a fixed concept coincident with the cultural identity the nation's ruling forces claim for themselves and the nation. Chinese culture, like American or French or British or Indian or Mexican culture, is that of the elite and ruling peoples of the nation. It is not the culture of every ethnic or linguistic group within modern China. Officially within China, there are Han Chinese and some fifty-six minority "Chinese" cultures. In the province of Yunnan, minority cultures account for the majority of the population. The People's Republic of China, like other nations of the world, including the United States, is trying to officially include its minority cultures within the dominant cultural construct without challenging the hegemony of the majority culture. In every respect but politically, China is multicultural. Politically, China is Han Chinese. What does this mean for its cultural property laws and attitudes toward "Chinese" antiquities?

As noted earlier in chapter 1, the Chinese government's request to the United States for import restrictions includes all manner of artistic artifacts over thousands of years until 1911, only some of which are antiquities in the conventional use of the term (most are objects made for the trade or by imperial command). I argued against the Chinese request before the U.S. State Department's Cultural Property Advisory Committee in the spring of 2005.[7] The Chinese request included, but was not limited to, all metal, ceramic, stone, painting and calligraphy, textiles, lacquer, bone, ivory, and horn objects from the Paleolithic period to the Qing dynasty—in other words, millennia of human artistic production within the geographic area of today's Chinese borders.[8] The request stated that the pillaging and smuggling of cultural artifacts (it did not distinguish between archaeological and cultural ones) is rampant and destructive to Chinese heritage. It notes specifically that since the mid-nineteenth century, "through invasion and other means, foreign powers have looted Chinese archaeological artifacts," that "[f]rom the beginning of the 20th century, adventurers came into China to pillage sites and illicitly remove countless artifacts," and that in the last ten years looting has again become a serious problem. It assumes that all of these objects were pillaged from and thus caused damage to archaeological sites, resulting in the loss of knowledge. The latter may not be the case, as such material, particularly the easily transportable items like textiles, ceramics, painting, and calligraphy, had often been made for the market and circulated in the trade since at least the Han dynasty more than 2,000 years ago. Equally, it presumed that restricting imports of such material to the United States would stop or at least significantly reduce such pillaging and smuggling. I argued that this would not be the case so long as there are markets for such material elsewhere in the world, including within the People's Republic of China itself. And there are. The total Chinese art auction sales in 2005 inside the People's Republic of China (excluding Hong Kong) more than doubled over the 2004 total to US$1.5 billion.[9] (For scale, this is more than 25 times Christie's and Sotheby's combined U.S. sales of Chinese art in 2005.) Today there are more than eighty Chinese auction houses and hundreds of private dealers within the People's Republic of China handling the same items China requested U.S. Customs to embargo.

I argued before the CPAC that the Chinese request was really an attempt to have the U.S. government help enforce China's nationalist retentionist cultural property laws. And I sketched a history of China's efforts to control the trade in its self-proclaimed cultural property.

As early as 1930, the government of China had laws on the books restricting access to and trade in designated Chinese cultural relics.[10] The law on the Preservation of Ancient Objects, dated June 7, 1930, was passed in response to the removal of cultural artifacts from China—especially from the Silk Road, including, even specifically, from Dunhuang by Stein, Pelliott, and Warner—over the previous decades. The law forbade the export of cultural objects and the transfer of such goods to foreigners even within China. It also prohibited foreigners from engaging in any archaeological excavation in China. Soon after the founding of the People's Republic of China in 1949, the new government passed Provisional Measures Prohibiting the Exportation of Precious and Valuable Art Objects, Pictures, and Books and the Provisional Measures Governing the Investigation and Excavation of the Sites of Ancient Cultural Ruins and Ancient Graves and Burial Grounds (May 24, 1950). These measures governed access to and distribution of cultural property, which meant objects of revolutionary, historical, or cultural interest to the state. Other kinds of objects could be exported through designated ports, subject to inspection and sealing. Field research by foreigners was prohibited without government permission. Also in 1950, and again in 1953 and 1956, the Political Affairs Council of the central government issued various instructions concerning the protection of ancient sites, cultural buildings, and historical and revolutionary relics.[11]

In 1961, legislation was passed on the protection and administration of cultural heritage, including buildings, sites, and objects of historical interest which recall great events of the past, revolutionary movements or important figures, ancient sites, and "valuable works of art and applied art, regardless of the period to which they belong," as well as "representative objects which reflect the social system, social production and the life of society in all periods." The 1982 Cultural Relics Law uses similar terms and charges Peoples Committee at all levels with responsibility for protecting and administering cultural heritage. In addition, it declares all unearthed relics state property, prohibits their export without state authorization, and allows for their expropriation and confiscation in the case of illegal exports.

The 1982 law does allow for both state ownership and private ownership of cultural relics. Of the latter, it noted that "Ownership of . . . cultural relics handed down from generation to generation which belongs to collectives or individuals shall be protected by state laws. Owners of the cultural relics must abide by the relevant state regulations governing the protection and control of cultural relics." This reinstatement of private cultural property ownership rights in the People's Republic of China marked a very big change in Chinese law. In 1980, there were no art auctions in China. In 2006, almost $2 billion worth of art was sold at public auctions. The initial auctions were conducted by state-run auctioneers selling confiscated art from government warehouses. Private auctions quickly took over and now the P.R.C. auctions are all private enterprises loosely regulated by the government. And of course most of the successful Chinese bidders at the auctions are private individuals, with the result that private collections in China, including Hong Kong, are growing far more rapidly than public collections are enlarging.

The 1982 law also emphasizes the state's duty to "protect" cultural relics by prohibiting their sale except to the state and through the state sales apparatus and requiring their verification by the state. It prohibits private sales of cultural relics between individuals and to foreigners, although it allows for their being inherited by—and presumably gifted between—P.R.C. nationals. (This has been the letter of the law, but there was little enforcement of it as sales between individuals took place openly at large antiques "hyper markets" like *Guwancheng* in Beijing; and such "hyper markets" have only proliferated since 1982 in various metropolitan centers.) While the law does allow for export of cultural relics with state approval, the practice as of 1994 is not to allow for reasons other than a loan to a temporary exhibition, the export of any cultural relic that dates before 1795, or the sixtieth year of the reign of the Qing Emperor, Qianlong.[12]

Seeking to strengthen the 1982 law, which some considered too broad and lacking in means of implementation, a Circular on Cracking Down on Activities Involving Smuggling and Illegal Excavation for Cultural Relics was issued in 1987. It reinforced the 1982 principles regarding state ownership of undiscovered relics, the prohibition on private sales, and the propriety of severe punishment for those individuals, especially state personnel, caught breaking the law. In the same year, Provisional Regulations on Administrative Penalties for Speculation and Profiteering were passed to address the reselling of cultural relics as an act of speculation and profiteering. But still the central government felt a need to strengthen policy and regulations on cultural relics. And so for a third time since 1987 it issued an administrative circular, a Notice on Further Strengthening of Cultural Relics Work, which lamented that "the present development of the work on cultural relics is far from commensurate with the history of our motherland and the progress of our modernization programme. It is also way out of line with the task of reviving the great Chinese civilization."[13] These laws were not backed by enforcement mechanisms, however, and the internal art market has continued to grow at a dramatic pace.

The current Chinese economic boom began with Deng Xiaoping's economic reform plan in 1979. Care had to be taken to preserve cultural relics from damage during construction of major public works projects. Yet the pillaging of archaeological sites continued unabated, even as the nation was taking greater pride in its past as the foundation for its modern future, wanting to be certain that more and more of its cultural property remained within China as a means of reviving "the great Chinese civilization." Measures on the Administration of Export Verification for Cultural Relics were issued in 1989 to supplement the export provisions of the 1982 law. They increased the kinds of relics subject to verification before export. And they now included items not normally associated with cultural heritage: "All pottery, gold and silver wares, copper wares, other metal wares, jade articles, lacquerwares, glasswares, carvings of various materials, sculptures, furniture, painting and calligraphy, rubbings from stone inscriptions, books of stone rubbings, books, documentary materials, brocade, stationery, stamps, currency, appliances, utensils, handicrafts and artistic objects etc., made, produced or published by China and foreign countries before 1949 when the People's Republic of China was established; the works of late or contemporary famous painters or calligraphers, artists and crafters of the state, after 1949; paleovertebrates and paleoanthropoids, must be subject to verification for export."[14] Clearly the government was tightening its borders and widening its net for all items it considered cultural relics. Just how such items were to be verified or graded, judged worthy of restriction or allowed to be exported, was unclear. There were no objective criteria for making such determinations, and judgments in these cases were left to the various verification units.

As the Chinese economy continued to develop—by 1992 it was the world's fastest-growing economy, averaging 10 percent annual growth—and individual citizens and government-sanctioned industrial companies began to enjoy discretionary spending and alternative forms of capital investing (i.e., in works of art), the government began to release restrictions on the domestic market in cultural relics. This caused concern among critics of the commercial trade in such material, who in February 1992 called for greater controls on the illegal trade in domestic relics. The government responded with the Law of the People's Republic of China on the Protection of Cultural Relics, which sought to strengthen regulations over private ownership of and trade in "Precious" cultural relics, or those of the "First, Second, and Third grades."

Chinese interest in protecting and preserving cultural relics, and cultural property generally, has increased coincident with the nation's economic development.[15] Between 1979 and 1987, China devoted RMB300 million to cultural relics protection, more than was spent in all of the first thirty years of the People's Republic of China. The amount budgeted for 1992 was RMB120 million, an increase of RMB70 million over 1991, with even more spent in subsequent years. At the same time, much more was being spent on economic development, often resulting in the destruction of archaeological sites. The Three Gorges Dam is only the most famous incidence of this. Often described as "China's biggest construction project since the Great Wall," the dam is expected to produce as much electricity as eighteen nuclear power plants and to tame the notoriously dangerous Yangtze River, which through flooding has claimed more than 1 million lives over the past one hundred years. The project is expected to be completed in 2009 and flood nearly four hundred square miles of land, which some archaeologists have estimated contain as many as 1,300 important archaeological sites, including some relating to the Ba, an ancient people who settled the region over 4,000 years ago. The government has recognized this and has supported salvage archaeology in the area. But while the dam itself cost billions of dollars and was set to a relentless construction schedule, only a tiny budget and short period of time were allocated to "emergency" archaeology.

As of mid-1993, the government claims to have restored 1,000 ancient palaces, caves, buildings, and sites, and to have examined a further 350,000 sites, many of which contain several hundred tombs.[16] It promises soon to open hundreds of new museums, including some dedicated to the presentation and preservation of cultural relics and ethnic minority artifacts. These initiatives are not only the result of considerable concern over the pillaging of archaeological sites and the looting of cultural relics for both domestic and foreign markets, but also the result of increasing pride in China's cultural heritage and excitement about the potential for commercial and cultural tourism development. A 1993 news article praised advances in cultural relics training and conservation by noting that "The efforts have paid off. In 1992 forty-four historic and cultural cities earned an equivalent of RMB10.33 billion in tourism."[17]

With economic development has come calls for discouraging export of cultural relics to foreign markets and buying back "for China" Chinese cultural relics "held" abroad. Among the Chinese companies most active in the domestic and international markets for Chinese relics is the Poly Group, a conglomerate with its own museum of Chinese antiquities, mostly unprovenanced and unexcavated.

The Poly Art Museum in Beijing opened in December 1999. It is an exemplary facility, with modern environmental systems, security measures, and installation design comparable to any museum anywhere in the world. And its scholarship is equally advanced. Its permanent collection catalogues are handsome and thorough: fully illustrated, with interpretive essays, full and accurate descriptions of individual objects, and line drawings and photographs of details when appropriate.[18] The museum is also highly acquisitive. Early in 2000, it spent $4 million to purchase three Qing dynasty bronze heads of a monkey, ox, and tiger that had originally been part of a zodiac fountain at the Chinese Emperor's Old Summer Palace (Yuanmingyuan) outside Beijing. The relics had been looted by British and French soldiers in the middle of the nineteenth century during a punitive expedition following the end of the second Opium War. The bronze heads eventually ended up in European collections, and when Christie's and Sotheby's auction houses announced their intention to sell the works in Hong Kong, Chinese nationalists in both Hong Kong and the People's Republic of China rose up in opposition. Even the dissident Hong Kong–based April 5 Action Group, typically fiercely critical of the Beijing government, was outraged by the intended sale.[19]

The P.R.C. State Bureau of Cultural Relics objected to the sale of the bronze heads for fear that they would be purchased by foreign collections and thus remain outside China. But Hong Kong officials claimed they had to honor their commercial obligations and were not bound by any P.R.C. constraints on selling antiquities. The sale went ahead and the Poly Art Museum stopped at nothing to acquire the bronzes. Ma Baoping, curator of the museum, insisted he had no choice but to pay whatever was necessary to recover the works: "If there are 12 hostages and you can only save three, would you do nothing? We must pay regardless of the cost," he said. For him, and for many P.R.C. elite, the bronzes were seen as hostages, as rightfully belonging to the Chinese people and, as they were being put up for auction where they might be purchased by anyone from anywhere in the world, it was like they were being stolen again; or rather, having been stolen and now once again on view, it was like they were being held for ransom. Xie Da Tong, managing director of Poly Investment Holdings Ltd, which officially bought the relics for the museum, said "It is not right that somebody either looted your personal belongings or stole your personal belongings. They can keep it if there's no international rule or policing of these kind of activities, but it's not fair that they should come to your house [i.e., Hong Kong] and try to sell those products. This is a very bad impression on me and I think on many of the Chinese people."[20]

The purchase of the bronzes was in keeping with what the *New York Times* described as part of the museum's mission "to bring back

Chinese treasures that have been smuggled or sold out of the country."[21] The Chairman of the Poly Group, Shan Yihe, wrote in the preface to a catalogue of selected highlights of the museum's ancient bronzes in 2001: "Most of these pieces [the forty bronzes included in the catalogue], lost to overseas collections, have exchanged hands many times. . . . Their return not only makes us fondly recollect days of old, but is more importantly a source of great comfort." And the "rescue of three bronze animal heads, formerly of the Summer Palace, particularly aroused the patriotic passions of Chinese sons and daughters. Regardless of the difference in their political stands and religions, they all equally praised the rescue."[22]

The museum proclaims to seek only "the precious, the rare and the fine," searching "widely in Europe, Asia, and America, enabling a large amount of cultural relics on the level of national treasures to return to their native place, putting an end to their wicked fate of wandering without proper shelter." And its chairman goes on to declare proudly that the "Poly Art Museum greatly enhanced the movement to preserve the cultural relics of our motherland, and received wide praise from all fields." The nationalist rhetoric is obvious: the museum's mission is political, acquiring for China what it believes to be rightfully China's cultural heritage. How—and how *recently*—the antiquities of art got on to the domestic or international market is beside the point. As the *New York Times* noted, the museum has spent millions of dollars, mainly in Hong Kong and Taiwan, "where newly discovered relics tend to appear on the market after being smuggled out of China. Some of the most stunning bronzes were almost certainly unearthed and smuggled out in just the past several years, museum officials believe." "It's not a very cheerful job, buying these items back from overseas," Mr. Yu said. "But I think the Chinese people will be happy to know that at least we're getting them back." Mr. Yu toured the *New York Times* reporter through the museum and pointed out the rarest and most valuable bronze in the collection, from the Western Zhou period, 11th–8th century B.C., which he noted was probably unearthed in Shaanxi Province in the "recent past," and which he bought from a Hong Kong dealer.[23] (The Poly Group has many divisions, of which the Poly Art Museum is but one section of one division.

Another section of that same division is the Beijing Poly International Auctions Co., Ltd, which claims to be among the top five auction houses in the People's Republic of China).[24]

Critics of U.S. and European art museums would not approve of our purchasing unprovenanced antiquities likely to have been only recently and clandestinely unearthed and smuggled out of the source country. These critics hold that such purchases only encourage further looting and smuggling and that the only way to stop looting and smuggling is to not purchase unprovenanced antiquities. This is the basis too for the Chinese government's request to the U.S. government to prohibit import into the United States of what it claims to be its cultural property, including antiquities. It asks the U.S. government to not permit U.S. museums to acquire what Chinese art museums can acquire, both within China and elsewhere: unprovenanced and likely looted and recently smuggled antiquities. The Chinese justification is that these are rightfully Chinese property, wherever they may now be. Buying them back for China is a patriotic act regardless of any alleged incentivizing effect such acquisitions may have on the looting of archaeological sites. And the constraints they want the rest of the world to accept—that Chinese antiquities and cultural property proposed for acquisition be accompanied by documentation proving that they were legally removed from China and not excavated or looted—do not apply.

Two years after the Poly Art Museum purchased the Yuanmingyuan bronze heads, the China Cultural Relics Recovery Fund was established.[25] Chinese businesses making donations to the fund were allowed tax exemptions. The web site ChinaCulture.org described the fund as the "first and only art foundation in China that enjoys such a policy widely adopted in Europe and the United States." The director of the fund was quoted as saying that "the rise in the price of artwork in its home country, and the forthcoming return of the country's relics from overseas have been a natural result of the economic boom." He was also quoted as saying that there are three ways for a country to recover cultural relics from overseas collections: "to apply international conventions, to purchase them and to get them back as donations."[26]

In April 2005, ChinaCulture.org reported that the China Cultural Relics Recovery Program had announced a new project to reclaim China's national treasures from around the world. It reported that "Artifacts returned from overseas account for more than 50% of lots at domestic auctions, and 60% of total auction deals. By January 2005, nearly 40,000 returned cultural relics had been auctioned to Chinese buyers."[27] Two months later in an article on the China Cultural Relics Recovery Program, *China Daily* reported a senior cultural heritage preservation expert as saying "Cultural wealth can be shared by the whole world, but not the ownership, just like the property rights on software. Ownership of lost Chinese cultural treasures should lie with the Chinese people." In the same article it was also noted that the *Wall Street Journal* reported that the spring 2005 Christie's auction of Chinese relics totaled $10 million, most of the relics being purchased by Chinese.[28]

In early 2006, the (UK) *Guardian* newspaper reported on the British Museum's loan of more than 270 objects from its collection to the Capital Museum, Beijing. No Chinese objects were included. The director of the Capital Museum was quoted as saying that "If we exhibited these items it would imply that we recognized their ownership." In the same article, a spokesman from the Poly Group, which was credited with spending GBP 57 million to buy Chinese art from abroad, is quoted as saying, "Foreign friends should come to China to appreciate Chinese art objects, yet too often we end up going overseas to see them in foreign museums. Our national treasures should not be flowing beyond our borders. They are ours, part of our roots."[29]

The Poly Art Museum, for which the Poly Group purchased so much of its Chinese art, enjoys the closest relations with China's elite. At its founding, it was headed by He Ping, a son-in-law of Deng Xiaoping, and one of its primary consultants is Yu Weichao, until recently head of the National Museum of Chinese History in Beijing. The Poly Group itself is well connected. Officially China Poly Group Corporation, it was, according to its Web site, founded in 1984 with "acceptance by the central government, State Department and Central Military Commission, Poly Technology Co., Ltd was built up jointly invested by Furnishment flow of the General Staff and China

International Trust & Investment Corporation specializing in import and export of industrial equipments."[30] In 1992, upon "acceptance by the State Department and Central Military Commission, China Poly Group Corporation was founded on the basis of Poly Technology Co., Ltd." A year later it was "one of those corporations specifically designated in the state plan." In 1994, on its tenth anniversary, General Secretary Mr. Ziang Zemin acknowledged the national importance of the corporation by making the epigraph (a traditional kind of written declaration of value, like those found on important temples and monuments during Imperial times), "Solidification and Enterprising for Flourish of Poly." Premier Li Peng made the epigraph, "Learning from those advanced for enterprising and progress." Vice Premier Li Peng made the epigraph, "Sticking to the priority of quality and credit and keeping on enterprising for contribution to the career of foreign trade and cooperation." Vice President of Military Commission Liu Huaqing made the epigraph, "A Hard work having brought out 110–124 achievement and making persistent for more progress." And Minister of National Defense Chi Hoatian made the epigraph, "A Hard working and enterprising and dedication with selflessness." And in 1999, the same year as the founding of the Poly Art Museum, the Poly Group became "one of those 180 key state-owned enterprises directly under administration of central government."

Its Web site further notes that after twenty years of development, Poly Group has "shaped up two core businesses: defense products trading and real estate development and has cultivated and developed a cultural industry." It lists its total assets as of 2004 as 15.5 billion yuan ($2B), and its profit that year as 538 million yuan ($70M). A year later, as a result of an announced equity participation with Credit Suisse, the Swiss financial services company described the Chinese conglomerate as having business activities in trading, real estate, culture, and the arts with total assets estimated to be more than HKD20 billion ($7.8B).[31] Poly Group is no small business, and the Poly Art Museum is not without resources for buying Chinese antiquities at home or abroad.

Running throughout the various descriptions of the Poly Group cited is its relationship to the Chinese military and "defense products trading," or arms dealing. The *New York Times* article pointed this out up front. Its opening paragraph reads in full: "A much-needed little antiquities museum has been created in Beijing by a most improbable source: a giant state corporation that was long notorious for its global weapons sales and was until recently a branch of the People's Liberation Army." The article was published in July 2006. When the Archaeological Institute of America's popular magazine *Archaeology* reported on the purchase of the Yuanmingyuan bronze zodiac heads by the Poly Art Museum in 2000, it described the Poly Group simply as a "Beijing-based state owned corporation."[32] By then and by its own admission on its Web site, the Poly Group was a large industrial and commercial conglomerate with an extensive history in dealing arms.

The Canadian Security Intelligence Service report of August 27, 2003 (Commentary No. 84) described the production of arms in China like this:

> In order to increase funds for the military, in the 1980s the Chinese army was allowed to enter into profit-making businesses, under favourable tax and investment rules. By the mid-1990s, the so-called PLA Inc. [People's Liberation Army] included over twenty thousand companies in everything from agribusiness to electronics to tourism to arms exports. In 1998, because of concerns about corruption and discipline, the leadership ordered the PLA to divest itself of its profit-oriented businesses in exchange for increases to the military budget. . . . But the PLA has not completely withdrawn from the economy, nor have divested firms completely severed ties with the PLA. These issues are best illustrated by the example of Poly Technologies, founded in the 1980s by the son of a PLA marshal, and currently headed by the son in law of Deng Xiaoping. Before 1998, Poly was one of the major exporters of weapons and technology from China. It had several U.S. subsidiaries involved in technology acquisition. . . . Its employees were implicated in the 1996 attempt to smuggle AK-47s into the U.S. The effects of the divestiture order on Poly are not entirely clear. Its arms-trading entities are believed to have been retained by the newly created General Armaments Division of the PLA, where they are not easily subject to civilian control. Now known as China Poly Group, the divested Poly has diversified

into a broad conglomerate, active in tourism, infrastructure construction and real estate. . . . Poly is believed to have influenced defence production and procurement entities to over-supply the PLA arsenal, with Poly selling the surplus abroad at reduced prices.[33]

The Poly Group and its Art Museum are aggressively seeking to purchase—and the Poly International Auction Co., Ltd., is trying to sell—the very kind of material that the Chinese government is requesting the U.S. government to ban. This is clearly a case where retentionist cultural property laws are part of a nationalist cultural and political agenda. Cultural property laws are devised to serve the nationalist agenda of the state. And when antiquities are counted as cultural property—Western Zhou bronzes together with Qing dynasty bronzes—they are being used for the same purpose: to legitimize the current government by reference to an ancient Chinese culture, as if the People's Republic of China were the rightful, indeed *natural*, heir to Chinese dynasties of millennia past.

❖ ❖ ❖

But what of minority ethnic cultural property in China? How does a minority culture fit into the official P.R.C. view of what is and is not Chinese cultural property? To learn more about Chinese minority cultures, I flew northwest from Dunhuang to Urumqi, capital city of the Xinjiang Uighur Autonomous Region, in the fall of 2005. I returned a year later and traveled south from Urumqi to Kashgar, a major oasis town on the western edge of the Taklimakan Desert, still within Xinjiang but not far from the borders of Afghanistan, Tajikistan, and Kyrgystan.

The Dunhuang airport had probably tripled in size in the four years that separated my first and second visits to the Magao caves. But it was nothing like the Urumqi International Airport, which is only one of Xinjiang's seven major airports. (Xinjiang leads all Chinese provinces and autonomous regions in the number of airports; the Xinjiang Airline Company shipped a passenger volume of 1,340,600 passengers last year.)[34] For Urumqi is the capital of China's largest region, with a landmass of 1.66 million square kilometers, or roughly one-sixth of the entire landmass of the People's Republic of China and three times the size of France. Its population of about 20 million is almost half Uighur, local peoples of Turkic descent and for hundreds of years Muslim by faith. The ethnic makeup of the region is a matter of concern to both local Uighurs and the central P.R.C. government.

The name Xinjiang means "new frontier" or "new territory" in Chinese, and dates only from the eighteenth century, when the Emperor Qianlong extended the Qing Empire to its greatest extent by defeating the Zunghar Mongols and controlling much of present-day Xinjiang.[35] (The name was officially given the region later, only in 1884.) Xinjiang had been first inhabited thousands of years before by what appear to have been Indo-European peoples from the steppes north and east of the Black Sea. The celebrated "Loulan Beauty," the preserved remains of a female corpse unearthed in the Tieban River delta in 1980, dates from around 4,000 years ago.[36] During the second century B.C., the area was occupied by members of a confederation of Altaic-speaking tribes, called the Xiongnu, who formed an empire encompassing much of Mongolia, northwest China, and Zungharia. They were opposed by the Chinese during the Han dynasty, and ultimately divided much of the region with them. The Han dynasty fell in A.D. 221 and various tribal confederations ruled part of the region in succession for the next 350 years. Around A.D. 560, the Kök Türks rode out of Mongolia, defeated the local powers, and held control over much of the area until their defeat at the hands of the Chinese Tang, who controlled the area through military and diplomatic alliances with the Turkic peoples. The influence of the Kök Türks over the region only increased during this period, despite Tang sovereignty. Throughout much of the seventh and eighth centuries, the Tang Chinese lost control over parts of the region through rebellions in the west and control of the south by a Tibetan empire. The Tang finally retreated altogether from Xinjiang in the mid-eighth century to focus attention and resources on the An Lushan rebellion "back home," but not before it enlisted the help of the recently arrived Uighur peoples from the north to serve as its proxy in the Xinjiang region.

The Uighurs controlled much of the Xinjiang region for the next one hundred years until they were ultimately destroyed by the Kyrgyz peoples from the northwest in A.D. 840, and scattered throughout the region; the main group of Uighurs settled in what is now Urumqi and Turpan and the area in between. There, Uighur kings ruled from the nineth through the thirteenth centuries, or longer than any other power in the history of the area.

These early Uighurs were not Muslim but Mongols who embraced Manichaeanism and Buddhism and tolerated Christianity. They intermarried with Iranian and other Indo-European peoples who had made up the indigenous population of the area before the Türks arrived. It was the Karakhanid rulers, who had emerged following the Kyrgyz victory over the Uighurs in the western reaches of the area, who converted much of the western Xinjiang region to Islam by the eleventh century. The elite, primarily Buddhist, Turkic society centered in the south around Turpan became known as Uyghuristan from 932 to 1450, to distinguish it from the Muslim Türks living in the western parts of Xinjiang. The Buddhist Uighurs converted to Islam only in the fifteenth century. Thus, although the modern Uighur people take their name from the historical Uighur Empire, they take their religion from the Karakhanid Muslims. Of course, too, since the mid-eighteenth century, they have been "Chinese," part of the People's Republic of China since 1949, and officially the Xinjiang Uighurs Autonomous Region since 1959. (To complicate matters a bit more, the region was a satellite of the USSR from 1934 to 1941, during a period of political chaos in China, and the Eastern Turkistan Republic from 1933 to 1934 and again from 1944 to 1949, a distinctly multiethnic state.)

The Xinjiang region is and always has been a borderland. The historian Peter Perdue has written that "[t]he frontier zone was a liminal space where cultural identities merged and shifted, as peoples of different ethnic and linguistic roots interacted for common economic purposes. . . . The story of the eighteenth-century Qing empire is of an effort to seal off this ambiguous, threatening frontier experience once and for all by incorporating it within the fixed boundaries of a distinctly defined space, and by drawing lines that clearly demarcated separate cultures." But "since Chinese efforts to demarcate the frontier never succeeded, the zone was never stabilized. It always contained transitional social groups—sinicized nomads, semi-barbarized Chinese, Tibetans, Muslims, and peasants."[37]

Xinjiang is a conglomerate of different cultures—forty-seven different ethnic groups—mostly, as Perdue describes them, "separate and oriented toward their local environments." Ever since the Qing dynasty, at least, colonizing political entities have tried to dominate the region by changing the makeup of its ethnic identity. The Qing first sent military colonists, both Manchu and Han, then exiled criminals, then resettled Han Chinese from Gansu Province looking for agricultural opportunities, and finally Muslim settlers from the south to help clear new land in and diversify the population of the north. Modern Chinese historians have described the Qing settlement policies and practices as precursors to the modern multinationality nation-state of Xinjiang. But Xinjiang's multinationality remains of concern to the P.R.C. On the one hand, the central government in Beijing wants to promote local culture: hence the new Xinjiang Uighurs Autonomous Region Museum in Urumqi, dedicated to the preservation and presentation of local cultural relics. But it also wants to control it, knowing well the region's legacy of independent actions and movements. It is doing so by pumping development money into the region (hence the new, expanded airport).

The number of Han Chinese as a proportion of Xinjiang's population increased from 5 percent in 1949 to 40 percent in 1982 (it was still roughly 40 percent in 2000).[38] In the 1990s, the Beijing government developed a plan to relocate hundreds of thousands of inhabitants from the Three Gorges Dam area of Sichuan to Xinjiang. Today, according to *The Times of Central Asia*, the majority population of Xinjiang is Chinese.[39] This is a result of the Beijing government's "great development of the west" program, often referred to as the "Go West" policy, launched in January 2000. In part it is designed to overwhelm or at least balance the dominance of the Uighurs in the area, certainly in the urban areas. The capital city of Urumqi, for example, was 76 percent Han in 1998, as opposed to the small oasis town of Turpan, which was 71 percent Uighur. But it is also a natural result of wanting to shore up the far western border of the nation with large populations of politically stable citizens enjoying the fruits of the region's economic development. Within five years, Xinjiang is expected to become the country's biggest producer of crude oil and natural gas, sitting on 40 percent of the nation's proven oil reserves and 34 percent of its natural gas reserves. And it is expected to more than double its annual output of oil within a few years. It also borders on Russia, Kazakhstan, and Kyrgyzstan, energy-rich countries from which China wants to import as much oil and gas as possible. And there is talk of two east–west natural gas pipelines from Xinjiang to the southern Chinese province of Guangdong and from Xinjiang to Siberia, the latter to connect with a pipeline already between Xinjiang and Shanghai.[40] (The modern hotels of Kashgar are filled with Petro-China oil workers wearing smart red uniforms and driving white, modern, imported SUVs back and forth from Kashgar to the oil wells deep in the Taklimakan Desert. The contrast between the Chinese engineers and the local Uighur population is telling in appearance and financial resources, and the two groups rarely meet; the Chinese remain hotel guests uninterested in patronizing the local markets and bazaar. Petro China attracted $1 trillion in market capitalization at its first public offering of stock in China in November 2007.)

But such economic development hasn't solved the "Uighur Problem." The region, episodically fiercely independent, is thought still to be a separatist threat to the central government. Beijing has denounced the "three evil forces" of separatist, terrorist, and religious extremism in Xinjiang.[41] As an "autonomous region"—Xinjiang Uighurs Autonomous Region—the government must be led by Uighurs. But the Chinese Communist Party, which wields the real power in the region, is typically headed by Han Chinese (by one account, Uighurs make up only 37% of the CCP in Xinjiang).[42] The collapse of the Soviet Union and the emergence of independent states in Central Asia caused Beijing concern for the fate of Xinjiang. The Standing Committee of the CCP—the most powerful men in China—convened a special meeting in March 1996 to discuss the "Xinjiang question." The official record of the meeting was a secret document obtained by Human Rights Watch in late 1997.[43] The document suggested a variety of measures to curb current and potential terrorist, separatist problems in Xinjiang, including the transfer to the region of "reliable" Party cadres, the purging from the CCP of ethnic Uighur cadres who "believe in religion and refuse to change, mobilization of China's security apparatus, and the resettlement in the area of large numbers of Han Chinese." In the same year, the central government announced a "Strike Hard" campaign in Xinjiang, outlawing "illegal" religious activities and countering violent opposition with the imposition of long terms of imprisonment and executions (some 24 in 2000 alone).

The Chinese government has focused simultaneously on secular resistance and religious activities in the region, at times confusing the one for the other. On April 5, 1990, Uighurs were killed in clashes with Chinese police near Kashgar (in an incident known in Chinese as the Baren County Counter-Revolutionary Armed Rebellion). Five years later, in the southern oasis town of Khotan, a large number of Muslim worshippers left their mosque to block traffic. When the police tried to clear them, they revolted and hundreds were killed and even more arrested. And then in 1997, more than three hundred students were killed in Ili in conflicts with police and soldiers. Bombing incidents occurred later that year in Urumqi and in Beijing, where Uighur militants blew up a bus. Central government crackdown on Uighur violence and opposition only increased after the September 11, 2001, attacks on New York. The Chinese government charged that Uighur groups had links with the Taliban in Afghanistan and were supported by radical Islamist organizations abroad.[44] In August 2002, the government identified eight Uighur terrorist groups operating in Xinjiang, including the Eastern Turkish Islamic Movement and the more secular Eastern Turkistan International Movement.

A few weeks later, the U.S. State Department, China, and the United Nations announced that the Eastern Turkish Islamic Movement would be placed on the list of international terrorist organizations.[45] (The state-run press referred to all of them generally as "East Turkestan terrorists.") Antagonism to the Uighurs was not shared by all Washington politicians after the September 11 attacks; not even by all conservative Republicans. Senator Jesse Helms, for example, no friend of terrorists or enemies of the United States of any kind, wrote an op-ed piece in the *Washington Times* a month after the attacks declaring that if "the U.S. should end up receiving any kind of support from Beijing for our anti-terrorist efforts, it will almost certainly come at the price of acquiescence in China's crackdown on the Uighurs (as well as its attempt to crush Tibet and isolate Taiwan). That would be a moral clamity, for there is no justification in lumping the Uighurs with the murderous fanatics who demonstrably mean us harm. The Uighurs are engaged in a just struggle for freedom from Beijing's tyrannical rule." Helms was also a major supporter of Radio Free Asia's Uighur broadcasts, which had begun broadcasting in 1998 in a format similar to that of Voice of America. When in May 2000, the U.S. House of Representatives passed legislation establishing permanent normal trade relations with China, it attached a provision increasing funding for both Radio Free Asia and Voice of America.[46]

The New York–based Human Rights Watch claims that the "security problem that exists in Xinjiang is being manipulated by Chinese authorities for political ends. When it is expedient—for example, when trying to attract foreign investment for the multimillion Xinjiang-Shanghai pipeline—the authorities insist that only 'an extremely small number of elements' are engaged in separatism, and that the situation is stable. . . . On the other hand, when it desires international support for its crackdown on Uighur challenges to Chinese authority, including peaceful activities, the government raises the specter of Islamic terrorism."[47] Many Western observers do not see a serious Islamist threat within Xinjiang but do note the existence of a Uighur opposition-in-exile, which is based in Turkey, Germany, and the United States and comprises a federation of many Turkish and European Uighur associations. Human Rights Watch reports that these and pan-Turkic movements like the East Turkestan Party and the Uighur Liberation Organization are ethno-nationalist movements, "that is, articulated along ethnic lines, not religious ones. There is no significant cooperation among Xinjiang's different Muslim ethnic groups of Kazakhs, Mongols, Tajiks, and Uighurs." In addition, as with most nationalist and separatist groups everywhere, Uighur nationalist groups tend to be led most often by intellectuals rather than religious leaders. And Uighur intellectuals are less inclined than most

Uighurs to identify Islam as a key element in their personal identity. They see themselves as Marxists, even Kemalist republicans like the secular groups in Turkey. Nevertheless, as two scholars wrote recently, "Islam is likely to play an increasing role in the Uyghur [sic] nationalist movement in the future. The intensity of the nationalist movement will inevitably increase, for it is nourished by the single dominant and sinister reality for all Uyghurs—relentless, massive, and unceasing in-migration of Han Chinese that threatens virtually every aspect of the Uyghurs' communal existence across Xinjiang."[48]

Uighur identity is formed by the peoples' history as frontier or border people. (Xinjiang is bordered by Mongolia, Russia, Kazakhstan, Kyrgyzstan, Tajikistan, Afghanistan, Pakistan, India, and Tibet.) Their long and complicated history has weakened any sense of a unified identity. As one scholar put it, "a 'Uyghur' can be variously a Uyghur; a Muslim; a Turk who is part of a greater Turkic world and a speaker of a Turkic language; a resident of a specific oasis town, which has its own special local culture (e.g., Kashgar, Turpan, and Aksu); a citizen of China, however unsought this status might be."[49] For Uighurs, as for all individuals, which aspect of identity is most important at any one time depends on the issue at hand and its social context.

This is true for the Han Chinese just as much as it is for the Uighurs. And it makes one wonder when the Poly Art Museum chairman wrote that his museum's "rescue of three bronze animal heads, formerly of the Summer palace, particularly aroused the patriotic passions of Chinese sons and daughters," which sons and daughters he had in mind. The Han Chinese and all of the fifty-six ethnic minority peoples, the latter comprising nearly 10 percent of the Chinese population? Is it possible that all Chinese everywhere felt patriotic about the bronze heads from the zodiac fountain of the Qing Summer Palace? What could ever justify such a remark? Clearly a range of Chinese people likely felt differently about the purchase, if they knew of it at all. And the chairman must have known this was the case because he made the further point that "regardless of their differences in their political stands and religions, they all equally praised the rescue." Differences in politics and religions exist and are often sources for difficulties, even violence. The destruction and looting of the Old Summer Palace was no doubt an offense to official Chinese confidence at the time. But did the Uighurs care then? Do they care now?

It is hard to imagine, when driving the long, straight, recently paved road from Urumqi to Turpan, that many people there cared about the Yuanmingyuan sculptures when they were looted in the 1860s or "saved" for China and the Chinese in 2000. The drive is many hours long. The "Flaming Mountains" are off to the left, great red, sandstone hills that run for 100 kilometers, empty and foreboding. To the right, from time to time, oil wells and machinery appear like large, mechanical Bactrian camels moving rhythmically across the sand in the blinding light of the desert sun. Even in October and November, it is hot during the day. The ruins of the ancient city of Jiaohe look like so many melting forms only slightly reminiscent of buildings. Jiaohe was the capital city of one of the small kingdoms in the "Western Regions" during the Han dynasty. Perched high on a terrace with rivers on either side, it gave protection to local peoples and troops from raiding bands of Xiongnu horsemen. And it did so for hundreds of years, even for the Uighurs, until the Mongols destroyed most of it and it was abandoned during the Yuan dynasty in the fourteenth century. Walking among the ruins one gets a sense of the urban plan and scale of dwellings and public spaces, but not much else. It is a lonely place now and, I suspect, despite the nearby rivers and grapes and trees, it was always so. It was more a garrison town than a city, a place where, far from the rest of the world, local peoples worked hard to live and were always subject to the threats and violence of conquering armies.

Turpan is six miles to the east. It was an important oasis town along the Silk Road. One of its earliest names, "Land of Fire," derived from the intense, long summer temperatures. Grapes grow well here, and from grapes, raisins and wine are made. Turpan commanded the northern trade routes along the Tarim Basin. Caravans stopped here on their way from Dunhuang en route to Urumqi to the north or Kashgar to the west. It is still a market town. The markets are filled with local produce—grapes, raisins, melons, and pomegranates—and yogurt, cold rice noodles, kebabs, and delicious *nan* flatbreads filled with meat or plain. The markets also have stalls and stalls of modern, ikat-looking fabric, electric colors of feathered stripes flecked with golden, metallic thread, and machine-produced carpets and quilted jackets and caps. The ikat-like fabrics are like displays of exploding fireworks along the otherwise drab and dusty streets and recall the handmade, Central Asian ikats first produced and sold along the Silk Road in the eighth and ninth centuries and then sold in greater and greater numbers through the nineteenth century in Bukhara and Samarkand to the west.[50]

Turpan is a Muslim town today. Its Uighur residents were converted to the faith more than one thousand years ago. But for centuries before that it was a Buddhist center and was even visited by the celebrated, seventh-century Buddhist monk Xuanzang. The learned Xuanzang left Xi'an (Chang'an), the Tang capital, in A.D. 629, and headed west along the Silk Road toward Central Asia and India. He was in search of the true sources of Buddhism and wanted to meet and learn from the holy men of Magadha and the Mahabodhi temple at Bodh Gaya where the Buddha achieved enlightenment.[51] He traveled through the Gansu corridor to the sands of the Taklamakan Desert and the Tarim Basin, reaching Turpan in early 630. The local king was also a devout Buddhist, and upon hearing of Xuanzang's approach went out to greet him. The two men talked through the night. When Xuanzang rose to leave, the king refused to let him go and made him stay and preach in the oasis town for a full month. We know that Xuanzang visited the ancient city of Gaochang, southeast of Turpan and once a center of Manicheanism as well as Buddhism (German archaeologists have even discovered a Nestorian church outside the city walls). There, Xuanzang is said to have preached to three hundred people in a pavilion especially prepared for him by the king. He may also have visited Jiaohe and even walked in the "Flaming Mountains" and the Tian Shan Mountains to the Thousand Buddhist Caves in Bezelik, thirty-five miles northeast of Turpan.

The caves at Bezelik are lesser versions of those at Mogao. Xuanzang had chosen not to visit the Mogao caves on his way to Turpan. But he would visit them sixteen years later on his return. A mural painting there in Cave 103 commemorates his visit and depicts Xuanzang crossing the Pamirs accompanied by a white elephant, which he received as a gift from an Indian king.[52] When he finally returned to Chang'an, Xuanzang was received in triumph. He was carrying crates and crates of cultural relics: "150 pellets of the Buddha's flesh and a box of his bone relics," and seven statues of the Buddha, some as tall as four feet, some made of wood, others of silver; all from India. He also brought 657 books bound in 520 cases. These were classified as "224 Mahayanist sutras and treatises; writings from a number of Hinayanist sects that were for the most part unknown, and no less than 36 general works of logic and 13 works on grammar."[53] His ambition was to translate as many of these scriptures as possible. But the emperor required that he first write a Record of the Western Regions, which he completed in 646 and which still stands today as a compelling, first-person account of the life, cultures, and governments of the various towns and regions of Central Asia during the Tang dynasty.

The Emperor Taizong grew close to Xuanzang, and the monk served as his spiritual guide near the end of his life. His son and successor, Emperor Gaozong, built Xuanzang an Indian-style, five-story pagoda to house the scriptures and sculptures the monk brought back with him from India. The Big Wild Goose Pagoda, as it is called, still stands in modern Xi'an. It is a testament to Xuanzang's contribution to the dissemination and institutionalization of Buddhism within China. It is also a powerful marker of the history of foreign travel and the long legacy of cultural and artistic exchange. Xuanzang's sixteen-year, ten-thousand-mile journey along the Silk Road inspired—and continues to inspire—other travelers far west of China. Aurel Stein even wrote an account of the monk's earlier journey.[54]

It was in great part because of Xuanzang's report on his travels that Stein made his first expedition to Central Asia, which was reported on in the Times in 1901. On his way back to Central Asia, he stopped by Berlin and reported his findings to Albert Grünwedel, Director of the Indian Section of the Berlin Ethnological Museum. The following year, Grünwedel led the first German expedition to the area.[55] He published his finds four years later, documenting the contents of forty-four crates of sculptures, manuscripts, and wall paintings removed from the ancient city of Khocho. The manuscripts were in

Sanskrit, Uighur, Mongolian, Chinese, and Tibetan, betraying the international character of this borderland and crossroads region. The second German expedition was led by Grünwedel's deputy, Albert von Le Coq.[56] Le Coq arrived in Turpan in November 1904 and worked again in Khocho, where he found numerous manuscripts with texts in seventeen languages pertaining to Buddhism and other religions, including, especially, Manicheanism, of which he discovered illustrated pages that are the first pictorial records known of this religious community. In March 1905, Le Coq went to Bezelik. There he found the cave temples, long neglected, many of them filled with sand blown in from the deserts nearby. In addition, long, snowy winters filled the earth of the caves with moisture, damaging the surface of the wall paintings. Le Coq removed numerous mural paintings and other objects to Berlin. The expedition's finds were published in 1912. There would be two more German expeditions in the area—Pelliot would be working there too, and then would follow Stein to Dunhuang and the Mogao caves—and Le Coq would publish a narrative account of the second and third expeditions in 1926. All of the German finds were removed to the Berlin Ethnology Museum. Those that survived the travails of World War II form the core of Berlin's Museum of Indian Art in Dahlem and are installed in rooms devoted to the so-called "Turfan Collection."[57]

What is one to make of this history of travel in the western reaches of China? Xuanzang's travels were difficult. So too were those of Grünwedel, Le Coq, Stein, Pelliot, and Warner. All went in search of knowledge. And all removed local materials to faraway places for the benefit of others, who then and since have studied them and been inspired to search further for new knowledge about the people, cultures, and history of the western borderlands of China. Of course, now it is impossible to remove material from the region as the above-mentioned Europeans did; nor will India allow a pilgrim like Huanzang to remove items of significant cultural property to China (and of course China will not allow an Indian Buddhist pilgrim to remove such material to India). If today's retentionist attitudes toward cultural property had been operative during the Tang dynasty, China's culture would be all the poorer.

Nationalist retentionist cultural property laws like China's, while said to be aimed at protecting archaeological sites and the scientific knowledge they contain (this is the archaeologists' argument and the fig leaf worn by modern nations that impose such laws), are really intended to keep cultural heritage within the borders of the nation within which such property is found. They are national and *national-ist* laws. The Chinese request to the U.S. government for import re-strictions on Chinese cultural property is clear about this. And it, like the cultural property laws that lie behind it—and all other nations' cultural property laws—includes antiquities among cultural prop-erty and thereby nationalizes them. The Chinese government is in fact less concerned about the integrity of the archaeological sites within its modern borders than it is about holding onto cultural arti-facts of all kinds—including antiquities—for itself and restricting the world's access to them. Nationalist retentionist cultural property laws are not *archaeological sites protection laws*. They are *retentionist cul-tural property laws*, intent on keeping what they identify as national cultural property within the country for the nation, for the sake of affirming and strengthening claims on a *national* identity, on just what the nation is: a unique cultural entity identifiable by its forms and practices, coincident in reach with the extent of its current politi-cal borders, and that confirms a particular kind of identity on the people of the nation. It is, in China's case, what defines China and its people against all non-Chinese or foreign others. It is part and parcel with China's centuries-long preoccupation with cultural purity, what has for so long prevented it from accepting the idea that Chinese cul-ture developed not just from the central region outward—from the Yellow River region during the Xia and Shang dynasties almost four thousand years ago—but simultaneously from multiple centers north and south. It is also part of what is driving the Xia-Shang-Zhou Chro-nology Project: an effort to lengthen China's chronology and docu-ment its primacy among all distinguished world civilizations. *Cul-tural purity, longevity,* and *primacy*: the pillars of China's sense of itself as a once-and-always great nation.

But Chinese culture—indeed, every nation's culture—includes elements of foreign cultures with which its peoples have come into

117

contact over many centuries. Buddhism was introduced into China during the Han dynasty in the first century A.D. It traveled along the trading routes from India through Central Asia into China, brought by foreign merchants and missionaries. Dunhuang is early and lasting evidence of the influence and presence of Buddhism in China. The earliest paintings in the shrines of the nearby Magao caves date from the fourth century A.D. They depict Buddhist nuns and monks and betray motifs and styles of Indian and Central Asian origin mixed with local Chinese stylistic effects and motifs. Earlier evidence of sculpted forms of the Buddha appear as early as the second century: one on a pedestal for a Sichuanese money tree, which would typically represent mountains with winged or horned animals climbing on them and often the Queen Mother of the West and her magical land, elements unrelated to and predating Buddhism in China. Later images of the Buddha in China betray a distinctly Ghandaran (modern-day Afghanistan) stylistic influence, which itself was influenced by Hellenistic Greek art carried by Alexander the Great and his troops hundreds of years earlier.

Centuries later, along the same trade routes, Islam would come to China from the West and eventually become part of the rich diversity of "Chinese" culture. Xuanzang's Chang'an was a multicultural city with ninety-one Buddhist monasteries, two Nestorian Christian churches, and four Zoroastrian shrines. Emissaries from many foreign nations resided there; from India, Central Asia, Southeast Asia, and Japan. Distant customs, foods, social practices, beliefs, costumes, and art mingled with local ones, making the Chinese capital one of the most international cities on earth at the time. This would be equally true of Beijing under the Yuan dynasty four centuries later and subsequently under the Ming and the Ch'ing dynasties. China has for most of its history been engaged with the larger world and has borne the cultural imprint of these encounters. Communism itself of course came to China from the West. There is little today that one could say was "Chinese," if by that one means bearing no influences from other cultures. Shanghai, its merchants, industrialists, financiers, professionals, and artists—all engaged with foreign colleagues and practices—is a truly international city competing on a global scale. Beijing is hosting the 2008 Olympic Games and much of its newest architecture and largest architectural commissions are the work of European and North American architects. China is as international now as it has been at any time in its glorious history.[58]

Nationalist retentionist cultural property laws are contrary to the generative principles of artistic, commercial, and social development. The latter depend on exchange and encounters with new and distant phenomena. The former seek to define and preserve a particular vision of the past as evident in a fixed, closed set of cultural norms to serve as the foundation for a present national identity determined by the nation's dominant, elite cultural and political groups. China's efforts in this respect are not new. The historian Owen Lattimore has written of China's long-time preoccupation with its frontiers, the site of its engagement with foreignness. It built walls and guardposts and stationed armies all along its borders. It conjured images of foreigners as different and inferior. And yet it could never keep foreigners and foreign influences out of China. No country can. But still, China—like all countries—tries, if only figuratively; that is, if only by defining what is and what is not Chinese. And they always fail in the end. "China could never put an end to the ebb and flow of frontier history and maintain the civilization of China in the closed world that was its ideal."[59]

History and identity matter greatly to the Chinese. The People's Republic of China's efforts to restrict access to the artifacts of its historical culture (by imposing strict export laws) are aimed at correcting the past and propping up the illusion of a "closed world." It feels aggrieved by assaults on its historical culture by Europeans during the nineteenth century, its own political and social disorders in the early years of the twentieth century, the flight of the Nationalist government with much of the Imperial collection to Taiwan, the rampant violence and destruction of the Cultural Revolution during the late 1960s, and aggressive collecting of Chinese art by Western and Japanese institutions and individuals throughout all of these years. It wants to keep what it considers to be Chinese art within China. As the spokesman from the Poly Museum said: "Our national treasures should not be flowing beyond our borders. They are ours, part of our roots."

But how deep and wide do these roots go? Do they extend equally to all populations and all cultures of modern China, including the fifty-six ethnic minority cultures? Are their cultures Chinese too? Are their antiquities preserved equally as Han Chinese antiquities? Are their archaeological sites identified, excavated, researched, and published equally as those valued by the dominant and elite Han Chinese bureaucratic authorities? In the end, the state determines what is and what is not valued as national culture. Decisions are made in Beijing, and Beijing is a long way from Dunhuang and the Magao caves. When considering the paintings on the walls of the frescoed cave temples at Magao, one is aware more of India and ancient Sogdiana than of Beijing. In both the far west and the far east of China today, one is surrounded by cultural objects. But are they equally Chinese? That is the question. We should be suspicious of easy answers to this question. After all, it all depends on what you mean by Chinese. And any simple answer only cheapens our understanding of China and Chinese culture, and of course of culture itself and the way it has always worked, free of political boundaries, to give form to humanity's greatest hopes and aspirations.[60]

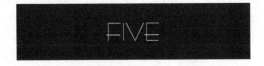

IDENTITY MATTERS

I want to insist that the terrible reductive conflicts that herd people under falsely unifying rubrics like "America," "The West" or "Islam" and invent collective identities for large numbers of individuals who are actually quite diverse, cannot remain as potent as they are, and must be oppressed.

—Edward Said[1]

Born in Jerusalem, raised a proud Palestinian and a Christian; educated in English and American primary schools in Cairo (in the first case, with Armenian, Greek, Egyptian, Jewish, and Copt students; in the latter, with American students almost exclusively) and then in a U.S. prep school and U.S. universities; by profession, a literary scholar (Western literature); by love, a music critic (European piano music and opera); and by commitment, a social critic (mainly of matters in the Middle East and how they are represented in Western media), Edward Said was no one simple thing. No one is, he would insist. He closed his memoir, *Out of Place,* by reflecting on the nature of identity. "I occasionally experience myself as a cluster of flowing currents. I prefer this to the idea of a solid self, the identity to which so many attach so much significance." In his published conversations with Daniel Barenboim, he spoke of identity as "a set of currents, flowing currents, rather than a fixed place or a stable set of objects."[2]

Surely this is how we all see ourselves, if we think about it. We are never only one thing, even if when asked we try to simplify ourselves to a few things: a married, white, professional, middle-aged father with a university education. The currents that flow through us originate in our genes, experiences, and imagination, and are constantly coursing through one another, intermixing and overlapping. The metaphor is apt: currents are never static and can only be separated with effort imposed from the outside. Said described them as "always in motion, in time, in place, in the form of all kinds of strange combinations moving about, not necessarily forward, sometimes against each other, contrapuntally yet without one central theme."

The journalist and novelist Amin Maalouf was born in Lebanon, raised speaking Arabic, lives in France, writes in French, and answers when asked whether he feels more French or Lebanese, "both!" And he means both *at once.* "You can't divide it up into halves or thirds or any other separate segments. I haven't got several identities: I've got just one, made up of many components in a mixture that is unique to me, just as other people's identity is unique to them as individuals." And yet social and political pressures assert themselves from time to time, we are "pressed to take sides or ordered to stay within [our] own tribe," and forced to reach down deep inside to some original, irreducible, undeniable core identity, as if all the rest—in Amin's words, "a person's whole journey through time as a free agent; the beliefs he acquires in the course of that journey; his own individual tastes, sensibilities, and affinities; in short his life itself"—counts for nothing.[3]

What were we originally? The children of our parents, surely. Part of a somewhat larger family, probably. Likely raised among still others in a local community. Possibly initiated into a particular faith practice. A boy or girl, at least. At what point then are we aware that we have a nationality? When we come into contact with the state. When we go to school and have to register our place of birth and residence. When we leave our birth country for travel and have to have passports or identification cards. When we reach our maturity and get married and have children and have to register our status and their birth with state authorities. When, in many countries, we are obliged to do national service. When we pay taxes.

We are born with a nationality, that's true. And likely we participate in national acts of observance—national holidays, recognition of the flag, oaths of allegiance—even before we come into direct contact with the state. But at the same time, even then we know that we don't only have a nationality. We have other identities, too: family member, townsman, black boy, white girl, vegetarian, blonde, clarinetist, Christian, Jew, Muslim, Buddhist. Some even contradict the claims of nationality and call for allegiance to a higher authority or greater good. And all of these hold nationality in suspension. Until we come up against the state. The state demands commitment. It forces us to take sides. At some point we have to answer the question, what nationality are we? Turkish? Chinese? Kurdish? Uighur? And then can we agree on what this means, precisely? Just who and what really are any of these "nation"-alities?

All too often in the modern world, our nationality is our identity. The Nobel Prize–winning economist Amartya Sen argues that this is not to our advantage: "The prospects of peace in the contemporary world may well lie in the recognition of the plurality of our affiliations and in the use of reasoning as common inhabitants of a wide world, rather than making us into inmates rigidly incarcerated in little containers."[4] I said it at the outset of this book, but it bears repeating here. Encyclopedic art museums are a counter argument to the prevailing tendency to divide the world—and us—into such little containers. They are dedicated to preserving and exhibiting the diversity of the world's common artistic legacy. They are repositories of things and knowledge, dedicated to the dissemination of learning and to serving as a force for understanding, tolerance, and the dissipation of ignorance and superstition about the world, where the artifacts of one time and one culture can be seen next to those of other times and other cultures without prejudice. They are based in the polymathic ideal of the Enlightenment museum: it is good for us, for our species, to experience the full diversity of human cultural industry in order to better understand our place in the world, as of but one culture and one time among many.[5]

Encyclopedic art museums introduce us to the larger world of which we are a part. They bear witness to the hybridity and interrelatedness of the world's cultures. Nationalist retentionist cultural property laws force national identities onto works of art, even works of art that were made long before nations—certainly specific nations—existed. Encyclopedic art museums are based on the eighteenth-century ideal of cosmopolitanism: "citizen of the cosmos," of the world, the universe (as Diderot wrote in his letter to Hume, a citizen of "that great city, the world"). Nationalist retentionist cultural property laws are based on the nineteenth-century idea of nationalism: that we are first and most important a national, a member of a tribe determined by language, ethnicity, and place. Emphasis in nationalism is on separateness: one nation separate from other nations. Emphasis in cosmopolitanism is on commonality: we are all branches of a single family, to whom we are obliged equally. Nationalism narrows its vision of the world. Cosmopolitanism expands it.

Nationalist retentionist cultural property laws segregate the world's cultural property within the borders of modern nation-states. Most often, as I have discussed them in this book, such laws are focused on antiquities; that is, on works of art made long before there were nations. National and international laws, regulations, and agreements typically define antiquities as works of art made at least 150 years ago. They claim antiquities found (or thought to have been found) within their national borders as a nation's patrimony, as important to that nation's identity and esteem, and not to our understanding of the world. Quite explicitly, they claim them as a nation's property, as bearing the imprint of a national identity.

Of course, this can not be true. As Kwame Anthony Appiah has written of Nok sculptures, which although made two thousand years ago are claimed by the modern state of Nigeria as part of its national patrimony: "We don't know whether Nok sculptures were commissioned by kings or commoners; we don't know whether the people who made them and the people who paid for them thought of them as belonging to the kingdom, to a man, to a lineage, to the gods. One thing we know for sure, however, is that they didn't make them for Nigeria."[6] And of course, this is true of all antiquities. Whomever they were made for, they were certainly not made for the modern nations now occupying the land of the ancient governing entities that ruled their makers, be they ancient Egyptians, Babylonians, Lydians, Persians, Athenians, Central Asian Turks of numerous kinds, or subjects of the Xia, Shang, or Han dynasties. If their makers made them with thoughts of their lasting, they were made "forever" and not for a particular unknown and unknowable modern nation-state.

Nationalist retentionist cultural property laws are based on false assumptions about art and culture: that the parameters of art and culture can be fixed—that the currents of influence can be stopped—and identified as national, as having *national* characteristics. Take the Italian government's request to the U.S. government to impose import restrictions on antiquities. It claimed that it—by which in the context of the request it means explicitly *antiquities*—is "a source of identity and esteem for the modern Italian nation," that it "constitute[s] the very essence of a society and convey[s] important information concerning a people's origin, history, and traditional setting," and that it is unique to a place: "these materials are of cultural significance because they derive from cultures that developed autonomously in the region of present day Italy." These assertions form the basis of all nationalist retentionist cultural property laws. Cultural property and national identity are said to originate from the same place: the country identified with the nation; that is, the stretch of land with which a group of people—the nation—identify themselves and whose boundaries are coincident with the sovereign authority of the state. Both are declared unique to that place, as having developed autonomously there: what is Italian is Italy's only and cannot be shared with any other nation; it is Italian by origin and identity.

In nationalist retentionist cultural property laws, sense of place is important. Cultural property originates from some place. It was made by people who once lived there (although of course their experience of the world was not limited to that place; no place is isolated from others for long). And that "some place" is now the territory of a modern nation (that the cultural property predates the modern nation is beside the point). As cultural property laws claim cultural property to be a source of national identity, that identity is located in that same place: in the country now occupied by the nation. But what if a national (a citizen or subject) is obviously not from that place?

Say, Italians born in North Africa, who may be Jewish or Muslim. Are their *origins* explained by—*is their identity founded upon*—cultural property that was made centuries ago in the region that is in fact not from where they *originate* but only where they now *live?* By the terms of Italy's request to the United States, North African–born Muslim or Jewish Italians can identify with Italian-ness only by adopting it as a foreign culture.

That is, they must come to their Italian identity (no small part of their individual identity, of course) by imagining a connection to some alleged pure other identity: from which only Italian identity comes—"from cultures that developed autonomously in the region of present day Italy." But of course, nothing was developed "autonomously" anywhere, and perhaps still less so in the region of present-day Italy than most places. Like every other culture in the world, Italian culture is a rich mixture of the cultures with which the inhabitants of its land have come into contact over many centuries. In the case of its ancient inhabitants, this meant virtually every then-known culture in the world, from China to Africa to Britain. In fact, what makes the ancient cultures of the region of present-day Italy so important is not that they have a particular relationship to modern Italians, but that they bear witness to so many early encounters with the larger world. They were cosmopolitan cultures from the beginning. Ironically, what the North African–born Muslim or Jewish Italian is being asked to identify with—Italian-ness—was, if Italians want to claim descent from the cultures of their land's ancient inhabitants, a polyglot, multiethnic world of overlapping cultures, which over the course of time included sustained encounters with the cultures from which the North African–born Italian has come, from which he *originated*.

Why then do national governments like Italy's make these claims? Because they justify the purpose and reach of their nationalist and retentionist cultural property laws. These laws mean to retain cultural property within the territorial borders of the nation-state for the benefit of the nation and not to share it with the world for the benefit of the world. If the Italian government were only concerned with preserving "Italian" cultural property, it would preserve it wherever it now is. If it were concerned about preserving it because it is "a source of identity and esteem for the modern Italian nation," it could still preserve it wherever it is. Aren't there Italians living outside Italy who deserve access to Italian national cultural property because it "constitute[s] the very essence of a society and convey[s] important information concerning a people's origin, history, and traditional setting" and not only so within Italy?

Of course, the Italian government argues that its cultural property laws are designed to prohibit the looting and destruction of archaeological sites within its borders. If one cannot own or export antiquities without the permission of the government, and if that permission is seldom ever granted, and if other nations, like the United States, agree not to import unprovenanced antiquities that might have come illegally from Italy, then looters will have no or at least a much-reduced market for their illicit trade, and archaeological sites will be preserved and the knowledge they contain made available to all interested parties through publication. But as I have already noted, such cultural property laws have not had the desired effect on the illicit trade in antiquities. Looting of archaeological sites continues at an ever-increasing rate, causing governments like Italy's to seek ever stricter bilateral agreements with other governments. If cultural property laws were an effective means of protecting archaeological sites, we would see signs of their success surely by now: nearly 150 nation-states have such laws and many of them have had them for decades. But the looting continues and, as archaeologists will tell you, has in fact increased. Where then have the looted antiquities gone? We can only assume on to the black market to private collectors around the world and to museums in countries that do not respect other nations' cultural property laws or international agreements. Cultural property laws have not reduced the market for illicitly traded antiquities. They have simply moved it around the world to ever newer markets, to wherever there is a buyer willing to take a chance on an antiquity with insufficient provenance and questionable export documents.

Italy's cultural property laws are indisputably nationalist and retentionist. They are concerned with keeping for Italians what the Italian government claims is Italy's national cultural property. And they are fighting to hold on to all of it. Yet, by any measure, Italy's museums are engorged with antiquities and their storerooms have long been filled to capacity with antiquities waiting to be catalogued, studied, and published. The promise is always that they will be published and thereby shared with the world. But Italy's record when it comes to publishing archaeological finds is poor (it is not alone in this respect). Finds languish in museum storerooms never to be published. And when those few are published, it is hardly done in a manner accessible to the general public. They almost always appear in reports prepared by specialists for specialists. Archaeological reports can never take the place of gallery presentations of antiquities. Only the object—the actual antiquity, the thing itself, there on view, ineluctably ancient, with the aura and facture of age—has the allure to attract the public's curiosity. If the Italian government is concerned about preserving antiquities because they are "a source of identity and esteem for the modern Italian nation," they can only have that effect if they are seen by Italian nationals. If they remain off view in storerooms for years or forever, they are mute and invisible and can hardly be said to exist for the purposes claimed by the Italian government.[7]

Let's say that antiquities are a source of identity and esteem and convey important information about a people's origin and history. Does each antiquity do this equally? Does one need every antiquity found within the borders of the modern Italian nation to remain within those borders, seen or unseen, in order to do these things? No, of course not. But that's not the point of Italy's cultural property laws. Other nations have laws that allow for restricting the trade in cultural property but permit the export of some things for the sake of sharing them with the world. Japan, for example, ranks its cultural property by quality and rarity and allows the export of much of it. (The rankings decline from National Treasures to Important Cultural Properties to Registered Tangible Cultural Properties; as of 2004, the nation's Agency for Cultural Affairs had ranked nearly 20,000 cultural properties and designated only some 1,000 as National Treasures, which in most cases are ineligible for export, leaving 95 percent of the cultural properties available for export.)[8] Britain can put a hold on the export of a property sold to an overseas buyer, giving a public museum a limited period of time to meet the property's sale price or let it go abroad. Italy is different. Nominally it allows for the export of cultural property, including antiquities, but in practice that almost never occurs. Italy's laws are retentionist for the sake of retaining its cultural property for itself and not for an international, global human history. They are also nationalist. They perpetuate the nationalist myth that Italy is a modern nation with a glorious and unbroken history stretching all the way back to ancient Rome and Etruria, when in the case of Ancient Rome "Italy" ruled much of the known world.

Let's be clear about this. Italy has been a republic only since 1946. It was a kingdom for less than one hundred years before that (for twenty-one years during this period it was ruled by a Fascist dictator), and thus has been a unified nation for less than 150 years. It has been a "nation" only since the age of nationalism. Much has been written about nationalism recently, encouraged by the rise of new nation-states following the breakup of the former Soviet Union. Some writers have praised it, others have been highly critical. Some philosophers have even argued that the boundaries of nations are morally irrelevant, made as they are from accidents of history with no rightful claim on our conscience.[9] Most writers agree that nationalism dates to the eighteenth century. The anthropologist Benedict Anderson locates its origins in the age of the Enlightenment and Revolution, when "the legitimacy of the divinely-ordained, hierarchical dynastic realm" was being destroyed.[10] The historian Eric Hobsbawm dates it to the age of the European and American revolutions, 1789–1848, when it came to represent "the common good against privilege" and common interests—especially political and economic liberty—which were best served and preserved politically.[11] And the political scientist Ernest Gellner dates it to the era of industrialization, when new technologies encouraged, even required, a more broadly educated population.[12]

It is also generally agreed that nationalism isn't what it seems to be, or what nationalist ideology claims that it is, or what nationalists believe. It is neither natural nor inevitable. It is not compelled by ethnic or linguistic purity, and it does not derive from below but from above, from the ambitions of the socially and intellectually elite power-holders. In Gellner's words:

> [N]ationalist ideology suffers from pervasive false consciousness. Its myths invert reality: it claims to defend folk culture while in fact it is forging a high culture; it claims to protect an old folk society while in fact helping to build an anonymous mass society. . . . Nationalism tends to treat itself as a manifest and self-evident principle, accessible as such to all men, and violated only through some perverse blindness, when in fact it owes its plausibility and compelling nature only to a very special set of circumstances, which do indeed obtain now, but which were alien to most of humanity and history. It preaches and defends continuity, but owes everything to a decisive and unutterably profound break in human history. It preaches and defends cultural diversity, when in fact it imposes homogeneity both inside and, to a lesser degree, between political units. Its self-image and its true nature are inversely related, with an ironic neatness seldom equaled even by other successful ideologies.[13]

Nationalism engenders nations, not the other way around. In Benedict Anderson's formulation, nationalism imagines a community—a nation—precisely because none exists naturally. A nation "is *imagined* because the members of even the smallest nation will never know most of their fellow-members, meet them, or even hear of them, yet in the minds of each lives the image of their communion."[14] Nationalism marks a change in the way people imagine their future, and imagine it for the better. But this does not apply to all of the people, of course. As a political principle, nationalism is the creation of the elite. It is not "the awakening of an old, latent, dormant force. . . . It is in reality the consequence of a new form of social organization, based on deeply internalized, education-dependent high cultures, each protected by its own state."[15]

A common language is crucial. It creates a community of people who can understand and identify with one another. But it is not a kind of popular *ur*-language, which lies dormant until released by cultural circumstances. It is an acquired language made standard and imposed broadly on "the people" through political and economic circumstances, including "deeply internalized, education-dependent high cultures, each protected by its own state."[16] Related ethnicities have been historically important, too, but they do not naturally create nations. They are related to the power relations that themselves create and sustain nations politically. Nationalism "is a theory of political legitimacy," Gellner tells us, "which requires that ethnic boundaries should not cut across political ones, and in particular, that ethnic boundaries within a given state—a contingency already formally excluded by the principle in its general formulation—should not separate the power-holders from the rest."[17]

During the Romantic era and then even more so through the second half of the nineteenth century, ethnicity and language became the central, decisive, or even the only criteria of potential nationhood. And in many cases this remains so today. Debates over the wearing of Islamic head coverings by public school teachers in Britain, legislators in the Netherlands, and public students in France are testament to the hold ethnicity has over nationalism still; and of course it plagues Turkey in its effort to join the otherwise "Christian" European Union. There was even the extraordinary moment recently when Mexican Americans and Mexicans in the United States took to singing the U.S. national anthem in Spanish, only to have their efforts roundly condemned by President Bush as separatist. To the president, the U.S. national anthem is not a set of ideas and beliefs, but a text that cannot be translated. It and the language it was written in—and officially is only sung in—are inviolate. Despite the hundreds of languages spoken in the United States today, there are still efforts to legislate English as the official national language. Ethnicity and language matter: they remain decisive in the formation of nations.[18]

This means of course that there are many more potential nations than there are possible viable states. And not all nationalisms can be satisfied, at least at the same time. As Gellner has noted, "The satisfaction of some spells the frustration of others." This is made all the more complicated by the fact that many of the world's potential nations live, or until recently have lived, not in compact territorial units but intermixed with other nations in complex patterns. It then follows that a territorial political unit can only become ethnically homogenous, in such cases, if it either "kills, or expels, or assimilates all non-nationals."[19] We witnessed violent incidents of such "ethnic cleansing" in the Balkans and Rwanda during the 1990s, and of course see them now in Timor, the Sudan and Darfur, and in Iraq, where Sunnis and Shiites are locked in mortal, sectarian conflict.

I do recognize that nationalistic feelings have bred beautiful music, poetry, and works of visual art and have often been powerful forces for human liberation from political oppression. But all too often they have also hardened into ideologies with roots in fear and hatred of the Other, often with racist affinities. They then become dangerous as reprehensible means of oppressing others, sources of vicious, even barbaric sectarian violence, persuading colossal numbers of people to lay down their own lives in an effort to kill others. The idea of the ultimate sacrifice is inspired by nationalism (or its cultural or religious equivalent) and it must be held accountable for untold acts of brutality.

Nevertheless, strong claims are made for the beneficial consequences of national identities, even among skeptics. Anthony Smith, a professor of Ethnicity and Nationalism at the European Institute, London School of Economics, allows that national identity can provide

> a powerful means of defining and locating individual selves in the world, through the prism of the collective personality and its distinctive culture. It is through a shared, unique culture that we are enabled to know "who we are" in the contemporary world. By rediscovering that culture we "rediscover" ourselves, the "authentic self", or so it has appeared to many divided and disoriented individuals who have had to contend with the vast changes and uncertainties of the modern world.[20]

Why does nationalism retain a hold on us, he asks?

> Perhaps the most important of its functions is to provide a satisfying answer to the problem of personal oblivion. Identification with the

"nation" in a secular era is the surest way to surmount the finality of death and ensure a measure of personal immortality.[21]

And perhaps, too, because it offers extraordinary promises that make nationalism so seductive in our modern era:

> Transcending oblivion through posterity; the restoration of collective dignity through an appeal to a golden age; the realization of fraternity through symbols, rites, and ceremonies, which bind the living to the dead and fallen of the community: these are the underlying functions of national identity and nationalism in the modern world, and the basic reasons why the latter have proved so durable, protean and resilient through all vicissitudes.[22]

Large claims indeed, but these are the kinds of claims made by many, and abused by many. Amartya Sen has acknowledged the double-edged sword of national identity (or for that matter all kinds of singular affiliations, national, religious, ethnic, linguistic, whatever) as also a source of richness and warmth as well as of violence and terror. But he points to the risks of limiting one's identity to one or a few categories and argues that "the force of a bellicose identity can be challenged by the power of *competing* identities" by the broad commonality of our shared humanity, ways of classifying people that can restrain "the exploitation of a specifically aggressive use of one particular categorization."[23]

Sen comes to these conclusions not only by analysis but by experience. In 1944, when he was eleven and living in Dhaka, the second city—after Calcutta—of Bengal, a man rushed into his family's garden bleeding profusely. He was a Muslim and had been attacked by rioting Hindus (this was during the communal riots that marked the end of the British Raj; Sen and his family were Hindus). Sen shouted for his parents and his father rushed the man to the hospital, where he died. The man had come into the neighborhood looking for work because his family had nothing to eat. He was killed by people who didn't know him but saw in him—his dress, his looks—something foreign and threatening.

At the time, Bengal was convulsed with sectarian hatred. A short while later it would be partitioned, with Dhaka the capital of what was then East Pakistan. Communal riots were replaced by Bengali patriotism, "with an intense celebration of Bengali language, literature, music, and culture" common to both the Muslims and Hindus of Bengal. But this was soon overshadowed by "the severe inequality of political power, linguistic status, and economic opportunities between the two halves of the imperfectly integrated Islamic state." Eventually Pakistan was partitioned and East Pakistan became Bangladesh with Dhaka as its new capital, but this occurred only after more carnage during the painful process of separation: "With the Pakistani army's frenzied attempt to suppress the Bengali rebellion, the identity divisions were along the lines of language and politics, not religion, with Muslim soldiers from West Pakistan brutalizing—and killing—mainly Muslim dissenters (or suspected dissenters) in East Pakistan."[24]

Sen witnessed these violent challenges as a young boy in Dhaka, and then when as a university student in Cambridge, United Kingdom, he worried about the fate of his family back home (his father taught at Dhaka University). But it was the powerful experience of that day in 1944 when he encountered the Muslim man—Kader Mia—that left its indelible mark: "That Kader Mia would be seen as having only one identity—that of being a member of the 'enemy' community who 'should' be assaulted and if possible killed—seemed altogether incredible. For a bewildered child, the violence of identity was extraordinarily hard to grasp. It is not particularly easy even for a still bewildered elderly adult."[25]

Mia was killed not only because he was a Muslim, of course, but also because he was poor. He had left the relative security of his home to look for work in an area swarming with Hindu thugs because his family was hungry. The poorest members of any community are the easiest to kill in sectarian riots: they have to go out unprotected in search of food. In the Hindu–Muslim riots in Dhaka, Hindus killed poor Muslims with ease, while Muslims "assassinated impoverished Hindu victims with equal abandon." And even though "the community identities of the two groups of brutalized prey were quite different, their class identities (as poor laborers with little economic means) were much the same." But no identity other than religious ethnicity was allowed to count. "The illusion of a uniquely confrontational reality had thoroughly reduced human beings and eclipsed the protagonists' freedom to think."[26]

The freedom to think and to choose our loyalties and priorities between different groups holds the promise to our overcoming such narrow, identity-based violence. But this presupposes that one can choose among identities, that there is not one identity that is undeniable because it is naturally, indelibly part of our origins, of who we are, really, "deep, down inside." Sen acknowledges that there are constraints restricting such choice, but points out that choices are always made within the limits of what are seen as feasible. "The feasibilities in the case of identities will depend on individual characteristics and circumstances that determine the alternative possibilities open to us." And even when we are clear about how we want to see ourselves, we may still have difficulty in persuading others to see us in just that way. The flowing currents of our ever-overlapping identities can only be separated with effort imposed from the outside, by others, often by the state: *what nationality are you?*

Still, the effort to insist on our ability to choose must be made. There is just too much at risk. "The point at issue is not whether *any* identity whatever can be chosen (that would be an absurd claim), but whether we do indeed have choices over alternative identities or combinations of identities, and perhaps more importantly, substantial freedom regarding what *priority* to give to the various identities we may simultaneously have."[27] And if this is true about human identities—and I am convinced it is—it is also true about cultural identities; that is, about the identities we give to works of art. Are they Italian because they derive from cultures said to have developed *autonomously* in the region of present-day Italy? Or have we simply chosen to identify them that way? They look like things we know to have been made by ancient peoples in the region of what is now, some nearly two thousand years later, Italy. Of course, they also look like things made in Greece, which in turn look like things made in Egypt, which themselves bear a resemblance to things made in the Ancient

Near East. And then too, we see resemblances to things made more or less at the same time in Persia, the Steppes of Russia, and central Asia, not to mention across the Levant and northern Africa and up into Europe by way of the Balkans. And of course, too, each of these influences comprises currents of others, such that we can trace the "identity" of "Italian" works of art through a series of artistic and cultural encounters over much of the known world and over hundreds and hundreds of years. To claim that these things came from cultures said to have developed autonomously in the region of present-day Italy is to willfully ignore the hybridity of culture and its multiple identities. It is to reach into a bag and pull out a single identity and declare it not only primary but singular—*the* defining characteristic of a particular cultural expression—and then to attach a modern *national* identity to it, to pronounce that characteristic *national*, as characteristic of its Italian-ness or Bangladeshi-ness or American-ness, or whatever *we* are or want to claim as most important to who we think we are and what we want others to see us as being, *our* national identity.

Cultural identities—both of things and of people—are tricky things. Sen admits that our cultural background (and in my argument, this includes works of ancient art and the way we come to identify with them as part of our culture and use them to define our culture as unique, autonomous) can have a major influence on our behavior and thinking. But the skepticism he holds "is not about the recognition of the basic importance of culture in human perception and behavior. It is about the way culture is sometimes seen, rather arbitrarily, as the central, inexorable, and entirely independent determinant of social predicaments." Our cultural identities can be important, "but they do no stand starkly alone and aloof from other influences on our understanding and priorities."[28] Class, race, gender, profession, and politics also matter. Culture is not a homogenous attribute, nor is it static. It perforce interacts with other determinants of social perception and action. Separating out any one determinant is a choice, a statement of one's priorities in determining one's own identity, and of course in determining the culture—and cultural limitations—of another's.

This is the grave danger in our affiliating with only one cultural attribute: it encourages us to see others the same way, as only a particular nationality or religion or ethnicity or class. This leads to personal acts of discrimination against other individuals and to shallow generalizations made against other cultures. Sen refers to cultural explanations of economic development as an example of these dangers, and he uses a recent book by Lawrence Harrison and Samuel Huntington. In his introductory essay to the book *Culture Matters*—the essay is entitled "Cultures Count"—Huntington, who received heavy criticism for his earlier book, *The Clash of Civilizations*, cites South Korea and Ghana as evidence that cultural differences do matter in national development. In the early 1960s, both nations had similar economies. Thirty years later, South Korea had grown to the fourteenth largest economy in the world with a per capita income approximately that of Greece, while Ghana's economy stayed flat, with a per capita income roughly one-fifteenth of South Korea's. Huntington admits that undoubtedly many factors played a role in the difference in the development between two economies, "but it seemed to me that culture had to be a large part of the explanation. South Koreans valued thrift, investment, hard work, education, organization, and discipline. Ghanaians had different values. In short, cultures count."[29] Sen responds by calling this causal story "extremely deceptive" and points out that there were many important differences between South Korea and Ghana in the 1960s, including class structures (with a much bigger role for the business classes in South Korea), politics, the close relationship between the Korean economy and Japan and the United States, and a much higher literacy rate and a much more expanded school system in Korea than in Ghana. And then he emphasizes: "This is not to suggest that cultural factors are irrelevant to the process of development. But they do not work in isolation from social, political, and economic influences. Nor are they immutable."[30]

Culture matters. But *cultural* matters can be misunderstood or manipulated to use cultural differences as a way of limiting our understanding and regard for other peoples.

Kwame Anthony Appiah points to the conflation of the two primary uses of the word "culture" in the context of the cultural patrimony/property debate. "On the one hand, cultural patrimony refers to cultural artifacts: works of art, religious relics, manuscripts, crafts, musical instruments, and the like. . . . On the other hand, 'cultural patrimony' refers to the products of *a* culture: the group from whose conventions the objects derives its significance. Here the objects are understood to belong to a particular group, heirs to a trans-historical identity, whose patrimony they are."[31] This is precisely how the Italian government sees cultural patrimony/property, and how nationalist retentionist cultural property laws inscribe it: "cultural property" is at once individual works of art—antiquities, in our case—and the property of a culture, the distinct, autonomous, immutable, national culture claimed by the modern nation and enforced by its state apparatus (laws, ministries, border agents, police, and school curricula). The influential, multinational convention UNESCO 1970 reinforces this point. It pronounces that a state's cultural heritage includes both work "created by the individual or collective genius of nationals of the State" and "cultural property found within the national territory."[32]

Appiah is a professor of philosophy at Princeton University. He was raised in Kumasi, the capital of Ghana's Asante region. On his father's side he was related to the first wife of the Asante king, Premph II; on his mother's side, to Sir Stafford Crips, Britain's Labour chancellor of the exchequer from 1947 to 1950. Appiah likes to recall that his father—friend and then opponent of Kwame Nkrumah (first prime minister and then first president of the newly independent and unified Ghana)—dressed in dark European suits and carried the white wig of the British barrister. He was a proud Ghanaian, a pan-Africanist (he was with Nkrumakh and W.E.B. Du Bois at the Pan-African Congress in Manchester, England, in 1945), a delegate from Ghana to the United Nations, a Methodist, and much more.

In Kumasi, young Kwame Anthony would wander down the main commercial street past Baboo's Bazaar, a food store run by an Indian (Mr. Baboo), get rice from the Irani Brothers, visit Lebanese and Syrian families, Muslims and Maronites, British and continental

Europeans, and hear stories of his English grandparents and Assante stories and folktales told by his father and others and fondly collected, retold, and published by his mother (he would also later publish with her a collection of Assante proverbs). His youth in Ghana was rich with national and multinational associations. It was a large world he lived in, in the town of Kumasi. And some fifteen years ago, not long after his father died, he wrote a book recalling what he had learned from his father about identity, about Africa, and about culture. He called it *In My Father's House: Africa in the Philosophy of Culture*, purposely referencing the Bible—"in my father's house, there are many mansions"—not only because the phrase would have come easily to his father and mother but also because it is a formulation appropriate to his view of culture and identity which he gathered from his rich life experiences:

> If my sisters and I were "children of two worlds," no one bothered to tell us this; we lived in one world, in two "extended" families divided by several thousand miles and an allegedly insuperable cultural distance that never, so far as I can recall, puzzled or perplexed us much. As I grew older, and went to an English boarding school, I learned that not everybody had family in Africa and in Europe; not everyone had a Lebanese uncle, American and French and Kenyan and Thai cousins. And by now, now that my sisters have married a Norwegian and a Nigerian and a Ghanaian, now that I live in America, I am used to seeing the world as a network of points of affinity.[33]

We all have similar stories. As Amin Maalouf says: "Isn't it characteristic of the age we live in that it has made everyone in a way a migrant and a member of a minority?" Isn't that the point, really?[34]

❂ ❂ ❂

The British Museum is the inspiration of all encyclopedic art museums.[35] A former director of the museum described its origins in the Enlightenment in England as a time that "can be characterized by a spread of the spirit of curiosity amongst newly developing classes of society, release from attitudinal constraints of the past, and a creative desire for knowledge which was satisfied in a variety of ways: by experimentation, by exploration, by books and by forms of public spectacle."[36] It was the age of the encyclopedia. Diderot's and Le Rond's *Encyclopédie* appeared in 1751, two years before the founding of the museum, and the English *Cyclopaedia* of Ephraim Chambers twenty-three years before that.[37] Both works sought to survey the state of knowledge, classify it, and provide informed public access to it. They were, as the British Museum would be, public archives intent on doing public good by sparking curiosity about and inquiries into the known world. This is why we call the British Museum, and all similar museums, *encyclopedic* museums: they comprise collections meant to represent the world's diversity, and they organize and classify that diversity for ready, public access. As a former director of the museum put it, "the Museum acted as though it were an encyclopaedia, or a dictionary based on historical principles, with sequences of rooms, their layout, and the juxtaposition of objects within them providing a means of understanding relationships within the three-dimensional world of objects and specimens."[38]

This was an Enlightenment ambition. Critics since have criticized this as an effort to control and dominate nature and humankind. Others more recently have argued to the contrary, that the Enlightenment was an age—and its legacy is still—of broad-minded tolerance and focused curiosity about the full richness of the world, "when these ways of thinking and behaving permeated all aspects of life—the interlacing pattern of history, arts, science, philosophy, politics and religion all reacting upon each other and in turn affecting people's attitudes to them."[39] We may acknowledge the limitations of our efforts, and the false pressures of classification. But the Enlightenment's ambition for universality—for discovering the underlying principles of all things and all knowledge—and its emphasis on unprejudiced and open inquiry about the world and its people should inspire us still. It is an argument against prejudice and specialization and for ideals that we can or should attempt to grasp and appreciate the whole of human knowledge in all of its untidy and glorious strangeness. And its museum—the British Museum and all encyclopedic museums since—should strive to be "a repository of the achievements of the human endeavour, and there is no culture, past or present, that is not represented within its walls. It is truly the memory of mankind."[40]

This is not a nationalist argument. It is an argument against narrow, proprietary notions of nationalist claims on the world's common artistic legacy. I have been arguing that nationalist retentionist cultural property laws are just such narrow, proprietary claims, and that they discourage our learning more about the diverse cultures of the world. They also perpetuate the falsehood that living cultures necessarily derive from ancient cultures. The latter, as I have argued, is a nationalist perspective. It does not allow for the building of encyclopedic collections. It segregates cultures and their artistic artifacts by a false, nationalist system of classification. In his recent book *The Myth of Nations: The Medieval Origins of Europe*, the historian Patrick Geary explores the role the academic discipline of history has played in defining nations and substantiating their nationalist claims:

> Modern history was born in the nineteenth century, conceived and developed as an instrument of European nationalism. As a tool of nationalist ideology, the history of Europe's nations was a great success, but it has turned our understanding of the past into a toxic waste dump, filled with the poison of ethnic nationalism, and the poison has seeped deep into popular consciousness. Clearing up this waste is the most daunting challenge facing historians today.[41]

And facing encyclopedic museums too, I would argue.

Works of art are made from encounters with new and startling things, and they encourage us to see further associations and to explore their implications. That is the nature of culture. And this is what encyclopedic museums can offer that no other kind of institution can: they reveal the truth about our nature as curious, sentient beings alive to the world of differences and similarities. Ours is a contaminated world of mongrel races. Appiah draws attention to Salman Rushdie, who described his novel *Satanic Verses*, which occasioned the *fatwa* against him, as celebrating "hybridity, impurity, intermingling, the transformation that comes of new and unexpected combinations of human beings, cultures, ideas, politics, movies, songs. It rejoices in mongrelization and fears the absolutism of the Pure. Mélange, hotchpotch, a bit of this and that is how new-ness enters the world. It is the great possibility that mass migration gives the world, and I have tried to embrace it."[42] Or, as Appiah has put it, "Cultural purity is an oxymoron."

⊠　⊠　⊠

Edward Said died in 2003. A few months earlier he had completed a new Preface to *Orientalism*, his classic study of Western representa-tions of the Middle East, which was first published twenty-five years earlier. Said had spent decades interpreting the way writers and orators in literature and the media used knowledge to gain and wield power over others, often explicitly over the Other. Knowing he would likely die soon, Said was precise about his concerns. He reflected on the state of what he called the humanist critique:

> I have called what I try to do "humanism," a word I continue to use stubbornly despite the scornful dismissal of the term by sophisticated post-modern critics. By humanism I mean first of all attempting to dis-solve Blake's mind-forg'd manacles so as to be able to use one's mind historically and rationally for the purposes of reflective understanding and genuine disclosure. Moreover, humanism is sustained by a sense of community with other interpreters and other societies and periods: strictly speaking, therefore, there is no such thing as an isolated humanist.[43]

He challenges us "to complicate and/or dismantle the reductive for-mulae and the abstract but potent kind of thought that leads the mind away from concrete human history and experience and into the realms of ideological fiction, metaphysical confrontation and col-lective passion."[44]

We who work in or care about the future of encyclopedic art museums should take up Said's challenge. We should argue against nationalist retentionist cultural property laws and international agreements and conventions that perpetuate nationalist orthodoxies

142

and ahistorical explanations of culture and its origins and development in the world. We should present our collections in ways that draw attention to the basic hybridity of culture and the interrelatedness of cultures. We should encourage our visitors to work against the conventional classification system by which we show our collections—sometimes by chronology (Ancient, Medieval, Modern, Contemporary), sometimes by geography (Asia, Africa, America, Europe), and sometimes by media (Prints and Drawings, Photography, Decorative Arts)—and to trace the currents of influence that course through the works in our collections. And, like Edward Said, we should always encourage a rigorous application of the humanist critique—by ourselves and among our visitors—"to introduce a longer sequence of thought and analysis to replace the short bursts of polemical, thought-stopping fury that so imprison us in labels and antagonistic debate whose goal is a belligerent collective identity rather than understanding and intellectual exchange."[45]

Much is at stake. Much of the world is at war. We live in an age of resurgent nationalism. And where the violence is not nationalist, it is sectarian. Identity matters proliferate, and identities matter more and more. We cannot be partners to ahistorical claims on the past and the cultural property laws that sustain them. We must always question them, challenge them, hold them up to humanist critique. And then "Rather than the manufactured clash of civilizations," as Said wrote in the final paragraphs of his final Preface, "we need to concentrate on the slow working together of cultures that overlap, borrow from each other, and live together in far more interesting ways than any abridged or inauthentic mode of understanding can allow. But for that kind of wider perception," he cautions us, "we need time and patient and skeptical inquiry, supported by faith in communities of interpretation that are difficult to sustain in a world demanding instant action and reaction."[46]

This is the challenge to encyclopedic art museums in the first years of the twenty-first century: Continue to build collections representative of the world's artistic legacy and argue against nationalist laws and international agreements that discourage this noble ambition. Some critics argue that this is a self-interested charge justifying the

143

transfer of cultural property from the Third World to the First. After all, they argue, encyclopedic museums are only in the developed world and mainly in the West. Although it is true that encyclopedic museums are primarily in the West, does that discredit the principle of their existence? If it is a good idea to have representative examples of all the world's cultures under one roof for curious people to see, to think about, to better understand and appreciate, to become more sensitive to the cultures of others, to the Other, to the expansive, rich, fecund diversity of the world's many cultures that over millennia have overlapped and influenced each other such that each has a claim on the other, then it is *a good idea, period.*

❋ ❋ ❋

I wrote in the Preface of this book about what we might learn from considering just six objects in neighboring galleries within the Art Institute. This is important not just in itself, of course, as I have argued, but it is also important because of the role the Art Institute plays in its host city, Chicago.

The Art Institute is Chicago's window on the world. It is where our citizens are introduced to, and are encouraged to engage with, cultures distant from their own in time and space. Increasingly, given the rapidly changing demographics of our city—already famously a city of immigrants—these distant cultures are coming home and moving next door. They are no longer only foreign. They are becoming local. Twenty-six different ethnic groups with at least 25,000 members each now live in our city; more Mexicans than any other U.S. city except Los Angeles, and more Asians than Honolulu. Africans are coming in great numbers too; from Nigeria especially, but also from Ethiopia, Somalia, and Tanzania. And of course there are hundreds of thousands of Irish, Germans, and Poles (more Poles than in Warsaw, it is often said). The more our citizens know about the world and the glories of its diverse artistic production and its distinguished history, the more likely they will develop respect and understanding for the different cultures of their neighbors in an ever-changing, increasingly multiethnic city. This is the promise of encyclopedic art museums:

they serve as a force for understanding, tolerance, and the dissolution of ignorance and superstition about *the world*. And they remind us of the connections that course through history and manifest themselves in the objects we prize for their beauty, eloquence, and fresh strangeness. The encyclopedic museum reminds us that culture is always *living* culture, always changing the way we see the world, and always transforming us, ourselves, into the bargain.

Encyclopedic museums gather the art of the world for the world at home and everywhere. They tell a cosmopolitanist story and should be encouraged. Individual governments and international organizations expend enormous amounts of time, effort, and money to enforce laws claiming that antiquities are a modern nation's cultural property and a source of identity and esteem for the citizens of that modern nation, and that such antiquities constitute the very essence of a society and convey important information concerning a people's origin, history, and traditional setting, and derive from cultures that developed autonomously in the region of a present-day nation. If all of that were spent instead to promote the understanding that antiquities are part of the world's common ancient heritage and a source of identity and esteem for all of us, and that they constitute the essence of our very humanity, and derive from cultures that have always influenced each other, that are hybrids and mongrels—*cosmopolitan*—we would all be much better off. We would be more likely to regard the cultural expressions of our neighbors and distant cousins as worthy of our respect and admiration, and the cultural expressions of ancient people not as patrimony of particular modern peoples but of all of us, as our common ancient heritage in which we all have a stake, and which we should preserve and make accessible to everyone.

The cultural property laws of Italy, Turkey, and China—just to name three nations—argue against these possibilities and claim antiquities to be not only the property and patrimony of particular nations but the manifestation of the "collective genius of nationals of the State." And therein lies the real danger: citizens of the state claimed by the state to be bound together by some collective genius that distinguishes them from everyone else in the world; and antiquities as bearing the imprint of some modern people's national genius, indelibly.

EPILOGUE

For Herodotus, the world's multiculturalism was a living, pulsating tissue in which nothing was permanently set or defined, but which continually transformed itself, mutated, gave rise to new relationships and contexts.

—Ryszard Kapuściński, *Travels with Herodotus* (2007)[1]

I have focused in this book on the question, *Who Owns Antiquity?* This is the real question, the one that lies behind the recent arguments between museums and archaeologists, and between museums and "source" countries' nationalist governments. I question the premise of nationalist retentionist cultural property laws: that it is the right of sovereign nations to legislate the protection of and access to whatever they consider to be *their* cultural property, that which they claim to be important to their national identities and self-esteem. Nationalist retentionist cultural property laws serve the interests of one particular modern nation at the expense of the rest of the world. Antiquities are ancient artifacts of times and cultures long preceding the history of the modern nation-state. And in all but a very few cases, they have no obvious relation to that state other than the accident of geography: they happen to have been found within its modern borders.

Antiquities are the cultural property of all humankind—of *people*, not *peoples*—evidence of the world's ancient past and not that of a particular modern nation. They comprise antiquity, and antiquity knows no borders. It is, as Ryszard Kapuściński says of human history, like "a great cauldron whose perpetually simmering surface sees incessant collisions of unnumerable particles, each moving in their own orbits, along trajectories that intersect at an infinite number of points."[2] It cannot be subdivided and nationalized. Its influence is boundless, uncontainable. We all have stake in its survival, in all of its forms, everywhere. We must find better ways to protect antiquity than by simply giving our unthinking endorsement to national retentionist cultural property laws.

What about an international trusteeship under the auspices of a nongovernmental agency? What would such an international authority be and how would it be constituted? There is one, of course: it is called the United Nations, or more specifically the U.N.'s Educational, Scientific and Cultural Organization (UNESCO), and it is already a large and well-established institution. According to its Web site, UNESCO functions "as a laboratory of ideas and a standard-setter to forge universal agreements on emerging ethical issues" and "promotes international co-operation" among its Member States and Associate Members. And it works "to create the conditions for genuine dialogue based on respect for shared values and the dignity of each civilization and culture," while its Culture Sector "builds on advances made in the recognition of cultural diversity for the sustainable development of peoples and societies, placing emphasis on a holistic approach to the protection and safeguarding of cultural heritage in all its forms, tangible and intangible." Among its "strategic objectives" for 2002–2007 is to "pursue further the updating of cultural policies and the development of cultural industries, taking into account the need to promote intercultural and interfaith dialogue," "to bolster cooperation in the domain of cultural heritage," "search for stronger linkages between cultural policy and intercultural dialogue [that] will have an emphasis on multi-ethnic environments and pre- and post-conflict situations," and "in the area of intercultural dialogue and pluralism, including inter-faith dialogue, will complement the development of cultural policies, notably through the support of national, regional and interregional initiatives and related research."

All of this sounds good and promising. But UNESCO has proven ineffectual in its efforts to promote greater understanding and pre-

servation of the world's common artistic heritage. This is the organization that by the terms of its charter had no grounds on which to act
to prevent the Taliban from shooting rockets at the Bamiyan Bud-
dhas and destroying much of the Kabul Museum's collection (in fact,
it refused to allow for the foreign acquisition of antiquities likely to
have been pirated from Afghanistan during the troubles, preferring
instead that they remain in Kabul, subject to the Taliban's senseless
destruction); or for protecting the Iraq Museum and the archaeological record of that vitally important part of the ancient world
(and calling for the return to Iraq of any undocumented antiquities
thought to have been improperly removed from that divided, failed
state); or for protecting the archaeological sites that will lie beneath
the body of water created by the Three Gorges Dam; and so much
more. And this is the same organization that brought us the 1970
Convention on the Means of Prohibiting and Preventing the Illicit
Import, Export and Transfer of Ownership of Cultural Property
(from its "Preamble"):

> Considering that cultural property constitutes one of the basic elements
> of civilization and *national culture*, and that its true value can be ap-
> preciated only in relation to the fullest possible information regarding
> its origin, history and traditional setting,/ Considering that it is incum-
> bent upon every *State* to protect the cultural property existing within
> its territory against the dangers of theft, clandestine excavation, and
> illicit export,/Considering that, to avert these dangers, it is essential for
> every *State* to become increasingly active to the moral obligations to
> respect its own cultural heritage and that of all *nations*, . . . /Considering
> that the illicit import, export and transfer of ownership of cultural
> property is an obstacle to that understanding between *nations* which it
> is part of Unesco's mission to promote by recommending to interested
> *States*, international conventions to this end,/Considering that the pro-
> tection of cultural heritage can be effective only if organized both *na-
> tionally* and internationally among *States* working in close co-operation."
> (italics added)

UNESCO unambiguously respects the nation-state and vests authority
in it. And yet, any state can denounce a UNESCO Convention "on its

own behalf or on behalf of any territory for which territorial relations it is responsible" and withdraw from it, or simply ignore it altogether.

In 1984, the United States did just that. We had long been frustrated with the workings of the U.N. agency. And we weren't alone. For years, many Western nations had accused UNESCO of inept management, unrestrained spending, and hostility toward Western interests.[3] In 1974, for example (and interesting in the context of this book), the UNESCO General Conference passed a resolution condemning Israel for "its persistence in altering the historical features of the City of Jerusalem and undertaking excavations which constitute a danger to its monuments subsequent to its illegal occupation of the city." And it invited the U.N. Secretary General to withhold assistance from Israel (approximately $25,000 of UNESCO grant-in-aid).[4] The U.S. Congress reacted swiftly and amended the Foreign Assistance Act of 1974 to neither authorize nor appropriate funds to UNESCO for the remainder of the year, nor for 1975 or 1976. And this was no small matter. When, in 1983, the United States threatened again to withhold funding, $47 million or 25 percent of UNESCO's $180 million budget was at stake.

In 1984, after more than a decade of unhappiness, twenty-four nations presented UNESCO's director general with a list of changes they wanted the agency to put into effect. (The nations included, among others, all ten of Western Europe's Common Market, plus the United States, Japan, Spain, Switzerland, and Turkey.) Chief among the changes was a proposal to amend the UNESCO voting system to give the Western contributors to UNESCO's budget greater control over how the money was to be spent. (UNESCO was managed by an Executive Board of fifty-five members, with resolutions adopted by the full General Conference of, at the time, all 161 members of the U.N. General Assembly, and most of the recent growth in U.N. Member States were among third world countries who tended to ally with the Soviet bloc against Western interests.) After giving due warning, the United States formally pulled out of UNESCO in January 1984. On February 29, Assistant Secretary of State Gregory Newell wrote a letter to Senator Charles Percy, Chairman of the U.S. Senate's Committee on Foreign Relations, explaining the reasons for the U.S. action:

"The Administration has judged that it is no longer worthwhile for the U.S. to remain a member of the organization in which negative considerations so far outweigh the technical benefits provided.... Our decision to withdraw from UNESCO involved a judgement that significant structural and programmatic change was not realistically possible in any reasonable time frame under existing circumstances."[5]

Key to the U.S. decision to withdraw from UNESCO was the determination that it simply was no longer in our *national self-interest* to remain part of it. As Newell explained in the Executive Review of the report that accompanied his letter: "UNESCO programs and personnel are heavily politicized and answer to an agenda that is often inimical to U.S. interests. The approach that UNESCO consistently takes to disarmament (which is not the proper concern of that body) too frequently coincides with that of the Soviet Union. Human rights programs and resolutions emphasize statist concepts of 'collective rights' in denigration of individual rights and freedoms recognized in the Universal Declaration of Human Rights."[6] And, quite specifically: "Most UNESCO programs are aimed almost exclusively at the Third World and have little or no direct impact on U.S. interests." In other words, the complaint was not only that UNESCO had become politicized, but that its politics were judged not to be in the best interests of the United States. And so we remained outside UNESCO until the spring of 2003.

By then, the political situation had changed significantly. The Cold War had come to an end, the Soviet Union no longer existed, third world countries were behaving less and less like a unified bloc, and the United States was seeking broad, U.N. support for a confrontation with Iraq. Suddenly, it was in our national self-interest to be part of UNESCO. As Mrs. Bush explained when she remarked upon the United States's return to U.N. agency at UNESCO's headquarters in Paris, "As the civilized world stands against terror, UNESCO's work can make an enormous difference. Together we can construct, as UNESCO's constitution states, the defences of peace in the minds of men."[7] A few days earlier, the U.S. Department of State's Bureau of International Organization Affairs posted the return to UNESCO on its Web site, noting just where UNESCO's mission was in concert with U.S. interests: its "Education for All" program advances "U.S. education goals worldwide and closely parallels the U.S. 'No Child Left Behind' program"; it advocates education that "promotes tolerance and civic responsibility" as a key "to building democracy and combating terrorism"; "helps countries protect their natural and cultural heritage," which is "important in maintaining a healthy balance between continuity and imperatives for change"; and "promotes press freedom and independent media, essential foundations of democracy." And it headlined President Bush's remarks that "As a symbol of our commitment to human dignity, the United States will return to UNESCO. This organization has been reformed and America will participate fully in its mission to advance human rights and tolerance and learning."[8] (President Bush nominated Louise V. Oliver, a Republican fund-raiser and former president of Gopac, the Republican political advocacy organization associated with the conservative pundit and former U.S. Congressman, Newt Gingrich, to serve as U.S. ambassador to UNESCO. Her appointment was approved and Ambassador Oliver serves in this capacity as I write.)[9]

Participation in the workings of UNESCO is determined by national political self-interest. If a country believes it is to the benefit of its political position in the world to participate in UNESCO, it will. If it believes it is not, it won't. This is true of the United Nations itself, of course. As the historian Paul Kennedy has written:

> The United Nations could never escape the central paradox of all international bodies. The paradox is this: Since the world organization was created by its member states, which acted like shareholders in a corporation, it can function effectively only when it received the support of national governments, especially those of the larger powers. Nations can ignore the world body . . . [and] the organization cannot pursue proposed actions if a Great Power—that is, one of the five countries possessing the veto—is opposed. This tension between sovereignty and internationalism is inherent, persistent, and unavoidable.[10]

At best UNESCO identifies issues of concern to the international community and raises awareness about them. It aspires "to build peace in the minds of men" by functioning as a "laboratory of ideas and a standard-setter to forge universal agreement on emerging ethical issues." But then, UNESCO is more. It wants to be, and often acts as, an operational agency. As its Web site states, "Through its strategies and activities, UNESCO is actively pursuing the Millennium Development Goals, especially those aiming to halve the proportion of people living in extreme poverty in developing countries by 2015, achieve universal primary education in all countries by 2015, eliminate gender disparity in primary and secondary education by 2005." To do this, UNESCO has a large bureaucracy. Its Executive Board comprises fifty-five members, divided among six world regions, and is charged with, among other things, executing the program adopted by the full General Conference and at times advising the U.N. Director-General on behalf of the General Conference, which comprises 193 Member States and six Associate Members. A twelve-member bureau of Executive Board members advises the Chairman of the Board. In addition, the Board has an eighteen-member Special Committee, a thirty-member Committee on Conventions, a twenty-four-member Committee on International Non-Governmental Organizations, and a Group of Experts on Financial and Administrative Matters, all of which are distributed more or less equally among the six world regions. The General Conference meets every two years. Its working languages are Arabic, Chinese, English, French, Russian, and Spanish. And the Executive Board meets twice a year. UNESCO's major fields of action and priorities include Education, Natural Sciences, Social and Human Sciences, Communication and Information, and Culture. In the latter field, its current cultural priorities include "promoting cultural diversity, with special emphasis on the tangible and intangible heritage; cultural policies as well as intercultural and interfaith dialogue and understanding; cultural industries and artistic expressions."

Among the committees in the field of Culture is the Intergovernmental Committee for Promoting the Return of Cultural Property to its Countries of Origin or its Restitution in case of Illicit Appropriation. The Committee was established in 1978 and held its first meeting in 1980. It recently held its fourteenth session. Its purpose is of an advisory nature, seeking "ways and means of facilitating bilateral negotiations for the restitution or return of cultural property to its countries of origin" as requested by the UNESCO Director-General, who shall have received requests for action from UNESCO Member States or Associate Members. It considers "cultural property" to denote "historical and ethnographic objects and documents including manuscripts, works of the plastic and decorative arts [i.e., sculpture, vases, bronzes], palaeontological and archaeological objects and zoological, botanical and mineralogical specimens." Among its declared successes are the return of 7,000 cuneiform tablets from Germany to Turkey and 12,000 Pre-Columbian objects to Ecuador from Italy after a seven-year litigation. Other cases still pending include Greece's request for the return of the Parthenon Marbles. It has also established a special Fund to support its efforts. The Committee has its own Web site, accessed through the UNESCO Culture field portal. There one can learn about the purpose, statutes, and procedures of the Committee, read texts of standing requests, and be advised on how to make requests for the return of cultural property. One can also find appeals for contributions to the Fund for the Return of Cultural Property to its Countries of Origin or its restitution in case of Illicit Appropriation, the purpose of which is to help claimant nation-states which "alone cannot solve the problem of recovering their lost heritage." Emphasis is everywhere on the *state*: claimant states; art-trading states party to UNESCO 1970; and states willing "to assist in the return of these objects to their creators."

It is time to question whether the nation-state bias of UNESCO and its Conventions has proven it to be a help or hindrance to the protection of the world's cultural and artistic legacy. To date, some thirty years after it was drafted, UNESCO 1970 has failed, and failed because it has no teeth: it cannot contradict the authority of its Member States. It can only offer to help mediate claims between Member States; and on the basis that culture is the property of nation-states. We are losing our common ancient heritage at an ever-increasing rate through theft and destruction, poverty, development, warfare, and sectarian violence. No amount of international conventions and agreements that declare the existence of, and then proclaim to respect, the "collective genius of nationals of the State" will be able to overcome the obstacle of nationalism. Nationalism is always a way out of international agreements. That's just the way it is.

Why do archaeologists accept this? Because they are dependent on nation-states to do their work. Nation-states hold the goods—antiquities and archaeological sites as national cultural property and cultural patrimony—and they control access to them. The history of archaeology as a discipline is deeply embedded in the history of the politics of the regions within which archaeology has been practiced. There is no denying this. And some would say there is no way out of it, either. It is the reality of the conditions within which archaeologists engage in the practice of their profession. But what if foreign archaeologists withheld their expertise until nation-states agreed to restore the practice of *partage*, or the sharing of archaeological finds, generally and generously? Host nations have always depended in great part on the work of foreign archaeologists for the raw material of their nationalist ideologies, not to mention the tangible property that fuels their tourism economies. Archaeologists should question their support of nationalist retentionist cultural property laws, especially those who benefit today from working among the finds in the collections of their host university museums, collections which could not now be formed, ever since the implementation of foreign cultural property laws. And they should join museums in pressing for the return of *partage*, the principle and practice by which so many local and encyclopedic museum collections were built in the past.

We should all work together to counter the nationalist basis of national laws and international conventions and agreements and promote a principle of shared stewardship of our common heritage. John Henry Merryman has already articulated a framework for reconsidering national and international cultural property laws: a "triad of regulatory imperatives"—preservation, knowledge, and access. Antiquities should be distributed around the world to better ensure their preservation, broaden our knowledge of them, and increase the world's access to them. And museums should share and exchange scholarly and professional expertise. Surely these are sounder principles on which to proceed than the nationalist ones enshrined in national laws and UNESCO's conventions.

Let's be clear about this: the argument between art museums and archaeologists is not over whether antiquities and archaeological sites should be preserved. It is over how best to preserve them and increase our knowledge of and public access to them for the benefit of all of us. This will not happen by emboldening nation-states and encouraging them to join forces to reclaim *their* self-proclaimed cultural property—Italy with Greece, Egypt with Italy and Greece, China with Peru, and more. Nation-states are feeling more confident now than ever. And the world's ancient artistic legacy is being held hostage to the nationalist ambitions of these nation-state governments.

The real argument is between museums and modern nation-states over the imposition of nationalist retentionist cultural property laws and their failure to protect our common ancient heritage and their perversion of that heritage by claiming the archaeological record as a modern nation's cultural property, important as a source of identity and esteem for modern nations and their nationals. It is imperative that we resolve this. The recent rise in nationalist and sectarian violence and the pervasive misunderstanding, even intolerance, of other cultures, and our ignorance of the very hybridity of culture and the interrelatedness of cultures such that we all have a stake in their preservation precisely because they are ours—both ancient and living cultures—because they are the mark of humanity, of what it means to be human, compels us to resolve our differences. Too much time has been wasted arguing the wrong issues. And in the meantime, our archaeological record is being destroyed.

We can do better than this. We need to encourage the sharing of the world's heritage, to allow people everywhere to learn from the kind of experience I described at the start of this book, when over just three galleries in one museum we were able to draw connections between cultures distant in time and space, and we realized that the ancient peoples of the Yellow River region of today's China ornamented their lives and engaged in ritual practices not unlike the peoples of medieval Europe and nineteenth-century Benin; and that the exquisite objects all of those people made resulted from contact between different cultures: a Christian monstrance with a crystal bottle made in the Islamic lands to hold perfume, now at its center and holding the tooth of the Baptist; and an ivory box likely made by Muslim artists living among Christians in Sicily and decorated with motifs, which derived from Middle Eastern metalware, and including the Arabic inscription, "May glory endure." This is the nature and promise of culure itself, and has always been.

⊠ ⊠ ⊠

I remember well my first visit to a museum. It was 1970 and I was nineteen. I hadn't come from a privileged family. My father was a career U.S. Air Force officer. I grew up on military bases. I was studying in Europe as a university sophomore and visiting Paris. I went to the Louvre for the obvious reason: it was what one did as a tourist. But as I walked from room to room I became profoundly aware of the strange, new universe I had entered. Most of the world was there before me, or so it seemed, on the museum's walls and in its cases: fragile artifacts from places of which I had never heard—Mesopotamia, Sumer, Akkad, Elam—some of them monumental, fragments of whole city walls (Susa in the time of Darius); mysteriously beautiful basalt sculptures and rapturously exotic gold- and other metalworks from New Kingdom and Pharoanic Egypt; Cycladic heads and ceramic vessels and metal sculptures from what I now know to have been the age of Homer; awe-inspiring, over life-size Greek and Roman sculptures from the Victory of Samothrace to the Venus de Milo; Roman silver and those all-too-serious portrait busts of emperors and republicans; Islamic ceramics, calligraphy, and metalwork; and of course the paintings of Renaissance Italy and Baroque France, both familiar and strange, from Leonardo to Poussin, the slaves of Michelangelo, and the modern monuments by David, Delacroix, Ingres, and Courbet. It was the Louvre before *le pyramid*. And on that winter afternoon I seemed to have the galleries to myself. I could wander at will, uninterrupted by crowds and commerce.

I remember being moved, powerfully. The largeness of the Louvre-as-universe—the "world under one roof," as the founders of the British Museum described their ambition for that museum—did not diminish my sense of being but enlarged it. I was not the lesser for not being "from" these magnificent cultures. They were not inaccessible to me, although in many cases I had never heard of them and in every case knew little if anything about them. They were not foreign, in the sense of being of another's culture. They were mine, too. Or, rather, I was theirs. They drew my attention and I looked long and hard at them. And I looked at them in wonder, too; in ways, I imagined, their original beholders looked at them. And then not just their original beholders but everyone since, everyone who has seen them, admired them, protected them until they came into the museum, where for almost two hundred years they have been kept safe for any and all to see, and be moved by.

And as I looked at them, I came to feel as if I were linked to—as if I could *identify with*—their makers and first beholders simply as a human being capable of being moved by beautiful works of art. It didn't matter that I was from a particular place and time distant from them, that I hadn't the preparation to know anything about them, that I was a middle-class Protestant kid from a U.S. military base background. It only mattered that I could identify with them, as exquisite works of human manufacture. There was no sense that they belonged to anyone. They were works of art, no more anyone's property than the great ideas that have come down to us over the centuries, and which we share and interweave into our particular belief systems. They weren't in any meaningful way possessible. They were fragile artifacts of humanity, of which I was a small part, but a small, *important* part as an heir to the diverse traditions of human creativity. In ways I didn't realize at the time, I left the Louvre that day a changed person.

That was in 1970, thirty-seven years ago. At the time, I was studying in Luxembourg and my parents were living in Germany, where my father was stationed with the U.S. Air Force. The previous year, while studying in the United States, I had had to write my parents to arrange a time when they could call me on the one dormitory telephone that could make and receive outside calls. It would take my letter about a week to get to them in Europe, and theirs about a week to get to me. But we didn't mind. That we could talk to each over the telephone at that distance was in itself remarkable. For the first trans-Atlantic telephone cable had been laid only a few years before, in 1957. Soon all of this would change.

In 1988, just fifteen years after I graduated from university, the first trans-Atlantic fiber-optic cable was laid, increasing the capacity for simultaneous telephone calls between the United States and London to 37,800, or nearly 800 percent over what it had been only five years earlier. In 1996, with more cables laid, some 1.3 million calls were possible between Europe and North America, and to Asia nearly one million more. With 150 communications satellites then operable, another 1 million calls could be made for a total capacity of over 3 million simultaneous calls. Thus, in just over ten years from 1983 to 1996, the number of simultaneous overseas telephone calls had increased exponentially from 4,300 to more than 3 million. And that was only the beginning. The Apple II home computer appeared in 1977 and the first IBM PC in 1981. The first version of Microsoft Windows operating system was launched in 1985, and its more powerful and quickly ubiquitous version—Windows 3.0—appeared in 1990. Personal computers could now create, store, search, and manipulate data, both verbal and numerical, as never before. Soon, with the invention of the Internet and World Wide Web in 1991, computers could communicate with each other and email became the communication means of choice for a rapidly ever-expanding universe of users. All that was needed was a tool for accessing the Web and communicating through the Internet free of proprietary protocols. This appeared in 1994 with the launch of Netscape, the first commercial Web browser. And then, four years later, the first super-powerful search engine, Google, appeared, allowing users to search the content of most pages on the Web for key words, directing them to specific pages and their content. Today, Google has more than 300 million users searching Web pages in more than one hundred languages. (Google is already so much a part of our lives that when I type it on my computer using Word, my spell check doesn't even question it: it did question me when I misspelled it as Gogle.)

Thus, in just a few years, we went from making phone calls to emailing, posting, searching, downloading, and sharing a universe of information almost instantaneously, anytime, from anywhere, 24/7/365. By 2006, close to 1 billion people, or one-sixth of the world's population, were connected to the Internet, capable of communicating with each other and with more than one person simultaneously by ever more powerful, faster, smaller, and more easily transportable computers over fiber-optic cables of increasing bandwidth. Had my father lived to see the Internet, and had he been so inclined to use it (my mother lived to see it and even sent an email or two), we could have dispensed with exchanging letters to arrange a time to call. We could have dropped each other an email anytime and from almost anywhere in the world and expected a reply in a matter of minutes or whenever we got around to it. Of course, too, we could have used our mobile telephones, on which we could also have received and sent email, surfed the Web, listened to music, watched movies, traded stocks: communicated with almost anyone in more ways than we could have dreamed of only twenty years earlier.[11]

This communication revolution has changed dramatically the world in which we live. And I have seen it occur in my lifetime; indeed, in my wife's and our children's lifetimes. We live in a globalized world my parents could never have imagined. Thomas Friedman has described this as "the inexorable integration of markets, nation-states and technologies to a degree never witnessed before—in a way that is enabling individuals, corporations and nation-states to reach around the world farther, faster, deeper and cheaper than ever before, and in a way that is enabling the world to reach into individuals, corporations and nation-states farther, faster, deeper, cheaper than ever before."[12] And he calls it Globalization 3.0. Globalizations 1.0 and 2.0 had over centuries shrunk the world from large to medium and medium to small, respectively driven by the muscle of nations and multinational companies. Globalization 3.0 had shrunk the world to tiny and flattened the playing field at the same time, and in just a matter of decades. Our world is now being driven by the power for *individuals* to collaborate and compete globally through the convergence of the personal computer with fiber-optic cable and the rise of workflow software. Individuals can now become the authors of their own content, access more and more digital content around the world at almost no cost, and collaborate on that same digital content from anywhere, regardless of the distances between them. Individuals from every corner of our now flat world are being empowered.[13]

I was thinking about all of this as I was finishing this book, and reflecting back on my first visit to the Louvre and my introduction to the wondrous universe of its encyclopedic collection, and how it made me feel, in my own small way (even if I couldn't have put it this way then) a part of it, with the dividers of time and space suddenly collapsed, non-existent: the diverse, interrelated cultures of antiquity no longer distant, one ancient culture from another, mine from theirs, hundreds, even thousands of years later. Between that visit (my first to an art museum) and my first email, twenty years passed. Between then and my constant use of email and frequent searches on the Web, ten years passed. And between then and now: downloads, uploads, podcasts, blogs, all manner of information-sharing reaching deeper and deeper into the lives of individuals all around the world.

We live in an age of globalization characterized by the potential of almost all of us to participate in and contribute to it. Whether we like it or not, we are part of a system of production and exchange which is tying us more closely together than ever before and implicating us all in the fate of the world's politics, economics, and culture. As Friedman put it: "Today, more than ever, the traditional boundaries between politics, culture, technology, finance, national security and ecology are disappearing. You often cannot explain one without referring to the others, and you cannot explain the whole without reference to them all."

We have always sought to expand our way in the world, ever since our common ancestors left the horn of Africa, likely in search of food fifty thousand years ago. There may have been only one hundred and fifty to two thousand of them then, but over the next thousands of years they covered the globe and established the first sedentary cultures centered on crop growing and animal husbandry. The spread of agriculture led to the exchange of crops for goods between communities of people as early as 7400 B.C. at Çatal Höyük in present-day Turkey. This led to the emergence of states with imperial ambitions in the area of Mesopotamia five thousand years later, which in turn led to ever larger states and empires from Egypt to Greece, Persia, China, Rome, the Mongols of Central Asia, and the Mughals of South Asia, until the modern states and empires of Europe and the Americas. And within and between them were the vast land and sea trading networks, which encouraged accidental and purposeful exchanges of culture and cultural artifacts to such an extent that we can speak rightfully of the world's culture—our *human* culture: nuanced in its differences, diverse yet wholly interrelated, generative and fecund.

It is a sad and even tragic irony that in the new age of globalization in which we live today, just as the world is getting smaller and smaller and more and more rapidly interconnected and interdependent, our common, ancient cultural heritage is being divided up and claimed by modern nation-states as theirs, the property of only some of the world's people, made by their alleged ancestors for them and deprived of its rich diversity of sources and evidence of cultural influences. Attempts by nation-states to restrict access to antiquity because they claim it to be *national*, the nation's culture, autonomously produced within the borders of the nation, the result of a collective, national intelligence, the living memory of the nation, essential for the development of the national identity and important to its self-esteem is a desperate, self-centered, political move and contrary to the facts of history: an attempt to deny the truth of our basic and inevitable cultural interrelatedness.

In his powerful and convincing book, *Bound Together: How Traders, Preachers, Adventurers, and Warriors Shaped Globalization*, Nayan Chandra, put it like this: "The result of all of [globalization] has been to intertwine peoples' lives across the globe ever more intimately. The process of reconnecting the dispersed human community that started more than ten thousand years ago is stronger than ever, and thanks to technology it is continuously accelerating, binding us together ever more tightly."[14] That is the truth we should never forget. And we should not let the modern ambitions of nation-states perpetuate a false reading of history for their personal, political gain. Globalization is and has always been inevitable. It is in the nature of our species to connect and exchange. And the result is a common culture in which we all have a stake. It is not, and can never be, the property of one modern nation or another. It is ours, all of ours. And it deserves to be preserved and shared for what it is: our common artistic legacy as human beings.

AFTERWORD TO THE PAPERBACK EDITION

In this book I question the efficacy and intentions of the current legal regime controlling the world's access to our ancient heritage. Originally published in 2008, the book met with mixed reviews. Some reviewers liked it. Others hated it. Some thought it provocative. Some called it self-serving. Some were downright hostile to it.

One reviewer called me "the pit bull of the American megamuseum establishment." Another called my book "an example of US cultural imperialism at its worst." My favorite review concluded with these words: "I assume that many will hope, and some I know will pray, that this book represents the last death throes of a failed traditional world-view: the dominance of the many by the (very) few; the dominance of a Western scientific tradition over all others; the dominance of a closed view clinging, perhaps subconsciously, to what one can only describe as colonial oppression." And then it closed with the funniest line yet written about the book: "Perhaps if a dinosaur could have written a book arguing against its extinction, it would have read like this."[1]

All in all I've been pleased with the book's reception. It struck a chord, which is why I wrote it. I wanted its readers to look again at the question of "Who Owns Antiquity," and to ask "why" and "to what purpose." And many have. This is not the place to respond to the book's critics, although I will reflect briefly on the charges of "imperialism" and "colonialism" below. I want first to update factual details that have changed since the book was first published.

At the time of the book's publication, the U.S. government had not yet responded to the People's Republic of China's 2005 request for import restrictions on a broad range of objects made in China from the Paleolithic period to the Qing dynasty (1644 A.D.), or some two million years of human manufacture. (The request was made through the U.S. President's Cultural Property Advisory Committee, as legislated by the 1983 Cultural Property Implementation Act [CPIA].) For the better part of four years, there was no action on the request. Then, on January 14, 2009, just days before the end of his presidency, and without public notice, George W. Bush accepted a modified Chinese request and agreed to prohibit the importation of monumental sculpture and wall art at least 250 years old and a broad range of categories of material dating from the Paleolithic period through the Tang dynasty (907 A.D.).

Just why President Bush responded as and when he did is not clear. It was the thirtieth anniversary of diplomatic relations between the two countries and the U.S.-Chinese relationship was (and of course still is) of the greatest importance to both nations. Diplomatic efforts were being made on multiple fronts: the United States was seeking China's help in containing North Korea and arguing for China to revalue the renminbi (pegged to the value of the weak dollar, the renminbi keeps Chinese exports artificially cheap); the United States was suspicious of China's reach into Africa, where China was trading aid and economic investments for political influence and access to much-needed raw materials; and the United States wanted China to join the American-led campaign to isolate Iran as a state supporter of terrorism with nuclear ambitions. (China imports crude oil from Iran to feed its booming economy and has large investments in Iran's oil and gas sector and thus remains critical of isolating Iran.)

There were many reasons that the Bush administration might have wanted to reply to China's request for import restrictions on what it claimed to be its cultural property. But almost certainly, protecting the archaeological record was not one of them. For governments do not make decisions on these terms. They do so for political reasons, because it is thought to be in their *political* advantage to make this or that decision. That was a principal argument of my book: governments define and police national cultural property for political reasons, not scientific ones. Retentionist cultural property laws are political instruments intent on restricting foreign access to what governments claim is their country's national cultural property as a means of strengthening the identity of the nation as defined by government. And in this, the laws are *nationalist* political instruments propagating a false ideology of cultural essentialism and national cultural purity: Chinese culture—and in particular, *Han* Chinese culture—not the world's.

The Chinese government's pride in China's long and distinguished history is sincere. Its sense of injustice done at the hands of the British and French during the Opium Wars of the nineteenth century, including the destruction of the Imperial Summer Palace, is equally sincere. So too are its feelings for the loss of much of its cultural property during the warlord years early in the twentieth century, when great quantities of ancient Chinese art were sold overseas. And of course the nationalists' transfer of much of the Imperial collection to Taiwan is the greatest loss of all. These instances mark moments of an imbalance of power, when a weakened China suffered losses at the hands of stronger, foreign governments. And now a resurgent China is seeking to recover what it claims is its *lost* cultural property through political and financial means and always with an emotional appeal to national pride.

The Chairman of the Poly Group, a Beijing-based industrial conglomerate with close ties to the Chinese military and a very handsome and important art museum, wrote in the preface to a catalogue of selected highlights of the museum's ancient bronzes in 2001, "Most of these pieces, lost to overseas collections, have exchanged hands many times. . . . Their return not only makes us fondly recollect days of old, but is more importantly a source of great comfort." And the "rescue of three bronze animal heads, formerly of the Summer Palace, particularly aroused the patriotic passions of Chinese sons and daughters. Regardless of the difference in their particular stands and religions, they all equally praised the rescue."[2]

The chairman was referring in the second sentence to the museum's purchase in 2000 of three bronze animal heads from the Zodiac Fountain of the Qinq dynasty Summer Palace (the heads were of the tiger, ox, and monkey figures). Designed by the French Jesuit Michel Benoist for the Qianlong emperor in the middle of the eighteenth century, the fountain once included twelve animals placed around a pool in two groups of six, each animal representing one of the twelve double-hours of the day and designed to spout water at its designated time during the day. A century later, in 1860, the Summer Palace was looted and destroyed by French and British troops. To date, seven of the animal heads have been located.

In 2003, the National Treasures Fund of China, a quasi-governmental group, purchased from a reported American collector the head of the pig figure. The purchase was made with a $1 million donation from Stanley Ho, a real estate and casino billionaire from Macao. Four years later Ho purchased from Sotheby's in Hong Kong the head of the boar and gave it to the Poly Museum. A year later, Christie's put up for auction two other bronze animal heads from the Summer Palace: the rat and the rabbit. They had belonged to the late French designer Yves Saint Laurent and his partner Pierre Bergé. The sale was condemned by China's State Administration of Cultural Heritage as having "damaged Chinese citizens' cultural rights." A spokeswoman for the Chinese Foreign Ministry said that the two bronzes should be returned to China because they had been taken by "invaders." And a Beijing lawyer seeking to block the sale, Liu Yang, declared that "the Summer Palace, which was plundered and burned down by Anglo-French allied forces during the Second Opium War in 1860, is our nation's unhealed scar, still bleeding and aching. That Christie's and Pierre Bergé would put them up for auction and refuse to return them to China deeply hurts our nation's feelings."[3]

The sale went ahead, and the successful bidder (at $40 million)— Cai Mingchao, who described himself as a collection advisor to the National Treasure Funds of China, an entity established under the administration of the China Foundation for the Development of Social Culture and registered under the name of the Ministry of Culture for the purpose of repatriating what it describes as looted Chinese artifacts—refused to pay, saying that his bid was made "on behalf of all Chinese people" and that the sculptures should be returned. At a news conference in Beijing following the auction, Cai said he had submitted his bids on moral and patriotic grounds: "I think any Chinese person would have stood up at that moment."[4] (It should be noted that at the time, diplomatic relations between China and France, where the auction occurred, were strained. A year earlier, the Chinese government had been angered by pro-Tibet and anti-China protests during the Olympic torch relay in Paris, and Chinese officials cancelled a trip to Paris after French President Nicolas Sarkozy met with the Dalai Lama in December.)[5] To date, the sculptures have not been returned.

Such statements as "on behalf of all the Chinese people" and "regardless of the difference in their political stands and religions, [all the Chinese sons and daughters] equally praised the rescue [of the Zodiac figures]" should give us pause. Who are the sons and daughters of China being spoken for? Certainly not the Uighur residents of China's western-most Xinjiang Uighur Autonomous Region, which came under Chinese control only under Qing Emperor Qianlong in the eighteenth century (the same emperor who built the Summer Palace). The Uighurs are Muslim and in number and cultural prominence historically dominated the region. But since the rise of the People's Republic of China in 1949, the percentage of Han Chinese in Xinjiang has risen from 5 to 40 percent (its capital city of Urumqi was 76 percent Han by 1998). The region is rich with crude oil and natural gas. Episodically fiercely independent, the region is considered a separatist threat. The Chinese government has denounced "three evil forces" in Xinjiang: separatist, terrorist, and religious extremism.

In chapter 4 of this book I noted reports of Human Rights Watch from the 1990s recounting Uighur uprisings and the Chinese government's police responses. While the book was in press, and during the run-up to the 2008 Beijing Olympic Games, violence broke out in Xinjiang when Uighur separatists first attacked and killed Chinese security personnel in Kashgar and then days later attacked government buildings in Kuqa city. In all, 197 people died. The region of some 400,000 Uighurs was cordoned off and tightened security was enforced.

The violence came amidst increasing Beijing-directed cultural change in Xinjiang. The location education system was being standardized on the Beijing model: the language of instruction was changing from Uighur to Mandarin, and Han Chinese teachers were replacing Uighur ones. Authorities were organizing public burnings of Uighur books. And traditional Uighur customs such as religious weddings, burials, or pilgrimages to the tombs of local saints were being prohibited. Most visibly, the Chinese government was accelerating the razing of old Kashgar for what Beijing claims are safety reasons: the historic buildings are condemned as too dangerous in the region's earthquake zone. The plan is to demolish 85 percent of old Kashgar and build in its place a mix of mid-rise apartments, plazas, avenues, and reproductions of ancient Islamic architecture "to preserve the Uighur culture," the city's Han Chinese vice-mayor, Xu Jianrong, was quoted as saying. (The government also plans to keep a section of old Kashgar as a tourist site, with actors performing traditional Uighur cultural practices.) No archaeologists are monitoring the razings. The government already knows everything about old Kashgar, the vice-mayor said.[6]

I make the point throughout this book that national domestic and foreign policies influence cultural policy: after all, they are government policies. For example, I point out how in 1984, during the first Reagan administration, the United States withdrew from UNESCO because our government had determined that "it is no longer worthwhile for the U.S. to remain a member of the organization in which negative considerations so far outweigh the technical benefits provided"; i.e., being part of UNESCO was no longer in our *self-interest*. The United States remained outside UNESCO until the spring of 2003, when, two years after 9/11, our foreign policy was directed at perceived threats of global terror around the world and we were looking for allies in our mounting "global war on terror." Suddenly we saw participation in UNESCO as *vital* to our national self-interest.

With the change in U.S. administrations in 2009, President Barack

Obama appointed David Killion U.S. ambassador to UNESCO. Formerly a senior member of the professional staff of the House Foreign Affairs Committee, Killion worked on the legislation that authorized our reentry into UNESCO in 2003. In his confirmation hearing before the U.S. Senate Foreign Relations Committee, Killion testified that "UNESCO is engaged in promoting a culture of peace and intercultural dialogue. This is critical because we face a common, global challenge to educate young people to resist violent ideologies, and to offer them tolerant, peaceful and constructive alternatives." He also emphasized that his agenda, and the Obama administration's, for UNESCO would include gender equality, freedom of expression and the press, and the addition of U.S. monuments to the list of World Heritage sites (he mentioned specifically Mount Vernon, the Virginia home of the first U.S. president, George Washington).[7] Is there any reason to think that this agenda indicates anything but that the appointment was political? Not if we take Killion's statement at face value: that his appointment ultimately advances the Obama administration's agenda.[8]

When I wrote this book, much of the debate between art museums and archaeologists in the United States centered on the terms by which museums should and should not acquire unprovenanced antiquities (those with incomplete recent ownership histories). Simply put, for years museums argued for more permissive terms and archaeologists for stricter terms. In footnote 7 of my introduction, I recounted the history of the position on this matter taken by the Association of Art Museum Directors (the organization representing the largest museums in North America). I concluded with the 2006 AAMD report calling for all AAMD members to work in conformity with U.S. law and in accordance with the 1970 UNESCO Convention when acquiring antiquities. And I pointed out that the report allowed for the acquisition of unprovenanced antiquities in certain circumstances: "AAMD recognizes that archaeological material and works of art, for which provenance information is incomplete or unobtainable, may deserve to be publicly displayed, conserved, studied, and published because of their rarity, historical importance, and aesthetic merit."

In 2008, AAMD adopted new guidelines advising member museums that they "normally should not acquire" an antiquity unless research substantiates that it was outside its country of probable modern discovery before 1970 or was legally exported after 1970.[9] That date of 1970 was chosen to acknowledge the authority (such as it is) of the UNESCO Convention of that year and to bring AAMD into alignment with certain museums in Europe and archaeological organizations like the Archaeological Institute of America. But 1970 is only a symbolic date. It has no juridical authority. It does not legalize a museum's acquisition of an object removed from its country of recent discovery after the establishment of laws restricting its ownership or export (whether those laws pre- or postdate 1970). It is meant to remove the financial incentive of looting: if the looter cannot sell the antiquity for forty or more years (and each year it will be one more year, for 1970 is a "bright line" date), he will not loot. But of course this applies only to museums, and only to museums that adhere to this principle.

It has become so difficult for museums to acquire antiquities that now they rarely do so. This is not to say that museums outside Europe and North America and private individuals anywhere are not acquiring unprovenanced antiquities, or that looting has been dramatically reduced. It is only to say that Western museums have almost stopped acquiring antiquities.

And this raises the issues of imperialism and colonialism. I argue in this book for the return of *partage*, the practice of sharing archaeological finds among foreign excavating institutions and local authorities. This is how the great archaeological research collections were built at Yale, Harvard, the University of Pennsylvania, and the University of Chicago, as well as the national museums in Cairo, Baghdad, and Kabul. But archaeologists tell me that *partage* will never return. It's a relic of colonialism, they say, a reminder of historic imbalances of power that allowed Western nations to take advantage of weaker, what we would now call Third World, nations. And it all hinges on the question of ownership. *Partage* allowed for foreign institutions to own a part of another country's past. And this should never—*will* never—happen again, they say.

I argue in this book against the premise that modern nation-states own the cultural remains of antiquity that lie within their borders simply because they are found there. I point out that those claims are motivated by nationalist politics intent on strengthening government claims of political legitimacy by appealing to racial, ethnic, and cultural pride. I argue instead that ownership is only a means of stewardship, a way of investing in the preservation of our common ancient heritage and encouraging broader access to it. But I am told that our ancient heritage is not common, but rather the heritage of particular peoples (*peoples* often confused with *nation-states*, which define and police cultural property on behalf of the people, often, as we have seen with the example of China, a particular subset of people, the ethnic and political elite of the nation). To claim common identity with the world's ancient past is, I am told, an act of imperialism or colonial oppression. And when I affirm the importance of encyclopedic museums as institutions dedicated to the dissipation of ignorance and superstition about the world and the promotion of inquiry and tolerance of *difference* itself, I am told that such museums are instruments of empire, evidence of colonial oppression, and the means of perpetuating Western hegemonic control over the world. (This is the "failed world-view" one critic accused me of clinging to.)

I disagree. In my view, encyclopedic museums are the result of the Enlightenment, not empire, evidence of curiosity about the world. It is true, of course, that in the intervening years since the first encyclopedic museum (the British Museum) opened its doors more than two hundred years ago, specific museum collections have grown due to imbalances of wealth and power. But this is not to say, as some critics do, that their collections were "stolen" from weaker countries. Overwhelmingly, their collections were acquired legally on the terms that applied at the time; that is, when former sovereign entities (e.g., the Ottoman Empire) granted permission for their removal, or when a transfer of power occurred as a result of war (e.g., from the French to the British), which was not illegal or uncommon. And their collections are still being built legally. Some critics argue that that may be true, but the moral thing to do is to return at least some key objects to the nations that are requesting them: the Parthenon Mar-

171

bles to Greece, the Rosetta Stone and Bust of Nefertiti to Egypt, and the Ishtar Gate to Iraq. And why? Because it is said that they belong there, where they were made and with the people who are said, by virtue of living there now, to have the only legitimate claim of identification with them.

I argue against using museum collections to redress historical imbalances of power. But more importantly, I argue that the Enlightenment principles that formed—and still inform—the work of encyclopedic museums offer the greatest promise for better understanding the truth about culture: that it has never known political boundaries and has always been mongrel and hybrid, evidence of contact between peoples and their intertwined history. For encyclopedic museums aspire to the condition of cosmopolitanism as articulated by Diogenes ("When anyone asked him where he came from, he said, 'I am a citizen of the world'"); the Roman emperor Marcus Aurelius, who famously urged his readers not to forget "the closeness of man's brotherhood with his kind; a brotherhood not of blood or human seed, but of a common intelligence"; and, during the Enlightenment, David Hume, who saw the cosmopolite as "a creature, whose thoughts are not limited by any narrow bounds, either of place or time."[10]

But to raise the ideal of cosmopolitanism is to tempt criticism from those who think cosmopolitanism itself is an imposition of Western values on others, values that allow Western dominance to slip in under the cloak of openness and curiosity about others. Certain postcolonial theorists are offering alternatives to the Enlightenment framing of cosmopolitanism, calling for a new cosmopolitanism in a context of "minoritarian modernity," which "is visible in the new forms of trandisciplinary knowledges.... Transdiciplinary knowledge, in the cosmopolitan cause, is more readily a translational process of culture's inbetweenness than a transcendent knowledge of what lies beyond difference, in some common pursuit of the universality of the human experience."[11] This is not the place to go into a larger investigation of the possibilities of a cosmopolitan view of the world today. But I would argue that encyclopedic museums are just the kind of institution where one can see evidence of cultural "inbetweenness" in the way objects bear witness to cultural influences and hybridity.

I believe as the philosopher Martha Nussbaum does, that fundamental to a cosmopolitan view of the world is compassion for the other. "Compassion begins with the local," she writes. "But if our moral natures and emotional natures are to live in any sort of harmony we must find devices through which to extend our strong emotions and our ability to imagine the situation of others to the world of human life as a whole."[12] And, like Nussbaum, I believe that a cosmopolitan view can be taught—"[s]ince compassion contains thought, it can be educated"—and that through cosmopolitan education (just the kind of education one can gain from the experience of encyclopedic museums), we learn more about ourselves:

> One of the greatest barriers to rational deliberation in politics is the unexamined feeling that one's own preferences and ways are neutral and natural. An education that takes national boundaries as morally salient too often reinforces this kind of irrationality, by lending to what is an accident of history a false air of moral weight and glory. By looking at ourselves through the lens of the other, we come to see what in our practices is local and nonessential, what is more broadly or deeply shared.[13]

In this respect, I argue that encyclopedic museums should be preserved where they exist and encouraged where they do not yet exist. (Some will respond, "Easier said than done. How will it be possible for poorer countries to compete in the marketplace for collections with richer countries?" But this presumes that ownership is the only way to build collections. Loans and exchanges of collections are the future of encyclopedic museums—and not loans of a limited duration, but loans for many years, so that visitors to such museums will be able to return again and again to explore the many nuances of a rich and diverse encyclopedic collection experience. But first there has to be curiosity about the world, a commitment to looking through the lens of the other to explore what is more broadly or deeply shared among us.)

⬚ ⬚ ⬚

Encyclopedic museums and their collections are not instruments of empire but witnesses to the *legacy* of empire, a fact of history dating back thousands of years and including the Babylonians, Egyptians, Chinese, Greek, Persians, Romans, Mongolians, Ottomans, Russians, British, Spanish, and Americans. Such museums hold, preserve, and present evidence of the intertwining of cultures, of the imperializer and the imperialized, for all time and for all to see. The history of empire didn't start with the British. It is a phenomenon as old as history itself, and culture bears its imprint. Culture has never been immune to—and in fact has thrived on—the imbalance of political power, just as it has thrived on the fruits of economic and cultural exchange. One sees evidence of this everywhere in the collections of the British Museum. Whatever has brought people into contact with one other has furthered the development of culture.

The legacy of empire is complex and needs to be considered carefully. Edward Said, to whom I referred in chapter 5 of this book, dedicated his professional life to examining the intentions and effects of empire through its representations in literature and the popular media. In numerous essays and books, he criticized our tendency to simplify the history of empire and reduce the complex and intertwined hybridity of culture and intellectual production to simplistic and reductive binary relationships.

Said was a professor of comparative literature, an academic field whose origin and purpose, like those of encyclopedic museums, he noted, "is to move beyond insularity and provincialism and to see cultures and literatures together, contrapuntally," a field in which "there is an already considerable investment in precisely this kind of antidote to reductive nationalism and uncritical dogma: after all, the constitution and early aims of comparative literature were to get a perspective beyond one's own nation, to see some sort of whole instead of the defensive little patch offered by one's own culture, literature, and history."[14] Ironically, as he noted, the study of comparative literature "originated in the period of high European imperialism and is irrecusably linked to it" (a fact that compromises its ideals no more than a similar history does those of the encyclopedic museum). Said then went on to trace the history of comparative literature and concluded by stating that "[i]f I have insisted on integration and connections between the past and the present, between imperializer and imperialized, between culture and imperialism, I have done so not to level or reduce differences, but rather to convey a more urgent sense of the interdependence between things."[15]

Seeing history as one-sided—as the richer, more powerful nations only exploiting the poorer, less powerful ones, taking from them their cultural treasures and imposing upon them a false culture, as if culture were something so distinct and pure as "ours" and "theirs" that the one can impose upon the other—is false and dangerous. As Said wrote of the legacy of empire, it is "so vast and yet so detailed . . . as an experience with crucial cultural dimensions, that we must speak of overlapping territories, intertwined histories common to men and women, whites and non-whites, dwellers in the metropolis and on the peripheries, past as well as present and future; these territories and histories can only be seen from the perspective of the whole of secular human history."[16]

And our task as servants of encyclopedic museums, just as it is the task of professors of comparative literature, is, as Said wrote of his lifelong intellectual project shortly before he died, "to complicate and/or dismantle the reductive formulae and abstract but potent kind of thought that leads the mind away from concrete human history and experience and into the realms of ideological fiction, metaphysical confrontation and collective passion."[17]

We must find ways to work together as nations and museums to encourage a greater curiosity about the world and a broader access to the world's cultural legacy through the development of encyclopedic museums: museums dedicated to the presentation of the world's many cultures without prejudice. This can come about only through a softening of the legal regime that restricts such access and perpetuates a false view of culture as pure and fixed, one nation's and not another's, to be policed, defended, and in the end, if necessary, fought over. In this respect, we need to remember the words of the Indian economic journalist Sanjay Subrahmanyam, who has written that "a national culture that does not have the confidence to declare that, like all other national cultures, it too is a hybrid, a crossroads, a mixture of elements derived from chance encounters and unforeseen consequences, can only take the path to xenophobia and cultural paranoia." [18]

We live in dangerous times. And the more we understand that we all have a stake in the preservation of the world's cultures as our *common* culture, that any and all forms of cultural expression produced at any time in any part of the world are all of ours to identify with and be inspired by, by dint of inheritance, of our being humans, individuals capable of surmounting the limitations of our national affiliations, the better off we will be and the greater will be the prospects for a safer world.

This is the argument of my book. And the argument I stand by.

NOTES

Preface

1. Benedict Anderson, *Imagined Communities*, 2d rev. ed. (London: Verso, 1991): 12.

2. Much of this is taken from Mary Beard's account of the Parthenon in her *The Parthenon* (Cambridge, Mass.: Harvard University Press, 2003). Also see Jeffrey Hurwit, *The Athenian Acropolis: History, Mythology, and Archaeology from the Neolithic Era to the Present* (Cambridge: Cambridge University Press, 1999); Eleni Bastéa, *The Creation of Modern Athens: Planning the Myth* (Cambridge: Cambridge University Press, 2000); John Henry Merryman, "Thinking About the Elgin Marbles," *University of Michigan Law Review* (1982) and William St. Clair, *Lord Elgin and the Marbles* (Oxford: Oxford University Press, 1998). On the larger question of the political implications and national ambitions of German archaeology from its founding until recently, see Suzanne L. Marchand, *Down from Olympus: Archaeology and Hellenism in Germany, 1750–1970* (Princeton, N.J.: Princeton University Press, 1996).

3. Much of this is taken from John Ray, *The Rosetta Stone and the Rebirth of Ancient Egypt* (Cambridge, Mass.: Harvard University Press, 2007). Also see Richard Parkinson, *Cracking Codes: The Rosetta Stone and Decipherment* (Berkeley: University of California Press, 1999). For the debate about publishing undocumented antiquities, see David Owen, "Censoring Knowledge: The Case for the Publication of Unprovenanced Cuneiform Tablets," in James Cuno, ed., *Whose Culture? On the Value of Museums and the Debate Over Antiquities* (Princeton, N.J.: Princeton University Press, 2009). The policy of the American Schools of Oriental Research governing the publication of undocumented antiquities can be found at www.asor.org/pubs/nea/instructions.html. In response to the destruction of Iraq during the current war, ASOR adopted a "limited exception" to its publication policy, effective November 20, 2004. This allows for the publication and presentation at

ASOR meetings of undocumented cuneiform tablets from Iraq if the State Board of Antiquities and Heritage (SBAH) of Iraq gives its consent and if the materials are returned to Iraq and "are in the ownership and custody of the SBAH." Given the circumstances in Iraq as of the effective date of this exception, ASOR interprets "return to Iraq" to include "temporary placement of the material on loan with an academic research institution in the United States which is approved by the SBAH, does not acquire undocumented antiquities, and commits in writing to transfer such material to Iraq at any time upon request from the SBAH." Further, "the ASOR Baghdad Committee can make a determination as to when conditions in Iraq permit the immediate return of materials to Iraq and this provision for temporary placement in a US institution would then no longer be applicable." See www .asor.org/textpolicy.htm for the full text of this "limited exception."

4. On Chen Mengjia's career, see Peter Hessler, *Oracle Bones: A Journey Between China's Past and Present* (New York: HarperCollins, 2006): 222–30, 243–8, 383–92, 431–4, and 454–5. Also see Charles Fabens Kelley and Ch'en Meng-Chia, *Chinese Bronzes from the Buckingham Collection* (Chicago: The Art Institute of Chicago, 1946). Elinor Pearlstein's unpublished manuscript on the chronology of Chen Mengjia's time and scholarship in the West is invaluable and available for consultation through the Art Institute's Department of Asian and Ancient Art.

5. In this respect there was an interesting exchange between Malcolm Bell, Professor of Art History at the University of Virginia and Co-director of U.S. excavations at Morgantina (Sicily) and Gary Wills, Professor of History Emeritus at Northwestern University in the June 28, 2007 issue of the *New York Review of Books*. Wills had reviewed the new installation of the Roman galleries at the Metropolitan Museum of Art ("We Are All Romans Now," *New York Review of Books*, May 31, 2007). Bell took exception to Wills's suggestion that, in Bell's words, "source countries of antiquities lay claim to them on the grounds of ethnic identity with ancient cultures, and that in this they are supported by archaeologists" (precisely what I argue in this book). Bell then declares that "whatever the rationale for national ownership claims, the position of archaeologists both inside and outside the source countries is that state ownership of antiquities from the soil is an effective way to protect archaeological sites from looting, the chief cause of which is the market demand created by museums and collectors. This is the real issue," Bell concludes, "not the claim of ethnic identity, that motivates archaeologists, who have constant firsthand experience of the destructive effects of market-driving pillaging." To this, Wills replied: "I am not sure as [Bell] is that *no* archaeologist is affected by ethnic nationalism in his or her laudable concern for protecting discovery sites." And then, responding to Bell's suggestion that the return of the Parthenon marbles to Athens is

justifiable, Wills replies: "The real argument for return of the Marbles is neither beauty nor integrity but ethnic nationalism—the Melina Mercouri argument." Needless to say, as this book demonstrates, I agree with Wills.

6. See Jay Xu, "Food Vessel (Fangding)," in *Notable Acquisitions at the Art Institute of Chicago* (Chicago: Art Institute of Chicago, 2006): 28–9. The caldron had previously been in the collection of Doris Duke, the noted American collector, who purchased it from the New York dealer, C. T. Loo. It was researched by the esteemed Chinese scholar, Chen Mengjia, in the 1940s and published by the Chinese government in the catalogue of *Shang and Zhou Bronzes Stolen by the American Imperialists.*

7. See Ma Chengyuan, "The Splendor of Ancient Chinese Bronzes," in *The Great Bronze Age of China* (New York: Alfred A. Knopf for the Metropolitan Museum of Art, 1980): 1–19, and Jessica Rawson: *Ancient China: Art and Archaeology* (New York: Harper & Row for the British Museum, 1980): 41–87.

8. The best source on the history and importance of oracle bones is David N. Keightley, *Sources of Shang History: The Oracle-Bone Inscriptions of Bronze Age China* (Berkeley: University of California Press, 1985).

9. The inscription was translated by Edward L. Shaughnessy of the University of Chicago. The *ding* has been published numerous times, including Renato Chen, *Jinkui lungu chufi* [Essays on Chinese Antiquities] (Hong Kong: Yazhou shi yin ju, 1952): cat. no. 6. See Jay Xu, "*Shi Wang Ding*," *Notable Acquisitions at the Art Institute of Chicago* (Chicago: Art Institute of Chicago, 2006): 30–31.

10. See Barbara Plankensteiner, ed., *Benin Kings and Rituals: Court Arts from Nigeria* (Vienna: Uitgeverij Snoeck Editions/Publishers, 2007). Its text offers the best single source of information about the history of the Benin Kingdom, its art and rituals, governance, sacking by the British, and current vitality.

11. See Barbara Winston Blackmun, "Icons and Emblems in Ivory: An Altar Tusk from the Palace of Old Benin," in *African Art at the Art Institute of Chicago, Museum Studies* 23, 2 (Chicago: Art Institute of Chicago, 1997): 149–63.

12. See Christine M. Nielsen in Karen Manchester, ed., *The Silk Road and Beyond: Travel, Trade, and Transformation, Museum Studies* 33, 1 (Chicago: Art Institute of Chicago, 2007): 72–3. On the Swahili, see Mark R. Horton, *Shanga: The Archaeology of a Muslim Trading Community on the Coast of East Africa*, Memoir 14 (London: British Institute in Eastern Africa, 1996). Generally, for the extent and effects of trade through the Indian Ocean from Europe to east Africa and across to southeast Asia and up to China, also see Anna Jackson and Amin Jaffer, eds., *Encounters: The Meeting of Asia and Europe, 1500–1800* (London: Victoria and Albert Museum, 2004).

13. On Ibn Battuta, see Ross E. Dunn, *The Adventures of Ibn Battuta* (Berkeley: University of California Press, 1986).

14. The privately owned, medieval ducal Guelph Treasure was in Brunswick, Germany until it was sold following World War I. An exhibition of much of it traveled through the United States to extraordinary press coverage and popular acclaim. It came to the Art Institute in March and April 1931. By the end of the tour, half of the objects were purchased and the rest were returned to Germany. Collectors close to the Art Institute purchased a number of objects from the Treasury, three of which Kate Buckingdom bequeathed to the museum in 1938. This monstrance was given to the museum by Mrs. Chauncey McCormick in 1962. See Christina M. Nielsen, *Devotion and Splendor: Medieval Art at the Art Institute of Chicago* (Chicago: Art Institute of Chicago, 2004): 13–15 and 53–4. On the Guelph Treasure, see Otto von Falke, Robert Schmidt, and Georg Swazenski, eds., *The Guelph Treasure: The Sacred Relics of Brunswick Cathedral Formerly in the Possession of the Ducal House of Brunswick-Lüneburg* (Frankfurt: Frankfurter Verlags-Anstalt, 1930).

15. The description is Al-Biruni's, an early-medival scholar and scientist from Persia. Quoted in Anna Contadini, *Fatamid Art at the Victoria and Albert Museum* (London: V & A Publications, 1998): 16–17. On the reuse of objects from the Islam lands by Christians in Europe, see Avinoam Shalem, *Islam Christianized: Islamic Portable Objects in the Medieval Church Treasuries of the Latin West*, Ars faciendi 7 (Frankfurt: Peter Lang, 1996).

16. See Stefano Carboni, ed., *Venice and the Islamic World* (New York: Metropolitan Museum of Art, 2006): 325–6.

17. Neil MacGregor, unpublished lecture, New York Public Library, New York (May 10, 2006).

18. See Jason DeParle, "In a World on the Move, a Tiny Island Strains to Cope," *New York Times* (June 24, 2007): A1 and 8. Also see Peter N. Stearns, *Cultures in Motion: Mapping Key Contacts and their Imprints in World History* (New Haven Conn.: Yale University Press, 2001).

Introduction: The Crux of the Matter

1. Neil Asher Silberman, "Nationalism and Archaeology," *The Oxford Encyclopedia of Archaeology in the Near East*, vol. 4, ed. Eric M. Meyers (Oxford: Oxford University Press, 1997): 103.

2. Among only the most recent such studies are Kate Fitz Gibbon, ed., *Who Owns the Past? Cultural Policy, Cultural Property, and the Law* (New Brunswick, N.J.: Rutgers University Press, 2005); Barbara T. Hoffman, ed., *Art and Cultural Heritage: Law, Policy, and Practice* (Cambridge: Cambridge

University Press, 2006); and John H. Merryman, ed., *Imperialism, Art and Restitution* (Cambridge: Cambridge University Press, 2006). Among U.S. law school journals with special issues on the subject, see *Cardozo Arts and Entertainment Law Journal* 19, 1 (2001), published by the Benjamin N. Cardozo School of Law, Yeshiva University, New York; and *Connecticut Journal of International Law* 16, 2 (Spring 2001), issued by the University of Connecticut School of Law. Among the more sensational book-length publications are Roger Atwood *Stealing History: Tomb Raiders, Smugglers, and the Looting of the Ancient World* (New York: St. Martin's Press, 2006); Matthew Bogdanos and William Patrick, *Thieves of Baghdad* (New York: Bloomsbury Publishing, 2005); Colin Renfrew, *Loot, Legitimacy and Ownership: The Ethical Crisis in Archaeology* (London: Duckworth, 2000); Peter Watson and Cecilia Todeschini, *The Medici Conspiracy: The Illicit Journey of Looted Antiquities, from Italy's Tomb Raiders to the World's Greatest Museums* (New York: Public Affairs, 2006). The McDonald Institute for Archaeological Research at Cambridge University, United Kingdom, publishes frequently on its Web site (mcdonald.cam.uk) and in print on looted archaeological sites and the illicit trade in antiquities. Among its projects was the Illicit Antiquities Research Centre, headed by Neil Brodie, Jenny Doole, and Peter Watson. The IARC published a newsletter, *Culture without Context.* Among the IARC's book-length projects, see especially, Neil Brodie, Jennifer Doole, and Colin Renfrew, eds., *Trade in Illicit Antiquities: The Destruction of the World's Archaeological Heritage* (Cambridge: McDonald Institute for Archaeological Research, 2001). The Centre closed in 2007.

3. The Metropolitan Museum of Art issued a press release on February 21, 2006, announcing that it had reached an agreement with the Italian Ministry of Culture, such that it would transfer the title of six antiquities, including a group of sixteen Hellenistic silver pieces, to Italy. In exchange, the Italian Ministry of Culture agreed that one of the antiquities, the so-called Euphronius krater, and the Hellenistic silver would remain on loan to the Metropolitan until January 2008 and 2010, respectively. The Italian Ministry of Culture agreed to provide the Metropolitan long-term future loans—up to four years each—"of works of art of equivalent beauty and importance to the objects being returned." The text of the press release can be found on the museum's Web site, www.metmuseum.org. Claims against the J. Paul Getty Museum have been registered (at least by statements made in the press) by both Italy and Greece. The Getty Museum was close to an agreement with Italy on the return of twenty-one antiquities, with Italy promising terms similar to those it gave the Metropolitan Museum, when the Italian government demanded an additional fifty-two; see Tracy Wilkinson, "Italy Widens Demands, Snarling Talks with Getty," *Los Angeles Times* (June 21, 2006).

At the same time, the Getty Museum agreed to return two antiquities to Greece; see Jason Felch and Ralph Frammolino, "Getty Will Return Two Greek Artfacts," *Los Angeles Times* (July 11, 2006): A1.

After months of negotiations, the Getty Museum agreed in July 2007 to return to Italy forty antiquities. This came after the Italians threatened a cultural embargo of the museum and its host J. Paul Getty Trust, which collaborates on conservation and research projects worldwide. For the politics of Italy's claim, and the political antics of its Cultural Minister, Francesco Rutelli, who has been leading the charge against foreign museums, see Christopher Knight, "The Grandstand Erected by Italy," *Los Angeles Times* (July 25, 2007): www.latimes.com/entertainment/news/arts/cl-et-getty25jul25,1,4603922.story?coll=la-util-entnews-arts. There Knight claims that "Rutelli's escalating anti-Getty posturing is old-fashioned political demagoguery, pitched to voters back home. The ultimatum symbolically proclaims that powerful American interests cannot push Italy around, making the government look tough. The emptiness of Italy's legal and ethical claims for the Getty Bronze are beside the point . . . [Rutelli's] ultimatum won't stop art smuggling or end the looting of archaeological treasures by nocturnal tomb raiders." The bronze statue, the so-called "Getty Bronze," was not included in the recent deal between Italy and the Getty Museum. Italy continues to claim that the sculpture was improperly removed from Italy's sphere of influence, even though the Italian government acknowledges that the sculpture was found by fishermen in international waters in 1964. Still, Rutelli claims it. "This is not a legal question, but a question of ethics," he wrote in the *Wall Street Journal* on January 17, 2007; even if it is generally thought that the sculpture is of Greek origin, perhaps sculpted by Lysippos, a favorite of Alexander's—*n.b.*, the Getty doesn't make this claim. For an account of the Italian claim, and its suit against a Getty Museum curator, Marion True, see Hugh Eakin, "An Odyssey in Antiquities Ends in Questions at the Getty Museum," *New York Times* (October 15, 2005).

In November 2005, Italian prosecutors claimed that the Museum of Fine Arts, Boston was in possession of twenty-nine antiquities they suspected were taken from ancient sites "largely throughout Italy." The museum officials claimed they had yet to hear from the Italian authorities. The museum's deputy director, who oversees curatorial departments, was quoted as saying, "We would be more than happy to hear directly from the Italian government and if, through that process, we find that any object in our collection has been stolen, we will absolutely return it to its prior owner." See Geoff Edgers and Sofia Celeste, "Case in Italy Suggests MFA Received Stolen Art," *Boston Globe* (November 4, 2005). Four months later, officials from the museum prepared to travel to Rome to meet with Italian officials over the matter, although the spokesperson for the museum still declared that "Absolutely no information has been given to us about what objects are in question, and there's no outline for discussions right now." See Randy Kennedy, "Boston Museum Chief Heads to Rome to 'Listen,'" *New York Times* (March 18, 2006): B8. Finally, on July 27, 2006, it was announced that the museum had reached a tentative agreement with the Italian authorities to return an unspecified number of antiquities "Italian authorities say were stolen and later sold to the museum." In a joint statement, the museum and Italian government noted that the agreement between them "will include the transfer of certain objects of Italian origin in the Museum's collection to Italy; the loan of significant works from Italy to the MFA's displays and special exhibitions program; and the establishment of a process by which the MFA and Italy will work together to ensure the viability of future acquisitions of Italian antiquities by the Museum." See Denise Lavoie, "Boston's Museum of Fine Arts Agrees to Return Art to Italy," *Associated Press* (July 27, 2006) and Christopher Reynolds and Livia Borghese, "Boston Museum Agrees to Return Artifacts, Italy Says," *Los Angeles Times* (July 28, 2006): E21. On September 29, 2006, the MFA formally turned over thirteen antiquities to Italy and announced an agreement to include the loan to the museum from Italy of "significant works" for exhibition and collaboration on other projects, including archaeological excavations. See Elisabetta Povoledo, "Boston Art Museum Returns Works to Italy," *New York Times* (September 29, 2006): B25, 33.

4. In a letter to the St. Louis Art Museum, dated February 14, 2006, Zahi Hawass, secretary general of Egypt's Supreme Council of Antiquities, charged the museum with possessing an Egyptian mummy mask improperly removed from Egypt and demanded its return. The contents of the letter were made public and appeared in the national and international press. The museum maintained that it had exercised due diligence in acquiring the mask and that it was confident the museum held good title on it. Hawass was quoted as saying that if the mask was not returned to Egypt by May 1, 2006, "I will make their [the St. Louis Art Museum] life hell." The museum's director, Brent Benjamin, was quoted in turn as saying, "Either provide us with the documentation" or end the attacks on the museum. To date, no documentation has been forthcoming to support Hawass's claim. He has pursued the claim only through remarks in the press. See David Bonetti, "Art Museum Won't Return Egyptian Mask," *St. Louis Post-Dispatch* (May 11, 2006) and Jeff Douglas, "Museum Refuses to Return Mummy Mask," *Washington Post* (May 12, 2006).

Other claims have been reported in the press against the Princeton University Art Museum and the Cleveland Museum of Art. This has emboldened authorities in Greece to declare, "Whatever is Greek, wherever in the world, we want back. . . . We're not talking about a handful, we're talking about hundreds of artifacts that have ended up in many different places." See Helena Smith, "Greece Demands Returns of Stolen Heritage," *Guardian* (July 11, 2006), http://arts.guardian.co.uk.

5. IFAR stands for the International Foundation for Art Research. It was founded in 1969 as an impartial, scholarly organization dedicated to educating "the public about problems and issues in the art world" and to researching "the attribution and authenticity of works of art." In 1970, it extended its purview to include "art theft and looting, and art and cultural property law and ethics." In 1991, it helped create the Art Loss Register, a commercial agency that registers stolen art and helps research claims of stolen art. See www.ifar.org and www.artloss.com.

6. Once again, see Eakin, "An Odyssey in Antiquities." See also Hugh Eakin's review of Peter Watson and Cecilia Todeschini, *The Medici Conspiracy: The Illicit Journey of Looted Antiquities, from Italy's Tomb Raiders to the World's Greatest Museums*, "Notes from Underground," *New York Review of Books* (May 25, 2006) and the exchange of letters between Watson/Todeschini and Eakin in *New York Review of Books* (July 13, 2006). See also Tracy Wilkinson and Livia Borghese, "Why Getty's Negotiations with Italy Are Tangled," *Los Angeles Times* (June 15, 2006): A1.

7. Statistics on the international traffic in antiquities are notoriously difficult to gather. Estimates range from $150 million to $5 billion annually. Even archaeologists who oppose museums' acquiring unprovenanced antiquities admit that such estimates are only guesses. Over 2005–2006, the Association of Art Museum Directors (AAMD), a membership organization representing more than 175 of North America's largest art museums, surveyed its membership regarding their purchases of antiquities. The results, released by AAMD, showed that member museums collectively spent only $1.5 million annually on unprovenanced antiquities. By any measure, this is a very small percentage of the world's traffic in such materials.

With regard to U.S. museums' participation in the market in antiquities, AAMD has regularly published professional guidelines and papers on the acquisition and loan of antiquities. Most recently, it issued the statement, "Art Museums and the International Exchange of Cultural Artifacts" (October 2001), which included the sentences, "While it is highly desirable to know the archaeological context in which an artifact was discovered because this can reveal information about the origin of the work and the culture that produced it, this is not always possible. Nevertheless, much information may be gleaned from works of art even when the circumstances of their discovery are unknown." It also suggests questions to ask when performing due diligence before acquiring an unprovenanced antiquity.

Three years later, AAMD issued a "Report of the AAMD Task Force on the Acquisition of Archaeological Materials and Ancient Art" (June 2004),

which included guidelines for making inquiries and conducting research before acquiring antiquities, and for promptly publishing information about
them after acquiring them. It included the sentence, "AAMD recognizes that
some works of art for which provenance information is incomplete or unobtainable may deserve to be publicly displayed, preserved, studied, and
published because of their rarity, importance, and aesthetic merit."

Two years later, AAMD issued the "Report of the AAMD Subcommittee
on Incoming Loans of Archaeological Materials and Ancient Art" (February
2006). As with the earlier reports and papers regarding the acquisition of
antiquities, this report called for all AAMD member museums to work in
conformity with U.S. law and in accordance with the 1970 UNESCO Convention, and it called for prior research and openness and transparency
when borrowing archaeological materials and works of ancient art for temporary and long-term loans. It also stated, "AAMD recognizes that archaeological material and works of ancient art, for which provenance information
is incomplete or unobtainable may deserve to be publicly displayed, conserved, studied, and published because of their rarity, historical importance,
and aesthetic merit. The display of such works in public museums may serve
to facilitate the discovery of further information regarding their ownership
and provenance history."

8. For an interesting collection of essays on the ethics of archaeology—its
principles and practices—see Chris Scarre and Geoffrey Scarre, eds., *The
Ethics of Archaeology: Philosophical Perspectives on Archaeological Practice*
(Cambridge: Cambridge University Press, 2006), especially, James O. Young,
"Cultures and the Ownership of Archaeological Finds" (15–31), and Julie
Hollowell, "Moral Arguments on Subsistence Digging" (69–96).

9. The statement is Irene Winter's: "At the heart of these conflicts is who
actually 'owns' the past. . . . That international challenges even arise must be
seen as part of a larger postcolonial universe. The successful negotiations
resulting in Denmark's return of a group of medieval manuscripts to Ice-
land opened the door to former colonies worldwide to petition for redress
against *historical imbalances of power* that permitted the removal of valued
moveable goods" (italics added). Irene J. Winter, Review of J. Greenfield, *The
Return of Cultural Treasures*, in *Art Journal* 52, 1 (1993): 103–7.

10. Bernard Lewis, *The Multiple Identities of the Middle East* (New York:
Shocken Books, 1998): 69. Lewis discusses the broad implications of this
over many pages; see especially 57–79. While touring a recent exhibition of
Egyptian antiquities at the Metropolitan Museum of Art, Zahi Hawass, the
aforementioned secretary general of Egypt's Supreme Council of Antiquities
(see note 4)—after saying that certain objects, although not looted, were
"icons of our Egyptian identity" and that "They should be in the motherland. They should not be outside Egypt"—was quoted as declaring "I am

Pharaoh!" See Sylvia Hochfield, "Descendent of the Pharaohs," *Artnews* (May 2006): 78–80. On the history of Pharaonism and its role in the nationalization of Eygyptology, see Donald Malcom Reid, "Nationalizing the Pharaonic Past: Egyptology, Imperialism, and Egyptian Nationalism, 1922–1952," in James Jankowski and Israel Gershoni, eds., *Rethinking Nationalism in the Arab Middle East* (New York: Columbia University Press, 1997): 127–49. Reid has written widely on this topic. See his "Cultural Imperialism and Nationalism: The Struggle to Define and Control the Heritage of Arab Art in Egypt," *International Journal of Middle Eastern Studies* 24, 1 (February 1992): 57–76; "Indigenous Egyptology: The Decolonialization of a Profession?" *Journal of the American Oriental Society* 105, 2 (April–June 1985): 233–46; and *Whose Pharaohs? Archaeology, Museums, and Egyptian National Identity from Napoleon to World War I* (Berkeley: University of California Press, 2002).

11. Lewis, *Multiple Identities of the Middle East*, 75.

12. The problem remains for Egypt. Recently the most senior religious scholar in Egypt condemned the display of figure sculpture—most of which was pharaonic—in the Cairo Museum in response to a layperson's call for a fatwa against such images. Mohamed al-Sayed Said of the al-Ahram Centre for Political and Strategic Studies in Cairo was quoted as saying, "This reflects the rising religiosity in Egyptian society.... What we are having at this point is an increasing gulf between secular and religious cultures." See Heba Saleh, "Egyptians Look to Islam for Answers," BBC News (May 10, 2006). A month later, the British newspaper *Daily Telegraph* reported "a religiously motivated attack" on statues at a museum in Cairo: a "veiled woman" screamed "Infidels, Infidels" and attacked three antiquities. The newspaper noted that the attack followed "a fatwa issued by the Grand Mufti of Cairo, Ali Gomaa, which banned all decorative statues of living beings." Nabil Abdel Fatah, of the al-Ahram Center for Political and Strategic Studies, was quoted as saying, "We are seeing an increase of conservative, Islamist feeling.... The Islamisation of Egyptian society is happening from the bottom up, and it has reached the middle classes." See Harry de Quetteville, "Statue Attack Fuels Fears of an Islamist Egypt," *Telegraph.co.uk* (June 18, 2006): www.telegraph .co.uk/news.

13. For an account of the role of archaeology in the formation of modern Iraq, see Magnus T. Bernhardsson, *Reclaiming a Plundered Past: Archaeology and Nation Building in Modern Iraq* (Austin: University of Texas Press, 2005). Nation building in Iraq has a primacy concern of Iraqi leaders since at least the end of the Ottoman Empire and the formation of the Hashemite Kingdom under British control. As Bernhardsson writes, "Ever since the establishment of the Hashemite Kingdom of Iraq in August 1921, the political leaders of

the state have been faced with a formidable task of nation-building among peoples of diverse religious and ethnic backgrounds. In the first few years of the nascent state, the Iraqi government and its British advisors had a diffi-cult time convincing 'Iraqis' of the legitimacy of the very idea of an 'Iraq'" (pp. 4–5). In the 1930s, following the British Mandate, and under the influ-ence of the Yemen-born, Lebanon- and Paris-educated, naturalized Iraqi, and nationalist Sati' al-Husri, who was appointed the government's director of antiquities in 1934, a year after the Iraqi King Faysal declared in frustra-tion that in "Iraq there is still no Iraqi people . . . but unimaginable masses of human beings, devoid of any patriotic ideal, imbued with religious tradi-tions and absurdities, connected by no common tie," archaeology was used to provide, as Bernhardsson writes, "a crucial foundation for the nation to build for itself a modern present based on a 'modern' past" (5; also see 164–210). On the role of Sati' al-Husri in the history of Iraqi archaeology, see William L. Cleveland, *The Making of an Arab Nationalist: Ottomanism and Arabism in the Life and Thought of Sati' al-Husri* (Princeton, N.J.: Princeton Univer-sity Press, 1971); Reeva Spector Simon, *Iraq Between the Two World Wars: The Militarist Origins of Tyranny* (New York: Columbia University Press, 2004 ed.): especially 69–78; and Sylvia G. Haim, ed., *Arab Nationalism: An Anthology* (Berkeley: University of California Press, 1976): especially 43–55 and 147–54. For an account of Iraqi archaeology in the context of Islamic ar-chaeology, see Stephen Vernoit, "The Rise of Islamic Archaeology," *Muqarnas* 14 (1997): 1–10.

14. Quoted in Anthony Shadid, "Lebanon, My Lebanon," *Washington Post* (April 16, 2006): B1.

15. In his prime time speech before the 1992 Republican National Con-vention, the conservative commentator and sometimes presidential aspi-rant Patrick J. Buchanan declared, "There is a religious war going on in our country for the soul of America. It is a cultural war, as critical to the kind of nation we will one day be as was the Cold War itself." The full text of the speech is available on the Patrick J. Buchanan official Web site, www .buchanan.org.

16. John Henry Merryman, "The Nation and the Object," *International Journal of Cultural Property* 1 (1994): 61–76.

17. Typically such loans are limited to no more than a year. As a result of its recent negotiation with the Metropolitan Museum of Art for the transfer to Italian jurisdiction of select antiquities, Italy agreed to extend loans of antiquities from its museums for a period of up to four years. See "Statement by the Metropolitan Museum of Art on Its Agreement with Italian Ministry of Culture," February 21, 2006, available online at www .metmuseum.org.

18. John Henry Merryman, "Cultural Property Internationalism," *International Journal of Cultural Property* 12 (2005): 11–39.

19. Amin Maalouf, *In the Name of Identity: Violence and the Need to Belong*, trans. Barbara Bray (New York: Penguin Books, 2000): 29.

Chapter One: Political Matters

1. Don D. Fowler, "Uses of the Past: Archaeology in the Service of the State," *American Antiquity* 52, 2 (April 1987): 241.

2. Carol Mattusch et al., *The Fire of Hephaistos: Large Classical Bronzes from North American Collections*, exh. cat. (Cambridge, Mass.: Harvard University Art Museums, 1996).

3. Aaron J. Paul, *Fragments of Antiquity: Drawing Upon Greek Vases*, exh. cat. (Cambridge, Mass.: Harvard University Art Museums, 1997).

4. Walter V. Robinson and John Yemma, "Harvard Museum Acquisitions Shock Scholars," *Boston Globe* (January 16, 1998): A1, Metro Section. The story was carried in full or in part on numerous Web sites. The Web site of the McDonald Institute of Archaeological Research of the University of Cambridge mentioned it prominently in its "Culture without Context: The Newsletter of the Illicit Antiquities Research Centre." It was also referred to a number of times in editorials and articles in *Archaeology*, the popular journal of the American Institute of Archaeology. See Ellen Herscher, "At the Museums: Tarnished Reputations," *Archaeology* 51, 5 (September/October 1998).

5. See James Cuno, "Art Museums, Archaeology, and Antiquities in an Age of Sectarian Violence and Nationalist Politics," in *The Acquisition and Exhibition of Classical Antiquities: Professional, Legal, and Ethical Perspectives* (South Bend, Ind.: University of Notre Dame Press, 2008): 9–26; "View from the Universal Museum," in John Henry Merryman, ed., *Imperialism, Art and Restitution* (Cambridge: Cambridge University Press, 2006): 15–36; "Museums, Antiquities, Cultural Property, and the U.S. Legal Framework for Making Acquisitions," in *Who Owns the Past? Cultural Policy, Cultural Property, and the Law*, ed. Kate Fitz Gibbon (New Brunswick, N.J.: Rutgers University Press, 2006): 143–58; "Museums and the Acquisition of Antiquities," *Cardozo Arts and Entertainment Law Journal* 19, 1 (2001): 83–96; "U.S. Art Museums and Cultural Property," *Connecticut Journal of International Law* 16, 2 (Spring 2001): 189–96.

6. The full text of the Convention can be found at www.unesco.org/culture/laws/hague/html. Also see, John Henry Merryman, "Two Ways of Thinking About Cultural Property," *American Journal of International Law* 80, 4 (October 1986): 837–38.

7. Etienne Clément, "Some Recent Practical Experience in the Implementation of the 1954 Hague Convention," *International Journal of Cultural Property* 1, 3 (1994): 12.

8. Clément, "Some Recent Practical Experience in the Implementation of the 1954 Hague Convention," 16–17. See also Keith W. Eirinberg, "The United States Reconsiders the 1954 Hague Convention," *International Journal of Cultural Property* 1, 3 (1994): 27, and Chip Colwell-Chanthaphonh and John Piper, "War and Cultural Property: The 1954 Hague Convention and the Status of U.S. Ratification," *International Journal of Cultural Property* 10, 2 (2001): 217–45.

9. UNESCO had been founded twenty-five years earlier out of concerns stemming from the destruction and trauma caused by World War II. Quoted from the "Preamble" to the 1970 Convention; for the full text, see www.unesco.org.

10. The "jeremiad" was the article, "Illicit Traffic of Pre-Columbian Antiquities," published in the College Art Association's *Art Journal* 29, 1 (Autumn 1969): 94, 96, 98, 114. Her recent reflections on that article and the moment in which it was written can be found in Clemency Chase Coggins, "Observations of a Combatant," in Kate Fitz Gibbon, ed., *Who Owns the Past?* 231–7.

11. Clemency Chase Coggins, "Archaeology and the Art Market," originally published in *Science* 175 (January 21, 1972): 263–6, reprinted in Kate Fitz Gibbon, *Who Owns the Past?* 221–9.

12. Paul M. Bator, "An Essay on the International Trade in Art," *Stanford Law Review* 34, 2 (January 1982): 280. Bator's essay was later published as a book, *The International Trade in Art* (Chicago: University of Chicago Press, 1983).

13. Clemency Coggins, "Illegal International Traffic in Art: Interim Report," *Art Journal* 30, 4 (Summer 1971): 384.

14. The full text of "The Pennsylvania Declaration" can be found in the museum's journal, *Expedition* 22, 3 (Spring 1980): 3, available on the museum's Web site, www.museum.upenn.edu.

15. The full text of the museum's acquisitions policy can be found in the museum's journal, *Expedition* 22, 3 (Spring 1980): 3, available on the museum's Web site, www.museum.upenn.edu.

16. Karl E. Meyer, "A Reporter at Large: The Plundered Past, I—The Flying Façade and the Vanishing Glyphs," *New Yorker* (March 24, 1973). The second and third parts of the article appeared in subsequent issues of the *New Yorker*: March 31, 1973, and April 7, 1973. The articles were published in book form in *The Plundered Past* (New York: Atheneum, 1973). Paul M. Bator has a good account of these years in *The International Trade in Art*, 4–9.

17. Bator, *The International Trade in Art*, 6, n.16.

18. *United States v. Hollinshead*, 495 F.2d 1154 (9th Cir. 1974). See John Henry Merryman and Albert E. Elsen, *Law, Ethics, and the Visual Arts*, 3rd ed. (London: Kluwer Law International, 1998): 167–9.

19. See Bator, *The International Trade in Art*, 69–70.

20. *United States v. McClain, et. al.*, 545 F.2d 988 (5th Cir. 1977) and *United States v. McClain, et. al.*, 593 F.2d 658 (5th Cir. 1979) See Merryman and Elsen, *Law, Ethics, and the Visual Arts*, 169–82.

21. Bator, *The International Trade in Art*, 73. Also see my "U.S. Art Museums and Cultural Property," *Connecticut Journal of International Law* 16 (Spring 2001):192–3.

22. The language is from the English language summary of the Italian request as reported in the *Federal Register Notices*: January 23, 2001; 66(15): 7399–7402, the text of which is available on the State Department's Web site, http://exchanges.state.gov/culprop/it01fr01.html.

23. Bator, *The International Trade in Art*, 33.

24. John Henry Merryman, "Cultural Property Internationalism," *International Journal of Cultural Property* 12 (2005):11–39.

25. Bator, *The International Trade in Art*, 72.

26. Bator, *The International Trade in Art*, 12. The National Stolen Property Act, 18 U.S.C. 2314–2315 (1976).

27. See James Fitzpatrick, "A Wayward Course: The Lawless Customs Policy Toward Cultural Properties," *N.Y.U. International Law and Policy* 15 (1983): 857, 860–61. See also "Proceedings of the Panel on the U.S. Enabling Legislation of the UNESCO Convention on the Means of Prohibiting and Preventing the Illicit Import, Export and Transfer of Ownership of Cultural Property," *Syracuse Journal of International Law and Commerce* 4 (1976): 97–139. The full text of the 1983 enabling legislation can be found on http://exchanges.state.gov/education/culprop//97–446.html.

The legislative process leading toward implementation of UNESCO 1970 was not an easy one. At issue was the right balance between concern for the international protection of archaeological sites and the right of U.S. citizens to participate in a legitimate trade in antiquities and other artifacts of cultural property. The State Department first opposed implementing legislation in 1973 and again in 1975. The House of Representatives approved an amended version of the legislation in 1977, but the bill was not reported by the Committee on Finance. Legislation was introduced again but no action was taken. The 1983 legislation is the successor to these earlier efforts.

In the end, after a decade of deliberation, Congress implemented only two of the convention's twenty-six articles: Articles 7(b)(i) and 9. The first article pertains only to objects that had been inventoried as having been in the collection of a museum or other public or secular or religious institution in a country that is a party to the convention. This is fairly straightforward and is dealt with as a matter of fact: such material is clearly owned by a foreign entity and cannot be alienated without documented permission. The second article is more complicated: it is concerned with undocumented materials which may have been looted from archaeological sites. The article emphasizes that any U.S. response must be part of "a concerted international effort to determine and to carry out the necessary concrete measures, including the control of exports and imports and international commerce in the specific materials concerned." States parties may negotiate a special, bilateral agreement with the United States—or request emergency import restrictions on specific materials—but only if the cultural property of the requesting state party is in real jeopardy from pillage, the state party has taken measures itself to protect its cultural property, and that the application of import restrictions is part of an international effort, is likely to help deter a serious situation of pillage, and less drastic remedies are not available.

Congress was especially concerned that any U.S. response be part of a concerted international effort. The legislative history recalls that "in previous years' consideration of various proposals for implementing legislation, a particularly nettlesome issue was how to formulate standards establishing that U.S. controls would not be administered unilaterally." Congress wanted to be certain that legitimate U.S. interests in the international movement of antiquities and cultural property would be respected. If states parties were not willing or able to protect their own cultural property, or if other nations were not willing to join forces with the United States in restricting the importation of undocumented materials, the United States would not go it alone. In "emergency" situations, the legislation allows for the president to act more unilaterally, but only after a review of a state party's request by CPAC, the State Department, and the U.S. Treasury, and then only for a period of no more than five years, with the possibility for one additional period of not more than three years.

The full text of the Convention can be found at www.unesco.org/culture/laws/1970/html. On the legislagive history of the U.S. enabling legislation, see S. Rep. 97–564, 1982 U.S. C.C.A.N. 4078.

28. Bator, *The International Trade in Art*, 52.

29. The museum members were William Lee Boyd (formerly of the Field Museum, Chicago; at the time professor of law at the University of Iowa) and John McCarter, President of the Field Museum, Chicago; the archaeologists and anthropologists were James Lorand Matory, professor of anthropology at Harvard, Joan Breton Connelly, Professor of Classical and Near Eastern Archaeology at New York University, and Nancy Wilkie, Professor of Archaeology in the Department of Sociology and Anthropology at Carleton

College and former President of the Archaeological Institute of America; the international sales experts were Meredith Long of Meredith J. Long & Co., James Wright Willis of James Willis Tribal Art, and Robert Bruce Korver of Heritage Numismatic Auctions; and the general public representatives were Aniko Gaal Schott, a philanthropist and Hungarian-born supporter of Hungarian causes, Marta Araoz de la Torre, a coin dealer from Florida, and Jay Kislak, a collector of Mesoamerican material. Kislak was chairman of the Committee. See the State Department Web site for information on CPAC, http://exchanges.state.gov/culprop.

30. A former CPAC member is quoted as saying of the CPAC staff director, Maria Kouroupas, "Her bureaucratic fiefdom has to reflect the wishes of her State Department superiors. And those wishes are clear: Cultural objects exist to make international friends and create better diplomatic relations." Steven Vincent, "The Secret War of Maria Kouroupas," *Art and Auction* (March 2002): 69. This article reviews the criticisms of CPAC, how it works, and the motivations of its staff director.

31. The full text of the bilateral agreement between the United States and Italy, which entered into effect on January 23, 2001, can be found on the CPAC Web site, www.exchanges.state.gov/culprop.

32. See Jeremy Kahn, "U.S. Delays Rule on Limits to Chinese Art Imports," *New York Times* (October 18, 2006): E, 2.

Chapter Two: More Political Matters

1. Bruce G. Trigger, "Alternative Archaeologies: Nationalist, Colonialist, Imperialist," *Man* 19, 3 (September 1984): 356.

2. The full text of the Convention can be found under the "Normative Action" pages of the "Culture" section of UNESCO's Web site, www.unesco.org/*culture*.

3. See Claire Leow, "Treasure from a Shipwreck Off Java Up for Auction," *International Herlad Tribune* (November 15, 2006): www.iht.com/bin.print.php?id=3543182. On September 4, 2007, the *New York Times* published an editorial on the subject of underwater cultural heritage. It was in response to Spain's recent claims on what is said to be seventeen tons of gold and silver on board the Nuestra Señora de las Mercedes, a Spanish galleon sunk by a British warship off the coast of Portugal in 1804. The *New York Times* argued that since the gold and silver coins on board were likely minted in Peru, and since Spain enriched itself by taking gold and silver from the Inca, Spain should cede any rightful claims on the loot to Peru, if only for moral reasons. After all, "if Greece can insist on the ownership of the Elgin Marbles, which Lord Elgin took from the Parthenon to ship to the British Museum in 1801—when Greece was part of the Ottoman Empire—Peru surely has a

shot at the gold from the Nuestra Señora de las Mercedes." *New York Times* (September 4, 2007): A22.

4. The full text of the Convention can be found under the "Normative Action" pages of the "Culture" section of UNESCO's Web site, www.unesco.org/culture.

5. The full text of the Convention can be found under the "Normative Action" pages of the "Culture" section of UNESCO's Web site, www.unesco.org/culture.

6. The full text of the Convention can be found under the "Normative Action" pages of the "Culture" section of UNESCO's Web site, www.unesco.org/*culture.*

7. The full text of the UNIDROIT Convention can be found on its Web site, www.unidroit.org.

8. Dr. Erica-Irene A. Daes, *Protection of the Heritage of Indigenous People* (New York: United Nations, 1997). Daes was Special Rapporteur, Chairperson-Rapporteur of the Working Group on Indigenous Populations, UN Office of the High Commissioner for Human Rights. Dr. Erica-Irene A. Daes, "Protecting Knowledge: Traditional Resource Rights in the New Millennium," keynote address for the conference, *Defending Indigenous Peoples' Heritage,* under the auspices of The Union of British Columbia Indian Chiefs, Vancouver, BC, February 23–26, 2000. The text of her address can be found at www.ubcic.bc.ca/Keynote.htm.

9. Laurajane Smith, *Archaeological Theory and the Politics of Cultural Heritage* (London: Routledge, 2004): 1.

10. Smith, *Archaeological Theory and the Politics of Cultural Heritage,* 3. Some archaeologists acknowledge that their work is inextricable from the specific, political circumstances under which the local people with or in whose proximity they work. As Caroline Steele has written in "Who Has Not Eaten Cherries With The Devil? Archaeology Under Challenge," in Susan Pollock and Reinhard Berbnbeck, *Archaeologies of the Middle East: Critical Perspectives* (Oxford: Blackwell Publishing, 2005), 45–65:

> By excavating the past and living in or alongside communities that are threatened in the present, archaeologists have within their remit both a tool for change and obligations to the people they work with. Archaeologists are participants in a social and political praxis that goes far beyond that of many other academics. (61)
>
> [And] whether on the level of personal conscience, in deciding whether or not to work under an oppressive regime, or at a community level, establishing ethical and fair relations with the people who live next to archaeological sites, participating in international campaigns that are far removed from immediate archaeological issues revolving around the local community, the praxis of archaeology challenges us to be self-reflexive but to resist turning that reflection into a

career tool. A starting point must be the local communities within which we work, both at home and abroad, and considered decisions that respect the rights of people to strive to achieve life economically, politically, and culturally. (61–2)

11. See especially Michel Foucault, *The Archaeology of Knowledge* (London: Tavistock, 1972), *The Order of Things: An Archaeology of Human Sciences* (New York: Vintage Books, 1973), and "Governmentality," in G. Burchell, C. Gordon, and P. Miller, eds., *The Foucault Effect* (London: Wheatsheaf Harvester, 1991). As it pertains to archaeology, see T. C. Patterson, "History and the Post-processual Archaeologies," *Man* 24 (1989): 555–66, and M. Shanks and I. Hodder, "Processual, Postprocessual, and Interpretative Archaeologies," in I. Hodder, M. Shanks, et al., *Interpreting Archaeology* (London: Routledge, 1995).

12. Smith, *Archaeological Theory and the Politics of Cultural Heritage*, 91, and R. C. Dunnell, "The Ethics of Archaeological Significance Decisions," in E. L. Green, ed., *Ethics and Values in Archaeology* (New York: Free Press, 1984): 64.

13. See especially D. D. Fowler, "Uses of the Past: Archaeology in the Service of the State," *American Antiquity* 52, 2 (1987): 229–48; M. Shanks and C. Tilley, *Social Theory and Archaeology* (Cambridge: Polity Press, 1987); P. Gathercole and D. Lowenthal, eds., "The Politics of the Past," *One World Archaeology*, vol. 12 (London: Unwin Hyman, 1990); B. G. Trigger, "Alternative Archaeologies: Nationalist, Colonialist, Imperialist," *Man* 19 (1984): 355–70; and B. G. Trigger, *A History of Archaeological Thought* (Cambridge: Cambridge University Press, 1989). See also Philip L. Kohl and Clare Fawcett, eds., *Nationalism, Politics, and the Practice of Archaeology* (Cambridge: Cambridge University Press, 1995); Margarita Díaz-Andreu and Timothy Chapman, eds., *Nationalism and Archaeology in Europe* (San Francisco: Westview Press, 1996); and John A. Atkinson, Iain Banks, and Jerry O'Sullivan, *Nationalism and Archaeology* (Glasgow: Cruithne Press, 1996).

"Nationalism and the Practice of Archaeology" was the topic of the American Anthropological Association meetings held in Chicago in 1991. The resulting publication demonstrates how nationalist politics work through archaeology in various ways: by setting the terms for archaeological practice, as noted above; by encouraging archaeological work on only some areas of archaeological evidence (those that strengthen a modern nation's claim on an ancient and pure pedigree); and by providing "data" that can be misrepresented and manipulated by the state in the service of its nationalist agenda.

14. Chris Heller, "Good News for Iraq," *Archaeology* 53, 4 (July/August 2000), www.archaeology.org/0007/newsbriefs/iraq.html.

15. Amatzia Baram, *Culture, History, and Ideology in the Formation of Ba'thist Iraq, 1968–89* (Houndmills, Basingstoke, Hampshire: Macmillan in association with St. Anthony's College, Oxford, 1991): 41–2.

16. Saddam Hussein in *Sumer* (1979): 9, quoted in Baram, *Culture, History, and Ideology in the Formation of Ba'thist Iraq*, 41.

17. Fa'iz Muhsin in *Jum* (February 4, 1970), quoted in Baram, *Culture, History, and Ideology in the Formation of Ba'thist Iraq*, 42.

18. See Magnus T. Bernhardsson, *Reclaiming a Plundered Past: Archaeology and Nation Building in Modern Iraq* (Austin: University of Texas Press, 2005): 41–2. Also see Mogens Trolle Larsen, *The Conquest of Assyria: Excavations in an Antique Land* (London: Routledge, 1996).

19. Zainab Bahrani, "Conjuring Mesopotamia: Imaginative Geography and a World Past," in Lynn Meskel, ed., *Archaeology Under Fire: Nationalism, Politics, and Heritage in the Eastern Mediterranean and Middle East* (London: Routledge, 2005): 162.

20. See Richard L. Zettler and Lee Horne, eds., *Treasures from the Royal Tombs of Ur* (Philadelphia: University of Pennsylvania Museum of Archaeology and Anthropology, 1998), especially 21–42.

21. See Georgina Howell, *Gertrude Bell: Queen of the Desert, Shaper of Nations* (New York: Farrar, Straus and Giroux, 2006) and Janet Wallach, *Desert Queen* (London: Weidenfeld & Nicolson, 1996).

22. Bernhardsson, *Reclaiming a Plundered Past*, 123–4.

23. William L. Cleveland, *The Making of an Arab Nationalist: Ottomanism and Arabism in the Life and Thought of Sat'i al-Husri* (Princeton, N.J.: Princeton University Press, 1971): 46. See also Adeed Dawisha, *Arab Nationalism in the Twentieth Century: From Triumph to Despair* (Princeton, N.J.: Princeton University Press, 2005): 49–75, and Sylvia G. Haim, ed., *Arab Nationalism: An Anthology* (Berkeley: University of California Press, 1976).

24. Bernhardsson, *Reclaiming a Plundered Past*, 181.

25. Bernhardsson, *Reclaiming a Plundered Past*, 185.

26. Bernhardsson, *Reclaiming a Plundered Past*, 188.

27. Bernhardsson, *Reclaiming a Plundered Past*, 194.

28. Bernhardsson, *Reclaiming a Plundered Past*, 204. See also Stephen Vincent, "The Rise of Islamic Archaeology," *Muqarnas* 14 (1997): 1–10.

29. Bernhardsson, *Reclaiming a Plundered Past*, 130. At the same time, Al-Husri was critical of attempts among the Arab states to emphasize their own, distinct heritage; even perhaps as he saw it among his intellectual and political peers in Egypt, to fabricate a link to a distant past for political purposes. William Cleveland writes of al-Husri's opposition to "Pharaonism": "Arousing further concerns on al'Husri's part were the attempts of certain Egyptian intellectuals to articulate a distinct modern Egyptian cultural

identity based on the Pharaonic heritage. Especially heated in this respect were his exchanges with Taha Husaynb in the late 1930s." Al-Husri asked if "Husayn's statement on the penetration of Pharaonic feelings into the hearts of the Egyptians meant that the language, civilization, and religion of the Pharaohs should be restored" (136–7).

30. Baram, *Culture, History, and Ideology in the Formation of Ba'thist Iraq*, 1–17.

31. *Th*, 6 (August 1980), quoted in Baram, *Culture, History, and Ideology in the Formation of Ba'thist Iraq*, 43.

32. See *Sumer* 33 (1977): 6–7 (in English) and *New York Times* (January 2,1980), cited in Baram, *Culture, History, and Ideology in the Formation of Ba'thist Iraq*, 43, n.15.

33. *Jum* (September 23, 1981): 6, quoted in Baram, *Culture, History, and Ideology in the Formation of Ba'thist Iraq*, 48.

34. *Jum* (September 23, 1981): 6, quoted in Baram, *Culture, History, and Ideology in the Formation of Ba'thist Iraq*, 49.

35. Baram, *Culture, History, and Ideology in the Formation of Ba'thist Iraq*, 49. Hammurabi was the king most associated with Babylonia's greatness. His name was given to the early code of laws, the "Hammurabi Code." See M.E.J. Richardson, *Hammurabi's Laws: Text, Translation, and Glossary* (Sheffield: Sheffield Academic Press, 2000), and H.-Dieter Viel, *The Complete Code of Hammurabi* (Munich: Lincom Europe, 2005).

36. Jamal Baban, *Afaq 'Arabiyya* (March 1980): 98, quoted in Baram, *Culture, History, and Ideology in the Formation of Ba'thist Iraq*, 98.

37. Saddam Hussein, "Hawla kitabat al-ta'rikh," *Afaq 'Arabiyya* (May 1978): 11, 13, quoted in Baram, *Culture, History, and Ideology in the Formation of Ba'thist Iraq*, 101.

38. See Baram, *Culture, History, and Ideology in the Formation of Ba'thist Iraq*, 97–111.

39. Ahmad Susa, *Hadarat al-'arab wa marahil tatawwuriha 'ibra al'-usur* (Baghdad,1979): 30–31, quoted in Baram, *Culture, History, and Ideology in the Formation of Ba'thist Iraq*, 106.

40. Susa, quoted in Baram, *Culture, History, and Ideology in the Formation of Ba'thist Iraq*, 106–7.

41. Heller, "Good News for Iraq," *Archaeology* 53, 4 (July/August 2000), www.archaeology.org/0007/newsbriefs/iraq.html.

42. "Experts' Meeting at UNESCO Issues recommendations to Safeguard Iraqi Cultural Heritage; April 17, 2003; full text of press release at www .unesco.org.

43. The full text of the Security Council resolution can be found at un.org/DOCS/SC/unsc_resolutions03.html.

44. Susan Breitkopf, "LOST: The Looting of Iraq's Antiquities," *Museum News* (January/February 2007), posted on www.aam-us.org/pubs/mn/MN_JF07_lost-iraq.cfm. See also Matthew Bogdanos with William Patrick, *Thieves of Baghdad: One Marine's Passion for Ancient Civilizations and the Journey to Recover the World's Greatest Stolen Treasures* (New York: Bloomsbury, 2005).

45. Quoted in Edward Wong, "Director of Baghdad Museum Resigns, Citing Political Threat," *New York Times* (August 28, 2006): A6.

46. The full text of the letter can be found on the AIA Web site, www.archaeological.org/webinfo.php?page=10374. See Martin Bailey, "International Archaeologists' Plea to Iraqi Government," www.theartnewspaper.com (October 25, 2006). See also Wong, "Director of Baghdad Museum Resigns, A6; Michael Garen and Marie-Hélène Carleton, "New Concern Over Fate of Iraqi Antiquities," *New York Times* (September 9, 2006): A17, A23. For a history of the Iraq Museum and archaeology in Iraq, see Bernhardsson, *Reclaiming a Plundered Past*, and Baram, *Culture, History, and Ideology in the Formation of Ba'thist Iraq*.

See Milbry Polk and Angela M. H. Schuster, eds., *The Looting of the Iraq Museum, Baghdad: The Lost Legacy of Ancient Mesopotamia* (New York: Harry N. Abrams, 2005). Professional organizations frequently respond to the outbreak of hostilities in archaeologically rich areas with statements. The full text of the letter can be found on the AIA Web site, www.archaeological.org. Recently, the Archaeological Institute of America (AIA) and the American Schools of Oriental Research (ASOR) issued a joint statement calling for quick resolution to the armed hostilities in the area. The statement concluded, however, almost in resignation, that "while the AIA and ASOR realize that not all parties to this conflict are nation-states and therefore not parties to the Hague Convention, we nonetheless urge all parties to the conflict to work within the terms of the Hague Convention and customary international law to minimize damage and destruction of these cultural sites, which are of great value to all humankind." The full text of the statement can be found on the AIA Web site, www.archaeological.org.

47. Frank Rich, "Stuff Happens Again in Baghdad," *New York Times* (September 24, 2006): Section 4, 12.

Chapter Three: The Turkish Question

1. Mehmet Özdoğan, "Ideology and Archaeology in Turkey," in Lynn Meskell, ed., *Archaeology Under Fire*, 113.

2. Bernard Lewis, *The Multiple Identities of the Middle East* (New York: Schocken Books, 1998): 12.

3. The name Turkey has long been given to Turkey by Europeans. It was originally a Western term used to describe a country which, as Bernard Lewis has reminded us, "the Turks usually called 'the lands of Islam,' 'the Imperial realm,' 'the land of Rum.'" The latter, he noted, "was used throughout most of the Ottoman Empire until in modern times it gradually gave way to 'the Ottoman Dominions.' In any case, these names were used to identify the full extent of the Empire, not just the area inhabited by the Turkish nation." Bernard Lewis, *The Emergence of Modern Turkey*, 2nd ed. (Oxford: Oxford University Press, 1961): 332.

4. See Caroline Campbell and Alan Chong, *Bellini and the East* (London: National Gallery, 2006): 78. Eighteen years earlier, Sigismondo Malatesta of Rimini sent his court artist, Matteo de' Pasti, to work for Mehmet II, but he was arrested in Crete and never made it to the Ottoman capital.

5. See Campbell and Chong, *Bellini and the East*, 98–105 and 125.

6. Campbell and Chong, *Bellini and the East*, 122–3. The two Safavid drawings are now in the collections of the Freer Gallery of Art in Washington, D.C. and the Kuwait National Museum. The recent exhibition, "Venice and the Islamic World," chronicles the history of the Italian port city's engagement with the Islamic world over almost one thousand years. See Stefano Carboni, ed., *Venice and the Islamic World, 828–1797* (New Haven, Conn.: Yale University Press for the Metropolitan Museum of Art, 2007), especially 12–119. Also see Deborah Howard, *Venice and the East: The Impact of the Islamic World on Venetian Architecture, 1100–1500* (New Haven, Conn.: Yale University Press, 2000); Rosamond E. Mack, *Bazaar to Piazza: Islamic Trade and Italian Art, 1300–1600* (Berkeley: University of California Press, 2002); and Lisa Jardine and Jerry Brotton, *Global Interests: Renaissance Art Between East and West* (London: Reaktion Books, 2000): 41–5.

7. Campbell and Chong, *Bellini and the East*, 82–3. Also see Julian Raby, "East and West in Mehmed the Conqueror's Library," *Bulletin du Bibliophile* 3 (1987): 296–318.

8. The medal of Mehmet II by Costanza da Ferrara bears the inscription "Sultan Mehmet of the house of Osman, emperor of the Turks" on the obverse and "This man, the thunderbolt of war, has laid low peoples and cities" on the reverse; it preceded a second medal designed by Bellini. As Stephen Scher writes in the Metropolitan Museum of Art's exhibition catalogue, *Byzantium: Faith and Power (1261–1557)* (2004), "As Byzantine emperors had been before him, [Mehmet II] was acutely conscious of the great Roman imperial heritage he was assuming, a heritage that included not only the local Byzantine and ancient Greek cultures but also the extraordinary accomplishments of the Italian Renaissance. . . . His was a new imperium built upon ancient foundations, and such an accomplishment needed to be marked by appropriate monuments. Thus, despite Muslim strictures against imagery, he

appreciated the effectiveness of, among other things, portraiture, which would support the crucial role he was playing" (536). See also Julian Raby, "Pride and Prejudice: Mehmed the Conqueror and the Italian Portrait Medal," in *Italian Medals*, ed. J. Graham Pollard (Washington, D.C.: National Gallery of Art, 1987): 171–94.

9. Melchior Lorich (or Lorch, the spelling varies) worked in Germany and Denmark and traveled to Italy and Constianople in 1556–57. His portrait of Selim I is dated 1559. See *Hollstein's German Engravings, Etchings and Woodcuts*, compiled by Robert Zijlma (Amsterdam: Ven Gendt & Co, 1978): cat. no. 35, 210–11. Also see Barnaby Rogerson, "A Double Perspective and a Lost Rivalry: Ogier de Busbeq and Melchior Lorck in Istanbul," in Gerald MacLean, ed., *Re-Orienting the Renaissance: Cultural Exchanges with the East* (New York: Palgrave Macmillan, 2005): 88–95. Pieter Coecke van Aelst was born near Antwerp and traveled to Constantinople around 1533. His *Ces Moeurs et Fachons de faire des Turcz* comprise fourteen woodblocks. See F.W.H. Hollstein, *Dutch and Flemish Etchings, Engravings and Woodcuts* (Amsterdam: Menno Hertzberger): cat. no. 4, pp. 198–9. For the twelve Venetian portraits of Ottoman sultans, see Carboni, *Venice and the Islamic World*, 110 and 308.

10. See Carboni, *Venice and the Islamic World*, 112 and 316–17. Also see Gülru Necipoglu, "Süleyman the Magnificent and the Representation of Power in the Context of the Ottoman-Hapsburg-Papal Rivalry," *Art Bulletin* 71, 3 (1989): 401–27. For an account of the rich, cultural world of Süleyman the Magnificent, see Esin Atal, *The Age of Sultan Süleyman the Magnificent* (New York: Harry N. Abrams for the National Gallery of Art, 1987). Also, more generally, but for a fascinating, personal account of trading within the Ottoman Empire and beyond during this period, see Nelly Hanna, *Making Big Money in 1600: The Life and Times of Isma'il Abu Taqiyya, Egyptian Merchant* (Syracuse, N.Y.: Syracuse University Press, 1998). For contacts between England and the Ottoman Empire during this period, see Gerald MacLean, *The Rise of Oriental Travel: English Visitors to the Ottoman Empire, 1580–1720* (New York: Palgrave Macmillan, 2004).

11. Encounters between the Islamic lands and Renaissance and early modern Europe have been the subjects of much recent literature. For a good sampling of it, with especially good citations in its footnotes, see Gerald MacLean, *Re-Orienting the Renaissance: Cultural Exchanges with the East* (New York: Palgrave, 2005). See especially the forward by William Dalrymple, the introduction by MacLean, and essays by Deborah Howard and Philip Mansel, from which the facts cited here were taken.

12. In John Freely, *Istanbul: The Imperial City* (London: Penguin Books, 1998): 245. See pages 188, 284, 302–3 of the same source for the figures of the censuses taken in 1477, 1886, and 1924.

13. From the CIA Factbook, www.cia.gov/cia/publications/factbook/ geos/tv.html#People. By 2000, the Istanbul province reported more than 2,500 mosques, with most Christian churches (Roman, Greek, or Eastern) closed or unoccupied for lack of attendance, and only sixteen synagogues serving a Jewish population of about 25,000.

14. Even the wearing of the traditional headscarf would be prohibited in Turkey's schools, universities, and parliament. First the *fez*, then the headscarf; head coverings, like language, fell on opposite sides of the secular/religious line. For an excellent, highly readable account of modern Turkey, in addition to Mango's *The Turks Today*, see Stephen Kinzer, *Crescent & Star: Turkey Between Two Worlds* (New York: Farrar, Straus and Giroux, 2003). Bernard Lewis has written that "To the Westerner, the enforced replacement of one form of headgear by another may seem comic or irritating, and in either case trivial; to the Muslim it was a matter of fundamental significance, expressing—and affecting—his relations with his neighbours and ancestors, and his place in society and in history. Islam was a faith and a civilization, distinct from other faiths and civilizations, uniting Muslim to other Muslims, and separating them both from his heathen forefathers and his infidel neighbours. Dress, and especially headgear, was the visible and outward token by which a Muslim indicated his allegiance to the community of Islam and his rejection of others." Lewis, *The Emergence of Modern Turkey*, 2nd ed. (Oxford: Oxford University Press, 1961): 267.

15. See Vali Nasr, *The Shia Revival: How Conflicts Within Islam Will Shape Its Future* (New York: W.W. Norton, 2006).

16. Ismet Inönü, Atatürk's prime minister at the time, and later president of the Republic, recalled the importance and difficulty of abolishing the caliphate: "It nourished the expectation that the sovereign would return under the guide of the caliph . . . and gave hope to the [Ottoman dynasty]. This is why the abolition of the caliphate . . . had deeper effects and was to become the main source of conflict." Ismet Inönü, *Hatiralar*, ed. Sabahattin Selek (Istanabu: Biligi, 1998): II, 188, quoted in Andrew Mango, *Atatürk: The Biography of the Founder of Modern Turkey* (New York: Overlook Press, 1999): 403. The abolition of the caliphate had two intentions: to weaken religious authority in the affairs of the state and to prevent the return of the Ottoman dynasty. A few days after the expulsion of Abdül Mecit II, 116 members of the dynasty followed him into exile. Most of them never returned to Constantinople. The ban on re-entering Turkey was lifted for female descendants of the dynasty in 1952, and for male descendants only in 1974. There has never been a significant movement to restore the Ottoman dynasty, but the secularization of the state was and remains controversial.

17. Quoted in Lewis, *The Emergence of Modern Turkey*, 353.

18. Lewis, *The Emergence of Modern Turkey*, 345–50, and Jacob M. Landau, *Pan-Turkism in Turkey: A Study in Irrendentism* (Hamden, Conn.: Archon Books, 1981): 1–2.

19. Lewis, *The Emergence of Modern Turkey*, 326–7 and 352–3.

20. Quoted in Lewis, *The Emergence of Modern Turkey*, 353.

21. These small, distinct kingdoms were within Anatolia already during the Early Bronze Age, ca. 3300–2000 B.C. In the early Middle Bronze Age (early second millennium), an Assyrian colony was established through trade with Mesopotamia. By 1700 B.C., the Indo-European peoples called the Hittites founded a kingdom in central Anatolia, in contrast with other Anatolian states, Mesopotamian powers, and Egypt.

22. See Mehmet Özdoğan, "Ideology and Archaeology in Turkey," in Lynn Meskell, ed., *Archaeology Under Fire*, 116–17. See also Lewis, *The Emergence of Modern Turkey*, 359.

23. See Mango, *The Turks Today*, 107–39, and Kinzer, *Crescent & Star: Turkey Between Two Worlds*, 59–81.

24. Quoted in Mango, *The Turks Today*, 98.

25. Mango, *The Turks Today*, 133.

26. This had already been the case under the earliest years of the Republic. The laws of 1924 made Islam a department of the state. A Presidency for Religious Affairs and a Directorate-General of Pious Foundations were established. The former was nominated by the prime minister and had responsibility for the administration of mosques, convents, and other religious offices; the appointment and dismissal of *imams*, preachers, *muezzins*, and other mosque functionaries; and the supervision of *muftis*. The latter was responsible for the maintenance of religious buildings. See Lewis, *The Emergence of Modern Turkey*, 413.

27. Burak Bekdil, a frequent critic of Erdoğan writing in the *Turkish Daily News*, often refers to his "Sunni genes" as an impediment in his relations with Washington. For just two examples, see Burak Bekdil, "Erdoğan vs. Erdoğan," *Turkish Daily News*, April 6, 2005 (turkishdailynews.com.tr), and "Perfect Allies—In Theory," *Turkish Daily News*, February 22, 2006 (turkishdailynews.com.tr).

28. For an account of the history of the Kurds under the Ottomans and more recently in Turkey, see Christopher de Bellaigue, "The Uncontainable Kurds," in *New York Review of Books* (March 6, 2007): 34–9.

29. To be accurate, the language of the agreement between Turkey and Greece, which set the terms for the exchange, spoke of the persons being exchanged as "Turkish subjects of the Greek Orthodox religion residing in Turkey" and "Greek subjects of the Muslim religion residing in Greece." Bernard Lewis described the exchange as "not an exchange and repatriation of ethnic or national minorities, but rather two deportations into exile of religious

minorities—of Muslim Greeks to Turkey, of Christian Turks to Greece." See Lewis, *The Multiple Identities of the Middle East,* 12.

30. See Lewis, *The Emergence of Modern Turkey,* 354–5.

31. Erdoğan's quote is from 32. "Turkish PM, President Agreeing on Unitary State, Equality," Sabah web site (November 11, 2004), on BBC Monitoring Europe-Political (November 14, 2004). Just recently, in August 2007, Turkey elected Abdullah Gul president. He first ran for Parliament in 1991 as a member of the openly Islamist, Welfare Party but with Erdoğan broke with the conservative party and formed the Justic and Development Party. He is an observant Muslim identified with Islamist politics with a doctorate in economics. He served for eight years in the Islamic Development Bank in Saudi Arabia before entering politics. And he was Turkey's foreign minister before being elected president. As foreign minister, he pressed for Turkey to join the European Union and called for changes in the law that punished writers for "insulting Turkishness." Still, for Turkey's secular class and the military, his ties to Islamist politics were too much. When he announced his intentions to run for president four months earlier, the military made clear its opposition. In the face of an imminent political crisis—the military had toppled four elected governments and has identified Islamist political groups as systematically trying to corrode the secular nature of the Turkish Republic—Gul stepped down from the election. Nevertheless, Turkey's secular elite won only a fifth of the votes. Emboldening and by law in the second election needing to win only a majority of the votes, Gul ran and won. He now holds the office Attaturk once held, and the government, with Gul as president and Erdoğan as prime minister, is squarely in the hands of young, reform-minded members of the Islamic middle class.

For all the talk of a modern, forward-looking Turkey, there is increasing interest in the glories of the imperial past—a kind of Ottomania—among the residents of Istanbul. Wooden, Ottoman buildings are being restored. Ottoman music and poetry are being revived. And Mehmet II's conquest of Constantinople is celebrated as an annual public festival. This year, the 533rd since the conquest, Istanbul Governor Muhammer Güler, city Mayor Kadir Topbaş, and the military commander Major-General Muzaffer Cengiz Arslan led the festival, which featured an Ottoman marching band and Jan-issaries re-enacting the storming of the city's walls, and a city employee impersonating the sultan. Hundreds of women went with their children up the Golden Horn to the tomb of Eyüp Ensari to have their children rub their hands against its silver plate for good luck (they were prevented from doing so by frantic officials). The tomb is particularly prized as an Ottoman site. Turkish Muslims rank Eyüp as the third most sacred place in the Islamic world, after Mecca and Jerusalem. It is the reputed burial place of Eyüp Ensari, who, as a friend and standard-bearer of the Prophet Muhammad, is said to have been among the leaders of the first Arab siege of Constantinople from A.D. 674 to 678. After the conquest of Constantinople in 1453, Mehmet II built a mosque on the presumed site of Eyüp's tomb, and until the end of the empire, Ottoman sultans traditionally assumed their throne there in a kind of coronation bearing the sword of Osman, the Ottoman founder.

Although not at the festival, Turkey's president, Ahmet Necdet Sezer, and Prime Minister Erdoğan, issued statements. These could be described as cautious, both approving of the popular festival, yet wanting to broaden its appeal beyond a mere nostalgia for the Ottoman era. Erdoğan is reported to have written that Istanbul has an important place in history as the capital of the Roman, Byzantine, and Ottoman Empires and that it "symbolizes the alliance of civilizations and was proof that people of different backgrounds could live in peace and harmony."

The description of Eyüp and its importance to the Ottomans can be found in John Freely, *Istanbul: The Imperial City* (London: Penguin Books, 1996): 187. And the account of this year's festival was taken from "553rd Anniversary of Istanbul's Ottoman Capture Celebrated, *Turkish Daily News* (May 30, 2006): 2.

The current political crisis in Turkey centers in many respects on the question of identity. Is Turkey religious or secular, of the Middle East or Europe? The cover of the May 5–11, 2007 *Economist* was emblazoned with the words, "The Battle for Turkey's Soul," the title also of the magazine's lead editorial. The Atatürk Society of America's Web site publishes regular opinion pieces. A recent one, written by Prof. Dr. Suna Kili of Bagazici University, is concerned with Turkey's national identity and is, as one would expect, forcefully Kemalist. "The Kemalist reforms constituted a turn of history for the Turkish nation: they involved the liberation of the nation from foreign control and influence, religious control, and theocratic allegiance. These reforms were directed, in the main, to strengthening the now central authority, to nation-building, to secularization of the Turkish state and society, to realizing political participation, and to bringing about changes in the socioeconomic structure of the country." Prof. Kili is critical of the Islamists' influence in Turkey: "The essence of the matter is whether Turkey is to be the secular Turkish Republic or the Islamic Turkish Republic?" He continues by saying that "Now and ultimately the solution between the Islamic and modernist groups in Turkey is not to be sought in the area of clash between these groups. Democracy is the answer. Tolerance for change, openness to dialogue and diversity, recognition and acceptance of the exigencies of modernity, enrichment of a pluralistic of life, and the strengthening of constitutional democracy would constitute the main elements of this solution." And then he concludes: "But if we do read Turkish history correctly and If [sic] we do understand the developments in Turkish political culture fully, we can unequivocally state that the secularist, modernist ethos of the Turkish Republic shall continue and shall be paramount." See www.ataturksociety.org/asa/voa/kili.html.

32. For an account of the history and ideology of the early years of the Imperial Museum (later the Archaeological Museum), see Wendy M. K. Shaw, *Possessors and Possessed: Museums, Archaeology, and the Visualization of History in the Late Ottoman Empire* (Berkeley: University of California Press, 2003).

33. Quoted in D. T. Potts, "The Gulf Arab States and Their Archaeology," in Lynn Meskell, ed., *Archaeology Under Fire*, 190.

34. Information on laws governing antiquities within Turkey can be found in Sibel Özel and Ayhan Karadayi, "Laws Regarding the Protection of the Cultural Heritage of Turkey," in Marilyn Phelan, ed., *The Law of Cultural Property and Natural Heritage: Protection, Transfer and Access* (Evanston, Ill.: Kalos Kapp Press, 1998): chap. 20, 1–14. Also see Shaw, *Possessors and Possessed*, 108–30.

35. See Alpay Pasinli, *Istanbul Archaeological Museums* (Istanbul: A Turizm Yayinlari, 2001): 69–110.

36. Mehmet Özdoğan, "Ideology and Archaeology in Turkey," in Lynn Meskell, ed., *Archaeology Under Fire*, 113.

37. Meskell, ed., *Archaeology Under Fire*, 4. Also see P. L. Kohl and C. Fawcett, eds., *Nationalism, Politics, and the Practice of Archaeology* (Cambridge: Cambridge University Press, 1995).

38. A. Bernard Knapp and Sophia Antoniadou, "Archaeology, Politics and the Cultural Heritage of Cyprus," in Meskell, ed., *Archaeology Under Fire*, 14.

39. Knapp and Antoniadou, "Archaeology, Politics and the Cultural Heritage of Cyprus," 16.

40. Mehmet Özdoğan, "Ideology and Archaeology in Turkey," in Lynn Meskell, ed., *Archaeology Under Fire*, 120–21. Kurds argue that the flooding of ancient sites for the Southeast Anatolia Project has hurt them inordinately, as in Hissarlik and Zeugma. See Stephen Kinzer, "A Race to Save Roman Splendors From Drowning," *New York Times* (July 3, 2000): A3.

41. The Kurdish question remains vexing to Turkey. Recent events in Iraq following the defeat of Saddam Hussein have increased the profile of Iraqi Kurds. *New York Times* described the increasing likelihood of Iraq breaking up into three self-governing regions: "An Iraq writhes in the grip of Sunni-Shiite violence, a de facto partitioning is taking place. Parts of the country are coming to look more and more like Iraqi Kurdistan, with homogenous armed regions becoming the norm." An autonomous Kurdish region would of course be very attractive to the Kurds across the borders in Turkey and Iran. The *Times* quoted Mahmoud Othnab, a senior Kurdish member of the

Iraqi Parliament, as saying "Both Turkey and Iran are not happy with what's going on in Iraqi Kurdistan—having a special region, having a government, having a Parliament, and so on. That's why they do those special operations, those bombings. It's a blow against the Kurdish government in Kurdistan." At the same time, the Turkish Prime Minister, Recep Tayyip Erdoğan, warned Tariq al-Hashemi, the Iraqi vice president and a Sunni Arab (like Erdoğan), that the Iraqi government needed to take "satisfactory steps" against the Kurdistan Workers Party, a guerilla group with hideouts in Kurdish Iraq. See Edward Wong, "For an Iraq Cut in 3, Cast a Wary Glance at Kurdistan," *New York Times* (August 27, 2006): 12.

42. Özdoğan, "Ideology and Archaeology in Turkey," 121.

43. Turkey has been calling for the return of the material uncovered by Heinrich Schliemann, the German archaeologist who excavated first in Hissarlik from 1868 to 1871, and then in Troy over four campaigns, the last from 1888 to 1890. He is famous—and often criticized—for uncovering "Priam's Treasure" and removing it to Berlin. ("Priam's Treasure" is the term given to the cache of gold and other objects Schliemann optimistically assigned to the Iliadic king of Troy, Priam.) He is also criticized for his early, unscientific excavating technique, which resulted in the loss of archaeological data, for which of course many other contemporary, early archaeologists could be—and are—also criticized.

By most accounts, Schliemann did remove finds from his digs without permission. They were acquired by the Imperial Museum of Berlin in 1880 and later transferred to the city's Pergamon Museum. There they remained until 1945, when the victorious Red Army of the Soviet Union removed them to Moscow. They are in the Pushkin today. (Much of Grünwedel's and Le Coq's finds from Turpan are, for similar reasons, in the State Hermitage Museum, St. Petersburg; see below, chapter 4).

To complicate matters, the heirs of Frank Calvert, the British archaeologist and diplomat, who preceded Schliemann at Troy and legally owned the eastern half of the Hissarlik Mound, are (or were at least in 1995) planning to file suit against Russia for their "share" of the finds. They accuse, and others now generally agree, that Schliemann also removed finds from the eastern half of the Hissarlik Mound—Calvert's property—in 1890. See Susan Heuck Allen, "Calvert's Heirs Claim Schliemann's Treasure," *Archaeology* 49, 1 (Jan/Feb 1996), www.archaeology.org/9601/newsbriefs/calvert.html. How exactly this claim falls within the law of the 1884 Ottoman Decree on Antiquities is unclear. That law decreed that all antiquities discovered through excavations belonged to the state, that one-half of any antiquities found accidentally on private land would be given to the landowner, and that all antiquities discovered in legal excavations are the property of the Imperial Museum in Constantinople (now the Archaeological Museum). Even if the

British Calvert owned the eastern half of the Hissarlik Mound in 1890, it would seem that Schliemann's finds, discovered through excavation, belonged to the Ottoman state, which of course no longer exists. In any case, they are now in Moscow, taken from Berlin as war booty.

On Schliemann, see Curtis Runnels, *The Archaeology of Heinrich Schliemann: An Annotated Bibliographic Handlist* (Boston: Archaeological Institute of America, 2002), and D. F. Easton, *Schliemann's Excavations at Troia, 1870–1873* (Mainz von Rhein: Von Zabern, 2002). Also see Suzanne L. Machand, *Down From Olympus: Archaeology and Philhellenism in Germany, 1750–1970* (Princeton, N.J.: Princeton University Press, 1996): 116–24.

44. Wendy Shaw argues that the formation of the Imperial Museum is part and parcel of the development of Ottoman political and cultural ideology. In the early years, coincident with the earliest expressions of Ottoman nationalism—itself influenced by European models—"the Ottoman Empire of the nineteenth century was attempting to reconfigure its identity as congruent with European practices and institutions. The collection of antiquities and the development of a museum to house them played a symbolic role in representing the new cultural aspirations of the Ottoman state" (68). Shaw notes the irony in this: "Ironically, the founders of the museum used the emulation of a European museum to counteract the physical incursion of Europe onto Ottoman territory. Through asserting its ownership of antiquities, the empire could reaffirm symbolically its control over its territories. . . . With its new name, Imperial Museum, its focus was not on these antiquities but on the concept of empire that the antiquities could represent" (86–7). Archaeological objects from around the empire, Shaw argues, "were not placed on display for the sake of antiquity but for the sake of modernity; they formed an essential part of retaining and constructing a modern Ottoman identity. In a time when nationalist uprisings threatened the unity of the empire, the museum attempted to promulgate the idea that the empire constituted a unitary state." The museum began to collect examples of Islamic art only in 1889, as the empire grew weaker under pressure from rebellious provinces and foreign governments: "The belated interest in Islamic antiquities at first seems ironic: the objects most readily accessible to Ottoman collectors—those in common use in mosques and elite households throughout the empire—were among the last to be collected" (not until 1889). "Unlike Helleno-Byzantine antiquities or military spoila, Islamic antiquities were not only part of the Ottoman past, they were also part of the Ottoman present. The establishment of an Islamic arts section in the museum near the end of the nineteenth century reflects the growing interest in the immediate past of the Ottoman territories as well as the awareness of the nationalistic implications of this past." It was under the ideology of the Young Turks that the museum was going "to transform the Islamic arts collection

into an overt means of nationalist expression and of resistance against European cultural subsumation" (209).

Chapter Four: The Chinese Question

1. Quoted in Jonathan Watts, "UK to Lend World Treasures to China," *The Guardian* (March 3, 2006), www.guardian.co.uk.

2. See Frances Wood, "Aurel Stein, The British Museum, and the India Office," in Susan Whitfield, ed., *The Silk Road: Trade, Travel, War and Faith* (Chicago: Serindia Publications for The British Library, 2004): 91–104. See also Annabel Walker, *Aurel Stein: Pioneer of the Silk Road* (London: John Murray, 1995) and Jeanette Mirsky, *Sir Aurel Stein, Archaeologial Explorer* (Chicago: University of Chicago Press, 1977).

3. See Jacques Giès, ed., *The Arts of Central Asia: the Pelliot Collection in the Musée Guimet,* trans. Hero Friesen (London: Serindia Publications, 1996).

4. See Roderick Whitfield, Susan Whitfield, and Neville Agnew, *Cave Temples of Mogao: Art and History on the Silk Road* (Los Angeles: Getty Conservation Institute and J. Paul Getty Museum, 2000), and Susan Whitfield, *The Silk Road: Trade, Travel, War and Faith.* For a highly critical account of Stein's and Pelliot's forays to the Mogao caves and into Central Asia, see Peter Hopkirk, *Foreign Devils on the Silk Road* (Amherst: University of Massachusetts Press, 1980): 68–97 and 156–89.

5. Langdon Warner, *The Long Old Road in China* (Garden City, N.Y.: Doubleday, Page & Company, 1926). See especially pp. 138–45 for his account of his time at the Mogao caves. For a description and photograph of the sculpture and an account of its historical importance, see Roderick Whitfield, "Kneeling Attendant Bodhisattva," in James Cuno, ed., *Harvard's Art Museums: 100 Years of Collecting* (Cambridge, Mass.: Harvard University Art Museums, 1995): 56–7.

6. For a photograph of the remaining sculptures in Cave 328 and the glaring absence of the attendant, kneeling bodhisattva now at Harvard, see Whitfield, Whitfield, and Agnew, *Cave Temples of Mogao,* 80.

7. The text of the Convention on Cultural Property Implementation Act, of which CPAC is a part, can be found at http://exchanges.state.gov/culprop/97–446.html. Texts of my statement to CPAC, together with those of seven other witnesses before the committee, can be found in *IFAR Journal* 7, 3–4 (2004 and 2005): 20–59. In October 2006, the U.S. State Department officially postponed a decision on the Chinese government's request. See Jeremy Kahn, "U.S. Delays Rule on Limits to Chinese Art Imports," *New York Times* (October 18, 2006): E2.

8. The Public Summary of the P.R.C.'s request can be found at http://exchanges.state.gov/culprop/cn04sum.html.

9. This information is from the P.R.C. art information Web site, Artron, at www.artron.net/auction/list1.php?dt=2005. The catalogues of those auctions are often very professional, accurate in their descriptions of the objects on offer, with and without provenance. See, for example, the 2005 Autumn auction catalogue for the Chongyuan auction house in Shanghai, at which the large Chinese archaic bronze ritual vessel from the Zhou dynasty (item 201) sold for more than $3 million, the highest price for an ancient Chinese bronze sold at auction anywhere in the world in 2006. The largest art and antiques fair devoted to Chinese art in the world in 2006—the Asia International Arts and Antiques Fair (AIAA)—was in Hong Kong and sponsored by the Palace Museum, Beijing, the National Museum of China, Beijing, the Poly Art Museum, Beijing, and the Shaanxi History Museum, Xi'an. Cheng Jian-zheng, director of the Shaanxi History Museum, wrote a preface to the Fair's catalogue, describing Hong Kong as being "at the heart of Asia, and has long been a melting pot of Sino-Western culture and the window of Sino-Western worlds. Since a long time, the Hong Kong art market has been growing and widening excellently. This fair should be an exceptionally grand and famous occasion. As the milestone of a significant stage in the cultural enrichment and art development of this land, it will leave deep and impressive memories for the honourable guests in the show." See the *Exhibition Directory, Asia International Arts and Antiquities Fair (AIAA 2006), May 26–29, 2006.* The fair was three times larger than the largest Asian art fair in the United States in 2006 and included 136 exhibitors, 72 of which were from China alone. The fair's published total sales volume was $23,225,000.

10. The best English-language source for Chinese cultural property laws is J. David Murphy, *Plunder and Preservation: Cultural Property Law and Practice in the People's Republic of China* (Oxford: Oxford University Press, 1995). See especially pp. 81–143 for the information I cite in my text. Regarding the nationalist agenda of Chinese archaeology, see Kwang-Chih Chang, "Reflections on Chinese Archaeology in the Second Half of the Twentieth Century," *Journal of East Asian Archaeology* 3, 1–2 (2001): 5–13; Enzheng Tong, "Thirty Years of Chinese Archaeology (1949–1979)," in Philip L. Kohl and Clare Fawcett, eds., *Nationalism, Politics, and the Practice of Archaeology* (Cambridge: Cambridge University Press, 1995): 177–97; and Lothar von Falkenhausen, "The Regionalist Paradigm in Chinese Archaeology," in Kohl and Fawcett, eds., *Nationalism, Politics, and the Practice of Archaeology*, 198–217.

11. These early laws under both the Republican and Communist governments are political statements reasserting Chinese control over what it identifies as its cultural property and a rejection of unequal treaties and a shameful history of foreign control inside China. This is still an important theme in P.R.C. cultural policy.

12. Murphy, *Plunder and Preservation*, 94.

13. Quoted in Murphy, *Plunder and Preservation*, 98.

14. Quoted in Murphy, *Plunder and Preservation*, 99–100.

15. See William H. Overholt, *The Rise of China: How Economic Reform Is Creating a New Superpower* (New York: W.W. Norton, 1993), and C. Fred Bergsten, Bates Gill, Nicholas R. Lardy, and Derek Mitchell, *China: The Balance Sheet* (New York: Public Affairs, 2006). Also see James Fallows, "China Makes, The World Takes," *The Atlantic* (July/August 2007): 48–72.

16. Murphy, *Plunder and Preservation*, 126–7.

17. Murphy, *Plunder and Preservation*, 128.

18. A set of four catalogues, selected bronzes in the collection of the Poly Art Museum in three volumes and Buddhist stone sculpture in one, were published in 2000–2001.

19. Yulanda Chung, "A Cultural Revolution: The International Debate Over Stolen Relics Shifts to Hong King," *Asiaweek* (May 19, 2000), www .asiaweek.com. The sacking, looting, and burning of Yuanmingyuan remains an outrage and humiliation to the Chinese. The Old Summer Palace was begun in 1707 under the Emperor Kangxi. It was extensively enlarged under the Emperor Qianlong, who instructed the Jesuits, Giuseppe Castiglione and Michel Benoist, to design European-style palaces and fountains for the palace grounds. It would become the center of Qing dynasty court life. The emperors lived and conducted the affairs of state there, leaving the Forbidden City in Beijing to be used only for formal ceremonies. With the destruction of Yuanmingyuan in 1860, the court moved back to the Forbidden City, where it remained until 1924. See Frances Wood, "Imperial Architecture of the Qing: Palaces and Retreats," in Evelyn S. Rawski and Jessica Rawson, eds., *China: The Three Emperors, 1662–1795* (London: Royal Academy of Arts, 2005): 61–2. Recently, Sotheby's announced plans to auction off another of the zodiac animal heads from Yuanmingyuan. The head of a horse is the featured item in a four-day sale in Hong Kong, to begin on October 6, 2007. The seller of the horse head is an unidentified, "well-known Taiwanese collector." The object is believed to sell for as much as HK$80 million ($7.7 million). Total sales at the auction may exceed HK$1 billion. See Le-Min Lin, "Looted Qing Dynasty Horse May Fetch HK$80 Million at Sotheby's," Bloomberg.com (September 6, 2007), www.bloomberg.com/apps/news?pid =20601115&sid=aQ2iQjT_YLEg&refer=muse.

20. "Zodiac Fountain Heads on Display in Hong Kong," Cnn.com (May 19, 2000), www.transcripts.cnn.com.

21. Erik Eckholm, "Bringing Treasures Back to China," *New York Times* (July 30, 2006), www.nytimes.com.

22. Shan Yihe, preface to *Selected Bronzes in the Collection of the Poly Art Museum* (Beijing: Poly Art Museum, 2001), n.p.

23. Erik Eckholm, "Bringing Treasures Back to China," *New York Times* (July 30, 2006), www.nytimes.com.

24. The Beijing Poly International Auction Co., Ltd., lists auction results and features upcoming auctions on its Web site, www.polypm.com.cn. In November 2005, a traditional-style painting by the 86-year-old living artist, Wu Guanzhong, fetched a record price of $3.7 million at a Poly auction. Li Da, the general manager of the auction house, was not surprised. More recently the auction house sold 270 oil paintings for a record $18.1 million. A China.org posting cited Li Da as describing the buyers as "mainly the nouveau riche, typically real estate developers, bankers and securities investors in their 30s and 40s." See www.china.org.cn, November 8, 2005 and June 8, 2006.

25. "Reclaiming Cultural Relics from Overseas," *China Daily* (June 14, 2005), www2.chinadaily.com.cn.

26. "Cultural Relics On Their Way Home," ChinaCulture.org (November 20, 2003), www.chinaculture.org.

27. ChinaCulture.org, www.chinaculture.org. Also see Karen Mazurkewich, "Collectors Look East," *Wall Street Journal* (March 24, 2006): W5.

28. "Reclaiming Cultural Relics from Overseas," *China Daily* (June 14, 2005), www2.chinadaily.com.cn.

29. Jonathan Watts, "UK to Lend World Treasures to China," *The Guardian* (March 3, 2006), www.guardian.co.uk.

30. See www.poly.com.cn.

31. "Equity Participation in Poly Finance Company Limited," *Credit Suisse Emagazine* (January 11, 2006), www.emagazine.credit-suisse.com.

32. Spencer P. M. Harrington, "China Buys Back Its Past," *Archaeology* (May 11, 2000), www.archaeology.org. The article also notes Elizabeth Childs-Johnson's view that China's success in buying back such cultural relics presents "a 'very, very good chance to improve the laws preventing the export of antiquities from the mainland.' Childs-Johnson likewise predicts changes that will tighten Chinese antiquities legislation."

33. The full text of the report, "Weapons Proliferation and the Material-Industrial Complex of the P.R.C.," is available on the Web site of the Federation of American Scientists, www.fas.org/nuke/guide/china/sources.htm.

34. See the region's official Web site www.xi.gov.cn. See also www.china.org.cn.

35. James A. Millward and Peter C. Perdue, "Political and Cultural History of the Xinjiang Region Through the late Nineteenth Century," in S. Frederick Starr, ed., *Xinjiang: China's Muslim Borderland* (London: M. E. Sharpe, 2004): 27–62. Also see James A. Millward, *Eurasian Crossroads: A History of Xinjiang* (New York: Columbia University Press, 2007).

36. See the catalogue of the Xinjiang Uighurs Autonomous Region Museum, one of China's newest museums (Urimqi: Xinjiang Baishiyuan Craft and Art Co., Ltd, n.d.): 192–96.

37. Peter C. Perdue, *China Marches West* (Cambridge, Mass.: Harvard University Press, 2005): 41–2.

38. Modern population and demographic statistics, unless otherwise noted, are taken from Stanley W. Toops, "The Demography of Xinjiang," in Starr, ed., *Xinjiang: China's Muslim Borderland*, 241–75.

39. Giorgio Fiacconi, "China Moves West: Booming Trade and Investment in Central Asia, Uyghur Problem Still Unsolved," *Times of Central Asia* (May 30, 2006). See also Colin Mackerras, "Why Terrorism Bypasses China's Far West," *Asia Times* (April 23, 2004), www.atimes.com. Also see Millward, *Eurasian Crossroads*, 306–10.

40. "Go West Policy Begins to Flourish," *Jakarta Post* (February 13, 2006). See also "Xinjiang to Build Largest Onshore Energy Channel in China," *SinoCast* (March 14, 2006), and "Xinjiang to Become China's Energy Base," *SinoCast* (March 13, 2006). The anticipated tourism benefits, double those of 2001–2005, are cited in "China Xinjiang Eyes $13.5 Bln Tourism Revenue, 2006–2010," *Chinese News Digest* (February 24, 2006). Also see Millward, *Eurasian Crossroads*, 300–301.

41. Olivia Ward, "Beijing Tightens Control on Uyghurs," *Toronto Star* (April 16, 2006): A12. Also see Millward, *Eurasian Crossroads*, 322–52.

42. Colin Mackerras, "Why Terrorism Bypasses China's Far West," *Asia Times* (April 23, 2004), www.atimes.com.

43. "Xinjiang, China's Restive Northwest," *Human Rights Watch World Report 2000: China and Tibet*, www.hrw.org.

44. "China: Human Rights Concerns in Xinjiang," *A Human Rights Watch Backgrounder* (October 2001), www.hrw.org.

45. See Justin Rudelson and William Jankowiak, "Acculturation and Resistance: Xinjiang Identities in Flux, " in Starr, ed., *Xinjiang: China's Muslim Borderland*, 317–18.

46. For an interesting account of recent developments for Uighurs in China and in exile, see Peter Hessler, *Oracle Bones: A Journey Between China's Past and Present* (New York: HarperCollins, 2006), especially pp. 119–21, 349–50, and 374–5.

47. This text and others can be found on the Human Rights Watch Web site, www.hrw.org/backgrounder/asia/china-bck1017.htm.

48. Graham E. Fuller and Jonathan Lipman, "Islam in Xinjiang," in Starr, ed., *Xinjiang: China's Muslim Borderland*, 344. Much information about Uighur nationalist, independence movements and activities can be found on Web sites like the Turkistan Newsletter (www.euronet.nl), Open Society

Institute (www.erasianet.org), the Uyghur Information Agency (www
.uyghurinfo.com), the Uyghur American Association (www.uyghuramerican
.org), and the *For Democracy, Human Rights, Peace and Freedom for Uzbekistan and Central Asia* (www.uzbekistanerk.org).

49. Justin Rudelson, quoted in Fuller and Lipman, in Starr, ed., *Xinjiang:
China's Muslim Borderland*, 338.

50. See Kate Fitz Gibbon and Andrew Hale, *Ikat: Splendid Silks of Central
Asia. The Guido Goldman Collection* (London: Laurence King Publishing,
Calmann & King, 1997), especially pp. 18–57.

51. Sally Hovey Wriggins, *Xuanzang: A Buddhist Pilgrim on the Silk Road*
(Oxford: Westview Press, 1996).

52. Whitfield, Whitfield, and Agnew, *Cave Temples of Mogao*, 25.

53. Wriggins, *Xuanzang*, 176–7.

54. Aurel Stein, "The Desert Crossing of Hsuan Tsang 630 A.D.," *Indian
Antiquary* 50 (1921): 15–25. For a powerfully written, recent account of a
travel *cum* spiritual quest inspired by Xuanzang, see Richard Bernstein, *Ul-
timate Journey: Retracing the Path of an Ancient Buddhist Monk Who Crossed
Asia in Search of Enlightenment* (New York: Vintage Books, 2001). Also see
Tansen Sen, *Buddhism, Diplomacy, and Trade: The Realignment of Sino-Indian
Relations*, 600–1400. (Honolulu: Association of Asian Studies and University
of Hawaii Press, 2003).

55. For an account of the expeditions, see Marianne Yaldiz, "The History
of the Turfan Collection in the Museum of Indian Art," *Orientations* 31, 9
(November 2000): 75–82.

56. See Peter Hopkirk, *Foreign Devils on the Silk Road* (Amherst: University of Massachusetts Press, 1980): 125–55.

57. See the English publication, which appeared two years after the German
one, Albert von Le Coq, *Buried Treasures of Chinese Turkestan*, trans. Anna
Barwell (London: George Allen & Unwin, 1928). The material comprises
mural paintings from Bezelik, paintings on silk and paper, sculptures, and a
full-scale reconstruction of a square temple with murals from Cave 123. In
1938, after the outbreak of the war in Europe, many of the artifacts were
crated and moved to less dangerous places. But many of the mural paintings
were too large and were left, sandbagged, in the museum. Together with the
museum buildings themselves, the murals were destroyed in 1945, or reduced
to fragments. Some of the artifacts were confiscated by the Soviet Red Army
and moved to Dresden and Leningrad. The Dresden material was returned
to Berlin in 1990. In 2002, State Hermitage Museum in St. Petersburg
acknowledged that it held 20 percent of the objects thought missing during
the war.

58. On China's early encounters with foreign cultures, see Valerie Hansen,
The Open Empire: A History of China to 1600 (New York: W. W. Norton,

2000); *China 5000 Years: Innovation and Transformation in the Arts* (New York: Guggenheim Museum, 1998), especially Jenny So, "Innovation in Ancient Chinese Metalwork" (pp. 75–88) and Helmut Brinker, "Transfiguring Divinities: Buddhist Sculpture in China" (pp. 144–58); Wu Hung "The Origins of Chinese Painting (Paleolithic Period to Tang Dynasty)," in Yang Zin et al., *Three Thousand Years of Chinese Painting* (New Haven, Conn.: Yale University Press, 1997): 15–86, and James C. Y. Watt, *China: Dawn of a Golden Age, 200–750 A.D.* (New York: Metropolitan Museum of Art, 2004), especially James C. Y. Watt, "Art and History in China from the 3rd through the 8th Centuries" (pp. 2–46), Boris Marshak, "Central Asian Metalwork in China" (pp. 47–56), and Angela F. Howard, "Buddhist Art in China" (pp. 89–99). For the history of more recent encounters, see Anna Jackson and Amin Jaffer, eds., *Encounters: The Meeting of Asia and Europe, 1500–1800* (London: Victoria and Albert Museum, 2004), and Evelyn S. Rawski and Jessica Rawson, eds., *China: The Three Emperors, 1662–1795* (London: Royal Academy of Art, 2005). On China's participation in the global adventure of contemporary art, see Wu Hung, *Chinese Art at the Crossroads: Between Past and Future, Between East and West* (New York: Chambers Fine Arts, 2003).

59. Owen Lattimore, *Studies in Frontier History: Collected Papers, 1928–1958* (New York: Oxford University Press, 1962): 113.

60. On the issue of Han identity in Chinese historiography, see Prasenjit Duara, *Rescuing History from the Nation: Questioning Narratives of Modern China* (Chicago: University of Chicago Press, 1995).

Chapter Five: Identity Matters

1. Edward W. Said, *Orientalism*, reprinted with a new Preface (London: Penguin Books, 2003): xxii.

2. Edward W. Said, *Out of Place: A Memoir* (New York: Vintage Books, 2000): 295, and Ara Guzelimian, ed., *Parallels and Paradoxes, Daniel Barenboim and Edward W. Said: Explorations in Music and Society* (London: Bloomsbury, 2004): 5.

3. Amin Maalouf, *In the Name of Identity: Violence and the Need to Belong* (New York: Penguin Books, 2000): 5.

4. Amartya Sen, *Identity and Violence: The Illusion of Destiny* (New York: W.W. Norton, 2006): xvii. Much of interest has been written on identity recently. In addition to the above cited works by Said and Maalouf, see especially Leila Ahmed, *A Border Passage: From Cairo to America—A Woman's Journey* (London: Penguin Books, 2000); Fouad Ajami, *The Dream Palace of the Arabs* (New York: Vintage Books,1999); Kwame Anthony Appiah, *In My Father's House: Africa in the Philosophy of Culture* (Oxford: Oxford University Press, 1992); Appiah, *The Ethics of Identity* (Princeton, N.J.: Princeton

University Press, 2005); Appiah and Henry Louis Gates, Jr., *Identities* (Chicago: University of Chicago Press, 1995); Anthony D. Smith, *National Identity* (Reno, Nev.: University of Las Vegas Press, 1991); Charles Taylor, *Sources of the Self and the Making of the Modern Identity* (Cambridge, Mass.: Harvard University Press, 1995); and Leon Wieseltier, *Against Identity* (New York: Drenttel, 1996).

5. On the formation of national (as opposed to encyclopedic) museums in the age of nationalism, see Gwendolyn Wright, ed., *The Formation of National Collections of Art and Archaeology*, Studies in the History of Art 47, Symposium Papers 27 (Washington, D.C.: National Gallery of Art, 1996).

6. Kwame Anthony Appiah, *Cosmopolitanism: Ethics in a World of Strangers* (New York: W.W. Norton, 2006): 119.

7. To encourage the publication of archaeological excavation reports, two New York philanthropists and collectors of antiquities, Shelby White and Leon Levy, established a special program at Harvard University's Semitic Museum in 1997. The Shelby White-Leon Levy Program for Archaeological Publications has awarded more than $7 million in grants to over 150 "archaeologists holding the doctorate, or to doctoral candidates conducting research on unpublished field work, provided they can devote full time to the publication project." To date, the program has seen twenty-two of its projects published—a remarkable record. See www.fas.harvard.edu/~semitic/wl/publications.html. The generosity and intentions of the donors have attracted controversy, however. In March 2006, New York University announced it had been given $200 million by White and Levy to establish an institute for the study of antiquity. Immediately members of the NYU faculty objected. Randall White, a professor of anthropology, resigned from the university's existing Center for Ancient Studies in protest. Other universities, including the University of Pennsylvania, the University of Cincinnati, and Bryn Mawr College, are reported to have adopted policies discouraging or banning the acceptance of what is called "Levy–White money." See Robin Pogrebin, "$200 Million Gift Prompts a Debate Over Antiquities," *New York Times* (April 1, 2006): A1.

Jane C. Waldbaum, former president of the Archaeological Institute of America, dedicated one of her monthly letters "From the President" in the AIA's popular magazine, *Archaeology*, to the issue of so many antiquities stored in museum basements. She admits that after an excavation is completed and published (of course she doesn't say how many have been "completed and published," sadly the number in each category is very low indeed), most finds are "in either museum basements or warehouselike depots belonging to antiquities departments." She then says, with obvious sarcasm, "Some dealers, collectors, and their apologists suggest that this material should be sold to make more space in these increasingly crowded storage areas, and also to satisfy the craving of tourists for 'souvenirs.' They claim that selling these unseen and unappreciated artifacts would help stem the tide of looting and illicit excavation by providing a legitimate source of excavated antiquities for the market. And besides, they say, these objects have been studied and published. They are no further use to science, right?" "Wrong!" she responds. Scholars work in basements among exhibition-unworthy artifacts all the time. She has herself "excavated" the basements and storerooms of the Israel Antiquities Authority, the Israel Museum, and "other institutions where material from 'finished' digs is housed." From this she gained a "much richer picture of the extent of contact between Greece and the Levant in the seventh through fourth centuries B.C." than she could have by studying "only published sources"—I gather this means that even "completed and published" excavations are not fully published—or "only the 'beautiful' pieces in museum display cases." See Jane C. Waldbaum, "From the President: Basement Archaeology," *Archaeology* (September/October 2003).

While at the Harvard University Art Museums, I was responsible for hosting the offices of The Archaeological Exploration of Sardis, an excavation jointly sponsored by the Harvard University Art Museums and Cornell University. The excavation is dedicated to ancient Lydia, now in a region of Turkey east of Izmir. It began in its current incarnation almost fifty years ago under Professor George M. A. Hanfmann of the Department of Fine Arts, Harvard University, and has been ably directed since 1977 by Crawford H. Greenewalt, Jr., Professor of Classical Archaeology at the University of California, Berkeley. Since then, some 11,000 artifacts have been found and two books and fifteen reports and monographs published (Professor Waldbaum wrote Monograph 8: *Metalwork from Sardis: The Finds Through 1974*, which was finally published in 1983 and is now out of print). Excavation reports are exacting and, given the number of illustrations they require and their small print runs, very expensive. This is why the White–Levy publication program is so important: it has funded more publications in seven years than Sardis alone has been able to publish in almost fifty.

8. Kate Fitz Gibbon, "Japan's Protection of Its Cultural Heritage—A Model," in Kate Fitz Gibbon, ed., *Who Owns the Past? Cultural Policy, Cultural Property, and the Law* (New Brunswick, N.J.: Rutgers University Press, 2005): 331–9.

9. See Appiah, *Cosmopolitanism*, xvi. In addition to Anderson's *Imagined Communities*, from which I quoted at the beginning of this chapter, among the many recent works on nationalism, see especially John A. Armstrong, *Nations Before Nationalism* (Chapel Hill: University of North Carolina Press, 1982); John Breuilly, *Nationalism and the State* (Chicago: University of Chicago Press, 1982); Partha Chatterjee, *The Nation and Its Fragments:*

Postcolonial Histories (Princeton, N.J.: Princeton University Press, 1993); Walker Connor, *Ethnonationalism: The Quest for Understanding* (Princeton, N.J.: Princeton University Press, 1994); Ernest Gellner, *Nations and Nationalism* (Ithaca, N.Y.: Cornell University Press, 1983); Eric Hobsbawm, *Nations and Nationalism Since 1780* (Cambridge: Cambridge University Press, 1990); Anthony D. Smith, *The Antiquity of Nations* (Cambridge: Polity, 2004); Anthony D. Smith, *The Ethnic Origins of Nations* (Oxford: B. Blackwell, 1986); and Anthony D. Smith, *Nationalism and Modernism: A Critical Survey of Recent Theories of Nations and Nationalism* (New York: Routledge, 1998).

10. Anderson, *Imagined Communities*, 7.

11. Hobsbawm, *Nations and Nationalism Since 1780*, 20.

12. Gellner, *Nations and Nationalism*, 35–8.

13. Gellner, *Nations and Nationalism*, 124–5.

14. Anderson, *Imagined Communities*, 6.

15. Gellner, *Nations and Nationalism*, 48.

16. Gellner, *Nations and Nationalism*, 48. Anderson locates these circumstances in the development of print capitalism, which "gave a new fixity to language" and "created unified fields of exchange and communication" such that people "gradually became aware of the hundreds of thousands, even millions, of people in their particular language-field, and at the same time that *only those* hundreds of thousands, or millions, so belonged. These fellow readers, to whom they were connected through print, formed, in their secular, particular, visible invisibility, the embryo of the nationally imagined community" (Anderson, *Imagined Communities*, 44). That said, progress was slow and nationalism did not wait for the numbers of "fellow-readers" to mount. Hobsbawm reminds us that in 1789, only 50 percent of the French spoke French and that the Italian language was the basis for Italian unification because it was spoken and read by the socially and intellectually elite; at the time of unification, only 2.5 percent of the Italian population used the Italian language for everyday purposes (Hobsbawm, *Nations and Nationalism Since 1780*, 44–62).

17. Gellner, *Nations and Nationalism*, 1.

18. The most recent number of languages spoken or signed in the United States that I can find is 337. Legislation to establish English as the nation's official language is pending in the U.S. House of Representatives (HR 300IH, January 2003; HR 931H, February 2003; and HR 997IH, February 2003). The latter is called the "English language Unity Act of 2003" and is intended "to declare English the official language of the United States, to establish a uniform English language rule for naturalization, and to avoid mis-constructions of the English language texts of the laws of the United Sates, pursuant to Congress's powers to provide for the general welfare of the United States and

to establish a uniform rule of naturalization under article I, section 8 of the Constitution." On May 25, 2006, the U.S. Senate passed an amendment to an immigration reform bill that would declare English the national language of the United States (the bill passed 62–36). Since 1981, twenty-two U.S. states have adopted various forms of "official English legislation."

19. Gellner, *Nations and Nationalism*, 2.

20. Smith, *National Identity*, 17.

21. Smith, *National Identity*, 160–61.

22. Smith, *National Identity*, 163.

23. Amartya Sen, *Identity and Violence*, 4.

24. The quotes in this paragraph are from Sen, *Identity and Violence*, 171–2.

25. Sen, *Identity and Violence*, 173.

26. Sen, *Identity and Violence*, 174.

27. Sen, *Identity and Violence*, 38. Appiah puts it similarly, though more expansively: "To create a life, in other words, is to interpret the materials that history has given you. Your character, your circumstances, your psychological constitution, including the beliefs and preferences generated by the interaction of your innate endowments and your experience: all these need to be taken into account in shaping a life. They are not constraints on that shaping; they are its materials. As we come to maturity, the identities we make, our individualities, are interpretive responses to our talents and disabilities, and the changing social, semantic, and material contexts we enter at birth; and we develop our identities dialectically with our capacities and circumstances, because the latter are in part the product of what our identities lead us to do. A person's shaping of her life flows from her beliefs and from a set of values, tastes, and dispositions of sensibility, all of these influenced by various forms of social identity: let us call all these together a person's ethical self" (Appiah, *The Ethics of Identity*, 163).

28. Sen, *Identity and Violence*, 112.

29. Lawrence E. Harrison and Samuel P. Huntington, eds., *Culture Matters: How Values Shape Human Progress* (New York: Basic Books, 2000), xiii, quoted in Sen, *Identity and Violence*, 107. The other book by Huntington is *The Clash of Civilizations and the Remaking of World Order* (New York: Simon & Schuster, 1996). There Huntington repeats the formula of identities (p. 21): "People and nations are attempting to answer the most basic question humans can face: Who are we? And they are answering that question in the traditional way human beings have answered it, by reference to the things that mean most to them. People define themselves in terms of ancestry, religion, language, history, values, customs, and institutions. They identify with cultural groups: tribes, ethnic groups, religious communities, nations, and, at their broadest level, civilizations. People use politics not just

to advance their interests but also to define their identity. *We know who we are only when we know who we are not and often only when we know whom we are against*" (italics added).

30. Sen, *Identity and Violence*, 107–8.

31. Appiah, *Cosmopolitanism*, 118.

32. Reference to the "collective genius of nationals of the State" is found in Article 4 of the Convention. The full text of the Convention can be found at www.exchanges.state.gov/culprop/unesco01/html.

33. Kwame Anthony Appiah, *In My Father's House*, viii.

34. Maalouf, *In the Name of Identity*, 37.

35. The Enlightenment term for such museums and aspirations was often "universal" rather than "encyclopedic." The term "universal museum" was used recently by a group of museum directors who signed a "Declaration of the Importance and Value of Universal Museums" (eighteen museums from Europe and North America were represented by their directors who wrote and signed the declaration in the Autumn of 2003 on behalf of their museums; the Art Institute was a signatory, but that was before I became director). The declaration addressed the current movement for repatriation of objects long in museums back to the countries from which they came (the Parthenon Marbles being just one case). It included the sentences: "Calls to repatriate objects that have belonged to museum collections for many years have become an important issue for museums. Although each case has to be judged individually, we should acknowledge that museums serve not just the citizens of one nation but also the people of every nation. Museums are agents in the development of culture, whose mission is to foster knowledge by a continuous process of interpretation. Each object contributes to that process. To narrow the focus of museums whose collections are diverse and multifaceted would therefore be a disservice to all visitors."

The British Museum was not among the eighteen signatories to the declaration. Its director, Neil MacGregor, nevertheless issued a statement, which was posted on the museum's Web site as a kind of preface to the declaration. MacGregor's statement reads: "This declaration is an unprecedented statement of common value and purpose issued by the directors of some of the world's leading museums and galleries. The diminishing of collections such as these would be a great loss to the world's cultural heritage." See www .thebritishmuseum.ac.uk/newsroom/current2003/universalmuseums.html for both the declaration and MacGregor's statement.

Geoffrey Lewis, Chair of the ICOM Ethics Committee, wrote an editorial opinion piece for *ICOM News*, 1 (2004) on this subject, in which he stated, "The concept of universality is embodied at the origin of museums. As we know them today, museums originated in the eighteenth century encyclopaedic movement of the so-called European Enlightenment. . . . The real purpose of the declaration was, however, to establish a higher degree of immunity from claims for the repatriation of objects from the collections of these museums. The presumption that a museum with universally defined objectives may be considered exempt from such demands is specious. The Declaration is a statement of self-interest, made by a group representing some of the world's richest museums; they do not, as they imply, speak for the 'international museum community.' The debate today is not about the desirability of 'universal museums' but about the ability of a people to present their cultural heritage in their own territory."

One can disagree with Lewis's statements. To my mind, the declaration does not imply that it speaks for the "international museum community." The only such mention of such a community is in its opening line: "The international museum community shares the conviction that illegal traffic in archaeological, artistic, and ethnic objects must be firmly discouraged." Surely Lewis agrees with this statement. Equally, it must be the case that the statement that the debate today is "about the ability of a people to present their cultural heritage in their own territory" is a statement of self-interest on the part of "source" nations and those who support their claims as represented by Lewis's statement.

Lewis's statement, and other statements by Peter-Klaus Schuster, General Director, State Museums of Berlin (in favor of the concept, "universal museum") and George Abungu, Heritage Consultant and Former Director General of the National Museums of Kenya (opposed), can be found together with a statement by Neil MacGregor on the ICOM website, www .icom.org, under "publications."

36. Robert Anderson, "Introduction," in R.G.W. Anderson et al., eds., *Enlightening the British: Knowledge, Discovery and the Museum in the Eighteenth Century* (London: British Museum Press, 2003): 2. Also see David M. Wilson, *The British Museum: Purpose and Politics* (London: British Museum Publications, 1989): 13–22 and 106–26.

37. See Richard Yeo, "Encyclopaedic Collectors: Ephraim Chambers and Sir Hans Sloane," in R.G.W. Anderson, et al., eds., *Enlightening the British*, 29.

38. Anderson, "Introduction," in R.G.W. Anderson et al., eds., *Enlightening the British*, 3.

39. Kim Sloan, "Aimed at universality and leonging to the nation': The Enlightenment and the British Museum," in Kim Sloan, ed., *Enlightenment: Discovering the World in the Eighteenth Century* (London: British Museum Press, 2003): 13.

40. Neil MacGregor, "Preface," in Sloan, ed., *Enlightenment*, 6.

41. Patrick J. Geary, *The Myth of Nations: The Medieval Origins of Europe* (Princeton, N.J.: Princeton University Press, 2002): 15.

42. Salman Rushdie, *Imaginary Homelands: Essays and Criticism, 1981–1991* (London: Granta Books, 1991): 394, quoted in Appiah, *Cosmopolitanism*, 112.

43. Said, *Orientalism*, xvii.

44. Said, *Orientalism*, xvii–xviii.

45. Said, *Orientalism*, xvii.

46. Said, *Orientalism*, xxii.

Epilogue

1. Ryszard Kapuściński, *Travels with Herodutus* (New York: Alfred A. Knopf, 2007): 109.

2. Kapuściński, *Travels with Herodutus*, 214.

3. See Mark F. Imber, *The USA, ILO, UNESCO and IAEA: Politicization and Withdrawal in the Specialized Agencies* (New York: St. Martin's Press, 1989): 96–120. Also see Harold K. Jacobson, "U.S. Withdrawal from UNESCO: Incident, Warning, or Prelude?" *Policy Science* 17, 3 (Summer, 1984): 581–85; and Richard Bernstein, "The UN versus the US, *New York Times Magazine* (January 22, 1984): 20–26, 68.

4. Imber, *The USA, ILO, UNESCO and IAEA*, 103.

5. Imber, *The USA, ILO, UNESCO and IAEA*, 108.

6. Imber, *The USA, ILO, UNESCO and IAEA*, 109.

7. "US Rejoins UNESCO," *Voice of America* (October 8, 2003), www .voanews.com/uspolicy/archive/2003-10/a-2003-10-08-1-1.cfm.

8. www.state.gov/p/io/rls/fs/2003/24189.htm.

9. Ambassador Oliver's April 19, 2007 address to the 176th UNESCO Executive Board is posted on the Web site of the U.S. Mission to UNESCO. It is a kind of report card on UNESCO, from the U.S. perspective, and includes a statement of U.S. interest in combating the illicit trafficking of cultural property and promoting cultural exchange. See http://unesco.usmission. gov/EB_04192007_Statement_04192007.cfm.

10. Paul Kennedy, *The Parliament of Man: The Past, Present, and Future of the United Nations* (New York: Vintage Books, 2007): xiii–xiv.

11. See Thomas L. Friedman, *The World Is Flat: A Brief History of the Twenty-First Century* (New York: Farrar, Straus and Giroux, 2005): 48–171.

12. Thomas L. Friedman, *The Lexus and the Olive Tree* (New York: Random House, 2000): 9.

13. Friedman, *The World Is Flat*, 10–11.

14. Nayan Chanda, *Bound Together: How Traders, Preachers, Adventurers, and Warriors Shaped Globalization* (New Haven, Conn.: Yale University Press, 207): 33.

Afterword to the Paperback Edition

1. Stephen L. Dyson, "Heritage Battles," *Apollo* (January 24, 2009); Roger Bland, "What's Yours Is Mine," *London Review of Books* (November 6, 2008); and Peter Stone, "Clinging on to their Marbles," *Times Higher Education* (July 3, 2008).

2. Shan Yihe, preface to *Selected Bronzes in the Collection of the Poly Art Museum* (Beijing: Poly Art Museum, 2001).

3. David Barboza, "China Pressures Christie's to Hand Over Sculptures," *New York Times* (February 17, 2009), www.nytimes.com/2009/02/17/world.

4. Mark McDonald, "Top Bid on Disputed Yves Saint Laurent Bronzes Was a Protest from China," *New York Times* (March 2, 2009), www.nytimes.com/2009/03/02/world; and Mark McDonald and Carol Vogel, "Twist in Sale of Relics Has China Winking," *New York Times* (March 3, 2009), www.nytimes.com/2009/03/03/world.

5. Katrin Bennhold and John F. Burns, "Protests Halt Olympic Torch Relay in Paris," *New York Times* (April 7, 2008), www.nytimes.com/2008/04/07/world.

6. Edward Wong, "Uighurs on Both Sides of Conflict in China," *New York Times* (September 3, 2008), www.nytimes.com/2008/09/03/world; Michael Wines, "To Protect an Ancient City, China Moves to Raze It," *New York Times* (May 28, 2009), www.nytimes.com/2009/05/28/world; and Nicholas Bequelin, "Behind the Violence in Xinjiang," *New York Times* (July 10, 2009), www.nytimes.com/2009/07/10/opinion.

7. http:/foreign.senate.gov/testimony/2009/KillionTestimony090728a.pdf.

8. It's too soon to get a sense of the Obama administration's position on U.S. cultural diplomacy, other than the statement made by Ambassador Killion. But the first test was the United States' opposition to the campaign to seat the Egyptian Farouk Hosni as the new director general of UNESCO (2009). Firmly backed by U.S. ally Egyptian President Hosni Mubarak, Hosni was finally not elected to the proposed position in part because he was quoted as saying to an Islamist member of the Egyptian parliament that he would personally burn any Israeli books found in Egyptian libraries. Although the matter was not officially acknowledged, the United States was said to oppose Hosni's election, and Killion was said to have worked "furiously in private to undermine his support." See Edward Cody, "Wrong Man for Top Job at UNESCO?" *The Washington Post* (September 9, 2009), www.washingtonpost.com.

9. The guidelines are on www.aamd.org.

10. As quoted in Martha C. Nussbaum, *For Love of Country?* (Boston:

Beacon Press, 2002), 2. Marcus Aurelius, *Meditations*, trans. Maxwell Staniforth (London: Penguin Books, 1964): Book 6, 44, p. 101; and Book 12, 26, p. 185. See also Karen O'Brien, *Narratives of Enlightenment: Cosmopolitan History from Voltaire to Gibbon* (Cambridge: Cambridge University Press, 1997).

11. Carol A. Breckenridge, Sheldon Pollock, Homi K. Bhabha, and Dipesh Chakrabarty, *Cosmopolitanism* (Durham, N.C.: Duke University Press, 2002), 6–7.

12. Nussbaum, *For Love of Country?*, xiii.

13. Nussbaum, *For Love of Country?*, 11.

14. Edward W. Said, *Culture and Imperialism* (London: Vintage Books, 1994), 49.

15. Said, *Culture and Imperialism*, 72.

16. Said, *Culture and Imperialism*, 72.

17. Edward W. Said, "Preface," *Orientalism* (London: Penguin Books, 2003), xvii–xviii.

18. Sanjay Subrahmanyam, "Golden Age Hallucinations," *Outlook India Magazine* (August 20, 2001), www.outlookindia.com.

SELECT BIBLIOGRAPHY

Ahmed, Leila. *A Border Passage: From Cairo to America—A Woman's Journey.* London: Penguin Books, 2000.

Ajami, Fouad. *The Dream Palace of the Arabs.* New York: Vintage Books, 1999.

Anderson, Benedict. *Imagined Communities,* 2d rev. ed. London: Verso, 1991.

Anderson, R.G.W., et al., eds. *Enlightening the British: Knowledge, Discovery and the Museum in the Eighteenth Century.* London: British Museum Press, 2003.

Appiah, Kwame Anthony. *Cosmopolitanism: Ethics in a World of Strangers.* New York: W. W. Norton, 2006.

———. *The Ethics of Identity.* Princeton, N.J.: Princeton University Press, 2005.

———. *In My Father's House: Africa in the Philosophy of Culture.* Oxford: Oxford University Press, 1992.

Appiah, Kwame Anthony, and Henry Louis Gates, Jr. *Identities.* Chicago: University of Chicago Press, 1995.

Armstrong, John A. *Nations Before Nationalism.* Chapel Hill: University of North Carolina Press, 1982.

Association of Art Museum Directors. "Report of the AAMD Subcommittee on Incoming Loans of Archaeological Materials and Ancient Art." February 2006, www.aamd.org.

———. "Report of the AAMD Task Force on the Acquisition of Archaeological Materials and Ancient Art." June 2004, www.aamd.org.

Atkinson, John A., Iain Banks, and Jerry O'Sullivan. *Nationalism and Archaeology.* Glasgow: Cruithne Press, 1996.

Atwood, Roger. *Stealing History: Tomb Raiders, Smugglers, and the Looting of the Ancient World.* New York: St. Martin's Press, 2006.

Bahrani, Zainab. "Conjuring Mesopotamia: Imaginative Geography and a World Past." In *Archaeology Under Fire: Nationalism, Politics and Heritage in the Eastern and Mediterranean and Middle East,* edited by Lynn Meskel, 159–74. London: Routledge, 1998.

Baram, Amatzia. *Culture, History and Ideology in the Formation of Ba'thist Iraq, 1968–89.* Houndmills, Basingtoke, Hampshire: Macmillan in association with St. Anthony's College, Oxford, 1991.

Bastéa, Eleni. *The Creation of Modern Athens: Planning the Myth.* Cambridge: Cambridge University Press, 2000.

Bator, Paul M. *The International Trade in Art.* Chicago: University of Chicago Press, 1983.

Bernhardsson, Magnus T. *Reclaiming a Plundered Past: Archaeology and Nation Building in Modern Iraq.* Austin: University of Texas Press, 2005.

Bogdanos, Matthew, and William Patrick. *Thieves of Baghdad.* New York: Bloomsbury Publishing, 2005.

Breuilly, John. *Nationalism and the State.* Chicago: University of Chicago Press, 1982.

Carboni, Stefano. *Venice and the Islamic World, 828–1797.* New Haven, Conn.: Yale University Press for the Metropolitan Museum of Art, 2007.

Chanda, Nayan. *Bound Together: How Traders, Preachers, Adventures, and Warriors Shaped Globalization.* New Haven, Conn.: Yale University Press, 2007.

Chang, Kwang-Chih. "Reflections on Chinese Archaeology in the Second Half of the Twentieth Century." *Journal of East Asian Archaeology* 3, 1–2 (2001): 5–13.

Chatterjee, Partha. *The Nation and Its Fragments: Colonial and Postcolonial Histories.* Princeton, N.J.: Princeton University Press, 1993.

Clément, Etienne. "Some Recent Practical Experience in the Implementation of the 1954 Hague Convention." *International Journal of Cultural Property* 1, 3 (1994): 11–26.

Cleveland, William L. *The Making of an Arab Nationalist: Ottomanism and Arabism in the Life and Thought of Sati' al-Husri.* Princeton, N.J.: Princeton University Press, 1971.

Coggins, Clemency Chase. "Archaeology and the Art Market," originally published in *Science* 175 (January 21, 1972): 263–66; reprinted in *Who Owns the Past? Cultural Policy, Cultural Property, and the Law,* edited by Kate Fitz Gibbon, 221–9. New Brunswick, N.J.: Rutgers University Press, 2005.

———. "Observations of a Combatant." In *Who Owns the Past? Cultural Policy, Cultural Property, and the Law,* edited by Kate Fitz Gibbon, 231–7. New Brunswick, N.J.: Rutgers University Press, 2005.

———. "Illegal International Traffic in Art: Interim Report." *Art Journal* 30, 4 (Summer 1971): 384.

———. "Illicit Traffic of Pre-Columbian Antiquities." *Art Journal* 29, 1 (Autumn 1969): 94, 96, 98, 114.

Connor, Walker. *Ethnonationalism: The Quest for Understanding.* Princeton, N.J.: Princeton University Press, 1994.

Cuno, James. "Art Museums, Archaeology, and Antiquities in an Age of Sectarian Violence." In *The Acquisition and Exhibition of Classical Antiquities: Professional, Legal, and Ethical Perspectives,* edited by Robin. F. Rhodes, 9–26. South Bend, Ind.: University of Notre Dame Press, 2008.

———. "View from the Universal Museum." In *Imperialism, Art and Restitution,* edited by John Henry Merryman, 15–36. Cambridge: Cambridge University Press, 2006.

———. "Museums, Antiquities, Cultural Property, and the U.S. Legal Framework for Making Acquisitions." In *Who Owns The Past? Cultural Policy, Cultural Property, and the Law*, edited by Kate Fitz Gibbon, 143–58. New Brunswick, N.J.: Rutgers University Press, 2005.

———. "Museums and the Acquisition of Antiquities." *Cardozo Arts & Entertainment Law Journal* 19, 1 (2001): 83–96.

———. "U.S. Art Museums and Cultural Property." *Connecticut Journal of International Law* 16, 2 (Spring 2001): 189–96.

Curtin, Philip D. *Cross-Cultural Trade in World History.* Cambridge: Cambridge University Press, 1984.

Daes, Dr. Erica-Irene A. *Protection of the Heritage of Indigenous People.* New York: United Nations, 1997.

Dawisha, Adeed. *Arab Nationalism in the Twentieth Century.* Princeton, N.J.: Princeton University Press, 2003.

Díaz-Andreu, Margarita, and Timothy Chapman, eds. *Nationalism and Archaeology in Europe.* San Francisco: Westview Press, 1996.

Duara, Prasenjit. *Rescuing History from the Nation: Questioning Narratives of Modern China.* Chicago: University of Chicago Press, 1995.

DuBoff, Leonard D., et al. "Proceedings of the Panel on the U.S. Enabling Legislation of the UNESCO Convention on the Means of Prohibiting and Preventing the Illicit Import, Export and Transfer of Ownership of Cultural Property." *Syracuse Journal of International Law and Commerce* 4 (1976): 97–139.

Dunn, Ross E. *The Adventures of Ibn Battuta.* Berkeley: University of California Press, 1986.

Eakin, Hugh. "Notes from Underground." *New York Review of Books* (May 25, 2006): Review of *The Medici Conspiracy: The Illicit Journey of Looted Antiquities, from Italy's Tomb Raiders to the World's Greatest Museums,* by Peter Watson and Cecilia Todeschini and the exchange of letters between Watson/Todeschini and Eakin in *New York Review of Books* (July 13, 2006).

Eirinberg, Keith W. "The United States Reconsiders the 1954 Hague Convention." *International Journal of Cultural Property* 1, 3 (1994): 27–36.

Elliott, Jeannette Shambaugh, and David Shambaugh. *The Odyssey of China's Imperial Treasures.* Seattle: University of Washington Press, 2005.

Fitz Gibbon, Kate, ed. *Who Owns the Past? Cultural Policy, Cultural Property, and the Law.* New Brunswick, N.J.: Rutgers University Press, 2005.

Fitzpatrick, James. "A Wayward Course: The Lawless Customs Policy Toward Cultural Properties." *N.Y.U. International Law and Policy* 15 (1983): 857, 860–61.

Fowler, Don D. "The Uses of the Past: Archaeology in the Service of the State." *American Antiquity* 52 (1987): 229–48.

Freely, John. *Istanbul: The Imperial City.* London: Penguin Books, 1998.

Friedman, Jonathan. "The Past in the Future: History and the Politics of Identity." *American Anthropologist* 94 (1992): 837–59.

Friedman, Thomas L. *The World Is Flat: A Brief History of the Twenty-First Century.* New York: Farrar, Straus and Giroux, 2005.

Friedman, Thomas L. *The Lexus and the Olive Tree.* New York: Anchor Books, 2000.

Fuller, Graham E., and Jonathan Lipman. "Islam in Xinjiang." In *Xinjiang: China's Muslim Borderland,* edited by S. Frederick Starr, 320–52. London: M.E. Sharpe, 2004.

Gathercole, P., and D. Lowenthal, eds. "The Politics of the Past." *One World Archaeology,* vol. 12. London: Unwin Hyman, 1990.

Geary, Patrick J. *The Myth of Nations: The Medieval Origins of Europe.* Princeton, N.J.: Princeton University Press, 2002.

Gellner, Ernest. *Nations and Nationalism.* Ithaca, N.Y.: Cornell University Press, 1983.

Greenfield, Jeanette. *The Return of Cultural Treasures.* Cambridge: Cambridge University Press, 1989.

Giès, Jacques, ed. *The Arts of Central Asia: the Pelliot Collection in the Musée Guimet.* Translated by Hero Friesen. London: Serindia Publications, 1996.

Goode, James. *Negotiating for the Past: Archaeology, Nationalism, and Diplomacy in the Middle East, 1919–1941.* Austin: University of Texas Press, 2007.

Guzelimian, Ara, ed. *Parallels and Paradoxes, Daniel Barenboim and Edward W. Said: Explorations in Music and Society.* London: Bloomsbury, 2004.

Haim, Sylvia G., ed. *Arab Nationalism: An Anthology.* Berkeley: University of California Press, 1976.

Hallman, Robert. "Museums and Cultural Property: A Retreat from the Internationalist Approach." *International Journal of Cultural Property* 12, 2 (2005): 201–25.

Hanna, Nelly. *Making Big Money in 1600: The Life and Times of Isma'il Abu Taqiyya, Egyptian Merchant.* Syracuse, N.Y.: Syracuse University Press, 1998.

Hansen, Valerie. *The Open Empire: A History of China to 1600* (New York: W.W. Norton, 2000).

Harrison, Lawrence E., and Samuel P. Huntington, eds. *Culture Matters: How Values Shape Human Progress.* New York: Basic Books, 2000.

Hobsbawm, Eric. *Nations and Nationalism Since 1780.* Cambridge: Cambridge University Press, 1990.

Hoffman, Barbara T., ed. *Art and Cultural Heritage: Law, Policy, and Practice.* Cambridge: Cambridge University Press, 2006.

Hopkirk, Peter. *Foreign Devils on the Silk Road.* Amherst: University of Massachusetts Press, 1980.

Howard, Deborah. "The Status of the Oriental Traveller in Renaissance Venice." In *Re-Orienting the Renaissance: Cultural Exchanges with the East,* edited by Gerald MacLean, 29–49. New York: Palgrave Macmillan, 2005.

———. *Venice and the East: The Impact of the Islamic World on Venetian Architecture, 1100–1500.* London: Yale University Press, 2000.

Imber, Mark F. *The USA, ILO, UNESCO and IAEA: Politicization and Withdrawal in the Specialized Agencies.* New York: St. Martin's Press, 1989.

Jackson, Anna, and Amin Jaffer, eds. *Encounters: The Meeting of Asia and Europe, 1500–1800.* London: Victoria and Albert Museum, 2004.

Jardine, Lisa, and Jerry Brotton. *Global Interests: Renaissance Art between East and West.* London: Reaktion Books, 2000.

Kaplan, Flora E. S. *Museums and the Making of "Ourselves": The Role of Objects in National Identity.* London: Leicester University Press, 1994.

Karsh, Efraim. *Islamic Imperialism: A History.* New Haven, Conn.: Yale University Press, 2006.

Kennedy, Hugh. *When Baghdad Ruled the Muslim World.* Cambridge, Mass.: Da Capo Press, 2005.

Kennedy, Paul. *The Parliament of Man: The Past, Present of the United Nations.* New York: Vintage Books, 2006.

Kepel, Gilles. *The War for Muslim Minds: Islam and the West.* Cambridge, Mass.: Harvard University Press, 2004.

Kinzer, Stephen. *Crescent and Star: Turkey Between Two Worlds.* New York: Farrar, Straus and Giroux, 2003.

Knapp, A. Bernard, and Sophia Antoniadou. "Archaeology, Politics and the Cultural Heritage of Cyprus." In *Archaeology Under Fire: Nationalism, Politics, and Heritage in the Eastern Mediterranean and Middle East,* edited by Lynn Meskell, 13–43. London: Routledge, 2005.

Kohl, Philip L., and Clare Fawcett, eds. *Nationalism, Politics, and the Practice of Archaeology.* Cambridge: Cambridge University Press, 1995.

Kouroupas, Maria Papageorge. "U. S. Efforts to Protect Cultural Property: Implementation of the 1970 UNESCO Convention." *African Arts* 28, 4 (Autumn 1995): 32–41.

Landau, Jacob M. *Pan-Turkism in Turkey: A Study in Irrendentism.* Hamden, Conn.: Archon Books, 1981.

Larsen, Mogens Trolle. *The Conquest of Assyria. Excavations in an Antique Land, 1840–1860.* London: Routledge, 1996.

Lattimore, Owen. *Studies in Frontier History: Collected Papers, 1928–1958.* New York: Oxford University Press, 1962.

Lewis, Bernard. *The Multiple Identities of the Middle East.* New York: Shocken Books, 1998.

———. *History Remembered, Recovered, Invented.* Princeton, N.J.: Princeton University Press, 1975.

———. *The Emergence of Modern Turkey.* 2d ed. Oxford: Oxford University Press, 1961.

———. "History-Writing and National Revival in Turkey." *Middle Eastern Affairs,* 4 (1953): 218.

Lowenthal, David. *The Heritage Crusade and the Spoils of History.* Cambridge: Cambridge University Press, 1998.

Lowenthal, David. *The Past Is a Foreign Country.* Cambridge: Cambridge University Press, 1985.

Maalouf, Amin. *In the Name of Identity: Violence and the Need to Belong,* translated by Barbara Bray. New York: Penguin Books, 2000.

MacLean, Gerald. *The Rise of Oriental Travel: English Visitors to the Ottoman Empire, 1580–1720.* New York: Palgrave Macmillan, 2004.

MacLean, Gerald, ed. *Re-Orienting the Renaissance: Cultural Exchanges with the East.* New York: Palgrave Macmillan, 2005.

Mack, Rosamond E. *Bazaar to Piazza: Islamic Trade and Italian Art, 1300–1600.* Berkeley: University of California Press, 2002.

Mango, Andrew. *The Turks Today.* New York: Overlook Press, 2004.

———. *Atatürk: The Biography of the Founder of Modern Turkey.* New York: Overlook Press, 1999.

Matar, Nabil. "Arab Views of Europeans, 1578–1727: The Western Mediterranean." In *Re-Orienting the Renaissance: Cultural Exchanges with the East,* edited by Gerald MacLean, 126–47. New York: Palgrave Macmillan, 2005.

Merryman, John Henry. "Cultural Property Internationalism." *International Journal of Cultural Property* 12 (2005): 11–39.

———. *Thinking About the Elgin Marbles.* London: Kluwer Law International, 2000.

———. "A Licit International Trade in Cultural Objects." *International Journal of Cultural Property* 1 (1995): 13–60.

———. "The Nation and the Object." *International Journal of Cultural Property* 4 (1995): 61–76.

———. "Two Ways of Thinking About Cultural Property." *American Journal of International Law* 80, 4 (October 1986): 837–8.

Merryman, John Henry, ed. *Imperialism, Art and Restitution.* Cambridge: Cambridge University Press, 2006.

Merryman, John Henry, and Albert E. Elsen. *Law, Ethics, and the Visual Arts.* London: Kluwer Law International, 1998.

Meskell, Lynn, ed. *Archaeology Under Fire: Nationalism, Politics, and Heritage in the Eastern Mediterranean and Middle East.* London: Routledge, 2005.

Messenger, Phyllis Mauch, ed. *The Ethics of Collecting Cultural Property: Whose Culture? Whose Property?* Albuquerque: University of New Mexico Press, 1989.

Meyer, Karl E. *The Plundered Past.* New York: Atheneum Press, 1973.

Millward, James A. *Eurasian Crossroads: A History of Xinjiang.* New York: Columbia University Press, 2007.

Millward, James A., and Peter C. Perdue. "Political and Cultural History of the Xinjiang Region Through the Late Nineteenth Century." In *Xinjiang: China's Muslim Borderland,* edited by S. Frederick Starr, 27–62. London: M.E. Sharpe, 2004.

Mirsky, Jeanette. *Sir Aurel Stein, Archaeologial Explorer.* Chicago: University of Chicago Press, 1977.

Murphy, J. David. *Plunder and Preservation: Cultural Property Law and Practice in the People's Republic of China.* Oxford: Oxford University Press, 1995.

————. "The People's Republic of China and the Illicit Trade in Cultural Property: Is the Embargo Approach the Answer?" *International Journal of Cultural Property* 3 (1994): 227–42.

Nasr, Vali. *The Shia Revival: How Conflicts Within Islam Will Shape Its Future.* New York: W. W. Norton, 2006.

Overholt, William H. *The Rise of China: How Economic Reform Is Creating a New Superpower.* New York: W.W. Norton, 1993.

Özdoğan, Mehmet. "Ideology and Archaeology in Turkey." In *Archaeology Under Fire: Nationalism, Politics, and Heritage in the Eastern Mediterranean and Middle East,* edited by Lynn Meskell, 111–23. London: Routledge, 2005.

Özel, Sibel, and Ayhan Karadayi. "Laws Regarding the Protection of the Cultural Heritage of Turkey." In *The Law of Cultural Property and Natural Heritage: Protection, Transfer and Access,* edited by Marilyn Phelan, 1–14. Evanston, Ill.: Kalos Kapp Press, 1998.

Pamuk, Orhan. *Istanbul: Memories and the City.* Translated by Maureen Freely. New York: Alfred A. Knopf, 2005.

Pasinli, Alpay. *Istanbul Archaeological Museums.* Istanbul: A Turizm Yayinlari, 2001.

Patterson, Thomas C. *Toward a Social History of Archaeology in the United States.* Fort Worth, Tex.: Harcourt Brace College Publishers, 1995.

————. "History and the Post-Processual Archaeologies." *Man* 24 (1989): 555–66.

Perdue, Peter C. *China Marches West.* Cambridge, Mass.: Harvard University Press, 2005.

Phelan, Marilyn, ed. *The Law of Cultural Property and Natural Heritage: Protection, Transfer and Access.* Evanston, Ill.: Kalos Kapp Press, 1998.

Polk, Milbry, and Angela M. H. Schuster, eds. *The Looting of the Iraq Museum, Baghdad: The Lost Legacy of Ancient Mesopotamia.* New York: Harry N. Abrams, 2005.

Pollock, Susan. "Archaeology Goes to War at the Newstand." In *Archaeologies of the Middle East: Critical Perspectives,* edited by Susan Pollock and Reinhard Bernbeck, 78–96. Oxford: Blackwell Publishing, 2005.

Pollock, Susan, and Reinhard Bernbeck. *Archaeologies of the Middle East: Critical Perspectives,* Oxford: Blackwell Publishing, 2005.

Pope, Hugh. *Sons of the Conquerors: The Rise of the Turkic World.* New York: Overlook Duckworth, 2005.

Potts, D. T. "The Gulf Arab States and Their Archaeology." In *Archaeology Under Fire: Nationalism, Politics, and Heritage in the Eastern Mediterranean and Middle East,* edited by Lynn Meskell, 189–99. London: Routledge, 2005.

Prott, Lyndel. "The International Movement of Cultural Objects." *International Journal of Cultural Property* 12, 2 (2005): 225–48.

Prott, Lyndel V., and Patrick J. O'Keefe. "'Cultural Heritage' or 'Cultural Property'?" *International Journal of Cultural Property* 2 (1992): 307–20.

229

Reid, Donald Malcolm. *Whose Pharaohs? Archaeology, Museums, and Egyptian National Identity from Napoleon to World War I*. Berkeley: University of California Press, 2002.

Reid, Donald Malcolm. "Nationalizing the Pharaonic Past: Egyptology, Imperialism, and Egyptian Nationalism, 1922–1952." In *Rethinking Nationalism in the Arab Middle East*, edited by James Jankowski and Israel Gershoni, 127–49. New York: Columbia University Press, 1997.

———. "Cultural Imperialism and Nationalism: The Struggle to Define and Control the Heritage of Arab Art in Egypt." *International Journal of Middle Eastern Studies* 24, 1 (February 1992): 57–76.

———. "Indigenous Egyptology: The Decolonialization of a Profession?" *Journal of the American Oriental Society* 105, 2 (April–June 1985): 233–46.

Renfrew, Colin. *Loot, Legitimacy and Ownership: The Ethical Crisis in Archaeology*. London: Duckworth, 2000.

Robson, Eleanor, et al. *Who Owns Objects? The Ethics and Politics of Collecting Artefacts*. Oxford: Oxbow Books, 2006.

Rudelson, Justin, and William Jankowiak. "Acculturation and Resistance: Xinjiang Identities in Flux." In *Xinjiang: China's Muslim Borderland*, edited by S. Fredrick Starr, 299–319. London: M.E. Sharpe, 2004.

Rushdie, Salman. *Imaginary Homelands: Essays and Criticism, 1981–1991*. London: Granta Books, 1991.

Said, Edward W. *Orientalism*, reprinted with a new Preface. London: Penguin Books, 2003.

———. *Out of Place: A Memoir*. New York: Vintage Books, 1999.

———. *Covering Islam: How the Media and the Experts Determine How We See the Rest of the World*. New York: Vintage Books, 1997.

———. *Culture and Imperialism*. New York: Vintage Books, 1994.

Scarre, Chris, and Geoffrey Scarre, eds. *The Ethics of Archaeology: Philosophical Perspectives on Archaeological Practice*. Cambridge: Cambridge University Press, 2006.

Sen, Amartya. *Identity and Violence: The Illusion of Destiny*. New York: W.W. Norton, 2006.

Sen, Tansen. *Buddhism Diplomacy and Trade. The Realignment of Sino-Indian Relations, 600–1400*. Honolulu: Association of Asian Studies and University of Hawaii Press, 2003.

Shanks, Michael, and I. Hodder. "Processual, Postprocessual, and Interpretative Archaeologies." In *Interpreting Archaeology: Finding Meaning in the Past*, edited by I. Hodder et al., 3–29. London: Routledge, 1995.

Shanks, Michael, and C. Tilley. *Social Theory and Archaeology*. Cambridge: Polity Press, 1987.

Shaw, Wendy M. K. *Possessors and Possessed: Museums, Archaeology, and the*

Visualization of History in the Late Ottoman Empire. Berkeley: University of California Press, 2003.

Silberman, Neil Asher. "Nationalism and Archaeology." *The Oxford Encyclopedia of Archaeology in the Near East,* vol. 4, edited by Eric M. Meyers, 103–12. Oxford: Oxford University Press, 1997.

———. *Between Past and Present: Archaeology and Nationalism in the Modern Middle East.* New York: Henry Holt, 1990.

———. "The Politics of the Past: Archaeology and Nationalism in the Eastern Mediterranean." *Mediterranean Quarterly* 1 (1990): 99–110.

Simon, Reeva Spector. *Iraq Between the Two World Wars: The Militarist Origins of Tyranny.* New York: Columbia University Press, 2004.

Sloan, Kim, ed. *Enlightenment: Discovering the World in the Eighteenth Century.* London: British Museum Press, 2003.

Smith, Anthony D. *Nationalism and Modernism: A Critical Survey of Recent Theories of Nations and Nationalism.* New York: Routledge, 1998.

———. *Nations and Nationalism in a Global Era.* Cambridge: Polity Press, 1995.

———. *National Identity.* Reno, Nev.: University of Las Vegas Press, 1991.

———. *The Ethnic Origins of Nations.* Oxford: Basil Blackwell, 1986.

———. *Nationalism in the Twentieth Century.* New York: New York University Press, 1979.

Smith, Bruce, ed. *Ethics in American Archaeology: Challenges for the 1990s.* Washington, D.C.: Society for American Archaeology, 1995.

Smith, Laurajane. *Archaeological Theory and the Politics of Cultural Heritage.* London: Routledge, 2004.

Starr, S. Frederick, ed. *Xinjiang: China's Muslim Borderland.* London: M.E. Sharpe, 2004.

Stearns, Peter N. *Cultures in Motion: Mapping Key Contacts and their Imprints in World History.* New Haven, Conn.: Yale University Press, 2001.

Steele, Caroline. "Who Has Not Eaten Cherries With the Devil? Archaeology Under Challenge." In *Archaeologies of the Middle East: Critical Perspectives,* edited by Susan Pollock and Reinhard Bernbeck, 45–65. Oxford: Blackwell Publishing, 2005.

Tong, Enzheng. "Thirty Years of Chinese Archaeology (1949–1979)." In *Nationalism, Politics, and the Practice of Archaeology,* edited by Philip L. Kohl and Clare Fawcett, 177–97. Cambridge: Cambridge University Press, 1995.

Trigger, Bruce G. *A History of Archaeological Thought.* Cambridge: Cambridge University Press, 1989.

———. "Prospects for a World Archaeology." *World Archaeology* 18 (1986): 1–20.

———. "Alternative Archaeologies: Nationalist, Colonialist, Imperialist." *Man* 19 (1984): 355–70.

Tubb, Kathryn W. *Antiquities: Trade or Betrayed? Legal, Ethical and Conservation Issues.* London: Archetype Publications, 1995.

Vernoit, Stephen. "The Rise of Islamic Archaeology." *Muqarnas* 14 (1997): 1–10.

Vincent, Steven. "The Secret War of Maria Kouroupas." *Art and Auction* (March 2002): 63–9.

Von Falkenhausen, Lothar. "The Regionalist Paradigm in Chinese Archaeology." In *Nationalism, Politics, and the Practice of Archaeology*, edited by Philip L. Kohl and Clare Fawcett, 198–217. Cambridge: Cambridge University Press, 1995.

Walker, Annabel. *Aurel Stein: Pioneer of the Silk Road.* London: John Murray, 1995.

Watkins, Joe. "Cultural Nationalists, Internationalists, and 'Intra-nationalists': Who's Right and Whose Right?" *International Journal of Cultural Property* 12, 1 (February 2005): 78–94.

Watson, Peter, and Cecilia Todeschini. *The Medici Conspiracy: The Illicit Journey of Looted Antiquities, from Italy's Tomb Raiders to the World's Greatest Museums.* New York: Public Affairs, 2006.

White, Jenny B. *Islamist Mobilization in Turkey.* Seattle: University of Washington Press, 2002.

Whitfield, Roderick, Susan Whitfield, and Neville Agnew. *Cave Temples of Mogao: Art and History on the Silk Road.* Los Angeles: Getty Conservation Institute and J. Paul Getty Museum, 2000.

Whitfield, Susan. *The Silk Road: Trade, Travel, War and Faith.* Chicago: Serindia Publications for The British Library, 2004.

Wilson, David M. *The British Museum: Purpose and Politics.* London: British Museum Publications, 1989.

Winter, Irene J. "Review of J. Greenfield, *The Return of Cultural Treasures.*" *Art Journal* 52, 1 (1993): 103–7.

Wood, Frances. "Aurel Stein, The British Museum, and the India Office." In *The Silk Road: Trade, Travel, War and Faith,* edited by Susan Whitfield, 91–104. Chicago: Serindia Publications for The British Library, 2004.

Wriggins, Sally Hovey. *Xuanzang: A Buddhist Pilgrim on the Silk Road.* Oxford: Westview Press, 1996.

Wright, Gwendolyn, ed. *The Formation of National Collections of Art and Archaeology,* Studies in the History of Art 47, Symposium Papers 27. Washington, D.C.: National Gallery of Art, 1996.

Wu, Hung. *Chinese Art at the Crossroads: Between Past and Future, Between East and West.* New York: Chambers Fine Arts, 2003.

Yaldiz, Marianne. "The History of the Turfan Collection in the Museum of Indian Art." *Orientations* 31, 9 (November 2000): 75–82.

INDEX

9 780691 148106